The National PTA,
Race, and Civic Engagement,
1897–1970

The National PTA, Race, and Civic Engagement, 1897–1970

Christine Woyshner

THE OHIO STATE UNIVERSITY PRESS
COLUMBUS

Library of Congress Cataloging-in-Publication Data
Woyshner, Christine A.
The national PTA, race, and civic engagement, 1897–1970 / Christine Woyshner.
    p. cm.
Includes bibliographical references and index.
ISBN 978-0-8142-0755-0 (cloth : alk. paper)
1. National PTA (U.S.)—History. 2. National Congress of Colored Parents and Teachers—History. 3. Education—Parent participation—United States—History. I. Title.
LC225.5.W69 2009
371.19'206073—dc22
                2008042261

This book is available in the following editions:
Cloth (ISBN 978-0-8142-0755-0)
CD-ROM (ISBN 978-0-8142-9190-0)

Cover design by Laurence J. Nozik
Text design by Juliet Williams
Typeset in Adobe Minion Pro
Printed by Thomson-Shore, Inc.

♾ The paper used in this publication meets the minimum requirements of the American National Standard for Information Sciences—Permanence of Paper for Printed Library Materials. ANSI Z39.48-1992.
9 8 7 6 5 4 3 2 1

CONTENTS

List of Illustrations   *vii*

Acknowledgments   *ix*

INTRODUCTION   The National PTA, Race, and Civic Engagement   1

CHAPTER 1   "No Hats to Be Worn":
Organizing the National Congress of Mothers   18

CHAPTER 2   "To Work More Effectively and Gain Better
Leadership Experience": The Founding of the National
Congress of Colored Parents and Teachers   52

CHAPTER 3   "For Convenience of a Better Education and
Training for My People": Organizational Growth and
Stability   85

CHAPTER 4   Making America "Strong from Within":
School Lunches, Civics, and Intergroup Relations   123

CHAPTER 5   Diminishing as It Advanced:
The Unification of the PTA   152

EPILOGUE   Civil Society and Public Education   195

Appendix   Archives   *203*

Notes   *205*

Works Cited   *257*

Index   *273*

ILLUSTRATIONS

FIGURE 1.1   The "Cabinet Ladies," or first Board of Managers of the
National Congress of Mothers, 1896   28

FIGURE 2.1   Comparison of PTA membership data, 1897–1925   61

FIGURE 2.2   Elementary school band at a Rosenwald school in
Stone Mountain, Georgia, n.d.   68

FIGURE 2.3   The Yonge Street Parent-Teacher Association, date unknown   79

FIGURE 3.1   Jeanes teacher and PTA organizer Narvie Harris, 1945   87

FIGURE 3.2   State units of the NCPT, 1902, 1912, 1922, and 1957   93

FIGURE 3.3   NCPT membership, 1930–55   94

FIGURE 3.4   NCCPT membership, 1930–55   99

FIGURE 3.5   State units of the NCCPT, 1926–28, 1932, and 1946   103

FIGURE 3.6   Groundbreaking for a new high school in Georgia, n.d.   115

FIGURE 5.1   State branches of the NCCPT, 1926–76   159

FIGURE 5.2   Atlanta PTA district workshop at Wheat Street
Baptist Church, 1959   167

FIGURE 5.3   Cover of NCCPT magazine, *Our National Family,* June 1968   179

FIGURE 5.4   NCPT President Pearl Price signing unification agreement,
Atlanta, June 22, 1970   189

ACKNOWLEDGMENTS

I AM ALWAYS astonished by the number of people it takes to bring a single-authored book to publication, and this work is no exception. This project has deep roots; its origins are found in my dissertation, in which I investigated the founding of the National PTA. Therefore, I must begin by acknowledging the guidance of my thesis advisors, Vito Perrone, Sally Schwager, Barbara Beatty, and Linda Eisenmann. These four pushed my thinking about schooling and the influence of women volunteers, and when I felt challenged as a newcomer to history, Vito would always remind me to just tell a story.

My early attempts at writing history involved a focus on biographical analysis, but these investigations took me only so far analytically. As luck would have it, I landed a position as a research assistant during the last two years of my graduate program that has shaped my thinking for this study. Working under the direction of Theda Skocpol and Marshall Ganz of the Civic Engagement Project at Harvard University compelled me to think in terms of networks, civic associations, and the connections that are created between and among historical actors. I am indebted to Theda, Marshall, and the rest of the CEP researchers for helping me strengthen the analysis and giving me the framework within which this study resides. More recently, Abigail Peck sent me additional data from the CEP as I was finalizing the manuscript.

When I finished my dissertation, I knew there was a larger story to be told about the racial policies and practices of the PTA, but uncovering the data and writing that history would take me well beyond my graduate school years. Presenting my emerging ideas at conferences as I continued to search for documentation on the National Congress of Colored Parents and Teachers proved to be a process that helped me develop the arguments and findings for this book. During the years I was developing those ideas, I benefited from the wisdom and encouragement of many colleagues, including Jim Anderson,

Nancy Beadie, Barbara Beatty, Susan Crawford, Bill Cutler, Linda Eisenmann, Michael Fultz, Vicki Gabriner, Ken Gold, Julia Grant, Val Littlefield, Margaret Nash, Dan Perlstein, Carol Rodgers, Wayne Urban, Vanessa Siddle Walker, Kathleen Weiler, Andrea Walton, Lynn Weiner, and Jon Zimmerman.

My writing group pals Alison Cook-Sather, Alice Lesnik, and Kristine Lewis helped at a most critical point in the manuscript, reading first drafts of chapters. Their suggestions and comments sustained me throughout the process, and their being outsiders to history has helped, I hope, make the narrative more accessible to readers in general. Additional projects I worked on during my pre-tenure years connected me with scholars who have come to be mentors and friends. My collaboration with Jane Bernard-Powers, Margaret Smith Crocco, Carole Hahn, and Joseph Watras has, I believe, helped me round out my repertoire of research skills.

A handful of grants supported this research, including a Radcliffe Grant for Graduate Women; a Grant-in-Aid from the Rockefeller Archive Center in Pocantico Hills, New York; and a Research Travel Grant from the Institute for Southern Studies at the University of South Carolina. I also appreciated the help of archivists Chuck Hill at Eastern Kentucky University, Annie Wang at the National PTA, Jason Kneip and Samantha McNeilly at Auburn University at Montgomery, the folks at the Library of Congress, and Ken Rose and the staff at the Rockefeller Archive Center. Several grants from my department at Temple University's College of Education and two summer research fellowships allowed me the time, freedom, and financing to work on the book and gather the hard-to-find black PTA data. I am especially grateful for the unwavering support of my department chair, Thomas Walker. A research and study leave from Temple University allowed me the time to draft the book manuscript, and several individuals helped me pull things together toward the end. I am indebted to Jim Gilmour for preparing the charts and tables for the book and to Claudia Keenan for her feedback on the complete manuscript. Jackie McCarthy at the National PTA and PJ Norlander and Joy Gilbert at Arcadia Publishing approved the use of photos from their collections. I am appreciative of the expert guidance of Sandy Crooms and the rest of the staff at The Ohio State University Press.

My parents have always been there as a source of support and strength. Losing my father and gaining a son while writing the manuscript has reminded me of the importance of keeping things in perspective and keeping me from thinking the book, as significant as it is to me professionally, was the only thing that mattered. As if that were not enough to remind me, Michael has been at my side, prodding me and encouraging me all the while, giving me the time and space to see this work come to publication. I dedicate this book to him.

INTRODUCTION

The National PTA, Race, and Civic Engagement

IN 1897 at a meeting of the National Education Association, General Federation of Women's Clubs (GFWC) president Ellen M. Henrotin gave a speech on the role of women's organizations in public education. She posited that the two major movements of the late nineteenth century—the "woman movement" and the development of popular education—were, in fact, interdependent, as women volunteers worked tirelessly to shape schools and the curriculum through their associations. She announced, "The work of the general federation from 1896 to 1898 will be devoted to furthering a knowledge of and an interest in the educational conditions of the United States, both in the state and public-school systems." Citing the duplication of organized women's work around the nation, Henrotin informed her audience of professional educators that superintendents and teachers are "often unable to secure needed reforms in this direction from the school boards. It needs an outside influence." The outside influence, women's federated associations, enabled women to wield public influence during a time when they were denied power through other means. Henrotin's speech foreshadowed women's educational activism for decades to come, through her own association and others, such as the National Association of Colored Women, the Woman's Christian Temperance Union, and the National Congress of Parents and Teachers, known colloquially as the PTA.[1] To Henrotin and her contemporaries, the benefits of organization were clear; they allowed for many members to unite around a common cause and to carry out work that relied on the strength of numbers. And no project was more important than education.

This book examines the history of what was arguably the largest voluntary organization in the twentieth century, the National PTA. The organization was founded in 1897 as the National Congress of Mothers to serve as a clearinghouse of information for parents. In 1908 its name was changed to the National Congress of Mothers and Parent-Teacher Associations, reflecting broader trends in parent-teacher organizing around the country. By 1924 it was called the National Congress of Parents and Teachers. Two years later, the National Congress of Colored Parents and Teachers was founded as a completely segregated branch, with separate national, state, and local units to serve the schools of the Jim Crow South. Despite an announcement to members shortly after the *Brown v. Board of Education* decision on May 17, 1954, that segregated state and local units were to work together toward integration, the two PTA branches did not unify until 1970, resulting in the dissolution of the black PTA and loss of black and white members in significant numbers nationally.

My focus is on organizational development, the networks that were forged, and how the rise and fall of PTA membership influenced schools in local communities, federal legislation, and, in particular, equity in education. I ask how legions of women came together to join a major federated organization and what they sought to accomplish by building such an extensive network dedicated to public schooling. Moreover, and what challenges the popular perception of the PTA, I posit that one cannot truly understand the history of the PTA until one gazes through the lens of race. In this book I contrast the work of the white and black PTA branches, showing how racial uplift and interracial cooperation served as guiding principles to the black association, while white PTA state and local branches did not have to consider either. In particular, I argue that the National PTA's inclusive racial policy often conflicted with its own and public schools' segregationist practices, and I demonstrate that what began in the Progressive era as an earnest, if not elitist, effort by organized white women to include all parents and citizens in membership based on the principles of child welfare became, during the Civil Rights movement, an embarrassing clash of principle and practice. Essentially, the federated design of the National PTA—modeled on the U.S. government—helped sustain segregationist practices, as local and state levels of the organization had the oversight of their own particular programs and activities.

The PTA was founded at the height of the women's club movement and was one of a long succession of voluntary organizations to shape the nation's political and social life; its membership drew on both the General Federation of Women's Clubs and the National Association of Colored Women. The tradition of women's and men's voluntary membership associations reaches back to the nation's early decades, on which French aristocrat Alexis de Tocqueville remarked, "Americans of all ages, all conditions, all minds constantly unite. . . . Everywhere that, at the head of a new undertaking, you see the government in France and a great lord in England, count on it that you will perceive an association in the United States." For Tocqueville as well as contemporary scholars, the voluntary organizations that made up civil society were a critical feature of civic engagement in a democracy, and were not entirely separate from the state and electoral politics. More recently, political scientist Theda Skocpol has reminded us that voluntary membership associations of many kinds peppered the American landscape, many of them forming in the post–Civil War years, and became increasingly connected to "translocal organizational networks" that ran parallel to the local-state-national structure of the U.S. state. Fraternal orders, women's organizations, and veterans' groups are just some of the kinds of networks that developed, overlapped, and shaped U.S. political, civic, and social life in the nineteenth and twentieth centuries.[2]

Americans' civic engagement throughout history has been expressed generally through formal party politics and voluntary associations. Arguably, voluntary associations have been more robust expressions of civic engagement, since they allow for a greater number of participants. They also allow for different kinds of civic work, day-to-day efforts that elicit more tangible results. Women thus could enact their political lives through organizations long before they had the vote, but as this study shows, women's voluntary efforts continued long after the passage of the Nineteenth Amendment. This research is based on the understanding that voluntary associations are at the heart of civil society, or the networks of groups and organizations within which people relate to one another and engage in community and political affairs. Civil society, in other words, operates in the space between individual citizens and the government.[3] Americans' propensity for forming voluntary membership associations has captured the interest of sociologists, historians, and political scientists but has been largely overlooked by educational historians.[4] Certainly, historians of education have studied such organizations as the Woman's Christian Temperance Union, the National Education Association, and the National Association for the Advancement of Colored Persons, but they have not investigated them as political entities or looked at the role of organized networks as institutions in the history of schooling and the curriculum. Some studies have argued significant determination on the part of African American parents and citizens, but these are local case histories that overlook the translocal networks of organized volunteers and how these state and national associations shaped and informed local activities.[5] Therefore, I argue that volunteers with a vested interest in public education were widely and deeply linked through voluntary organizations that wielded much power through fundraising, curriculum work, and political lobbying well beyond the Progressive era.

The research of Gabriel Almond and Sidney Verba explores the United States' "participant-civic culture," in which citizens believed themselves to be quite successful in influencing government at high levels. The same notion may be applied to the PTA's impact on public education. Among the most powerful groups in the twentieth century, the PTA, while leaving the management of the school to professionals, wielded a large measure of influence on school officials, the curriculum, and education in general. Black and white PTA workers were quite confident, in fact, about their ability to carry out their program and to shape public schools. They ran health programs, raised money for books and buses, and promoted international initiatives such as UNESCO to members in local units. Rather than employing a microanalytical approach that focuses on the relationships between and among individuals such as parents and teachers, this book views citizens' and volunteers' efforts to play a role in education as a form of civic engagement. Therein lies the book's contribution: acknowledging the important role that voluntary organizations, or civil society, played in education in the twentieth century.[6]

The PTA was more solid and durable than a loosely knit band of volunteers. Soon after its founding in 1897, it became an institution in American civic life that counted in its membership professional educators and administrators, especially in the segregated schools of the South. In the pages that follow I demonstrate how the development of its infrastructure worked to serve schools and communities in diverse regions and settings. By taking an institutional view, this organizational history examines the role of a federated network in and its impact on public education, rather than considering the role of scattered, disconnected citizens. In particular, I reveal how the organization was founded on the principle of including African American citizens, how black women worked to form their own segregated PTA units since they were not admitted into full membership in the white PTA, and the ways in which organizational leaders worked to unite the two PTA branches in the post-*Brown* years. I begin with the understanding that members worked together through networks, choosing to act based on organizational bylaws and guidelines and interpreting these rules according to their own goals within local communities. However, as Skocpol argues, an institutional perspective maintains that, just as much as trust, distrust is important to organizational vibrancy and, hence, a healthy democracy. Distrust and conflict were at the heart of the segregated PTA's development as members of marginalized groups found a place in the association and helped extend its institutional infrastructure through the American South. However, this distrust—or racism, really—resulted in the near-undoing of the association. As PTA leaders at the national level directed state and local units in the South to unify, the organization lost one-quarter of its membership during the 1960s and decreased to one-half its size by 1980. Many black parents no longer felt welcome in the desegregated units of local schools, and white members in some locations in the South did not want to be a part of an integrated association.[7]

Volunteer work through the PTA—organizing fundraisers, coordinating workshops and meetings, and running for office—shaped local schools and gave members, the vast majority of whom were women, leadership training in fundraising, parliamentary practice, and legislative matters. Such activities allowed women to enact their political lives before the passage of the Nineteenth Amendment. After 1920 the same association continued to help women serve the public. It helped white members play a leading role in helping pass the School Lunch Act and also provided a venue for black teachers to coordinate civil rights work when membership in the NAACP was perilous or even banned. Yet the PTA held great importance in black and white women's social and political lives, beyond political participation. Within the organization the average person rose to new levels of leadership, coordinated legislative and educational plans through a vast network, and relied on a clear system of order and rules in place to guide the program and activities of volunteers. Yet the PTA, like other voluntary associations, was not rigid and static, and in fact has always had much flexibility to allow for local units to conduct relevant and meaningful work not always directly related to the larger purposes expressed in the goals of the national association. A unifying issue bonded all members around one or more core issues: the welfare of children and young people. While the PTA did not focus solely on public education—or at least it did not intend to originally—it became an educational institution itself in the twentieth century.[8]

Lines of Inquiry

The history of American education has focused, in general, on two major themes: the development of formal schooling and the professionalization of teaching. In order to understand these foci, one must consider the context of significant economic, intellectual, and social changes, such as greater automation and a reliance on technology, urbanization and the transition from an agrarian economy, and the rise of science as a guiding principle in life and the economy. These changes called for greater attention to the education of youth and their preparation for life in a democracy. In this context, public schools took shape, and with them the school curriculum, which was remade to serve functional ends. This book adds yet another important context to the rise of popular education in the late nineteenth and early twentieth centuries: the role of civil society and voluntary organizations, in particular women's associations.

Historians have not only emphasized the professionalization of teaching and educational administration as a central interpretive thread in the history of American education but have also tended to examine the past from the perspective of professional educators. Some argue that the original impetus to form home-school groups came from within the school and that women volunteers, or parents, were concerned primarily with their own children. This interpretation overlooks civil society and the ability of organized women to mobilize a great number of volunteers around issues that were common to a diverse body of people, arguing that to do so was to serve the greater good. Therefore, existing scholarship not only gives a limited view but also tends to downplay and even denigrate citizens' contributions to public education. Thus, much of the history of education has omitted or marginalized the citizen, the volunteer, and the layperson. Were we to synthesize the many works on the history of schooling, we might come away with the impression that citizens and school volunteers were meddlers, rabble-rousers, or, worse yet, completely absent. As a result, the role that volunteers have played in the development of schools and the curriculum becomes trivialized in and tangential to the larger story of public education.[9]

My research takes a different view, looking from the perspective of associational ties to show how the women's club movement of the turn of the twentieth century and the rise of popular education during this era converged in the creation of the National PTA. In so doing, I reiterate William J. Reese's dialectic approach in that I investigate the role of outsiders to education. Yet I extend the time period covered by Reese to argue that the PTA had its greatest impact on schools and citizens after the Progressive era, when it grew to become a political and social reform behemoth. From the mid-1920s to the dissolution of the black PTA in 1970, the PTA was integrally involved in curricular decisions, school maintenance, and legislation on behalf of children and families. Viewing such efforts and the actors who coordinated them not as meddling masses but as efficiently organized citizens with intellectual, moral, and political motives expands the history of American education to consider the role and influence of civil society. In other words, I explore how a nationally networked voluntary organization sought to impose order from the outside of newly emerging school systems. It should not be underestimated that the PTA was networked nationally in a way public schools never were during the first three-quarters of the twentieth century.[10]

The PTA is commonly understood to be a white, middle-class women's organization. However, although the membership of the organization was not exceedingly diverse, it was more varied than we have understood it to be, for in its membership could be counted black and white, men and women, and volunteers and professionals. Other scholars to investigate the association have focused appropriately on its white female leaders' elitism and *noblesse oblige* in public and educational projects. I wish to move beyond this understanding, taking it as a given—that white middle-class women wished to control and manage the working classes and people of color—while investigating how those on the margins of the organization, African American teachers and community leaders, used the federated organization to their own ends. In particular, black members sought to have a voice in public education. They viewed the PTA as a means to gain decision-making power in schools and a way to fight for educational equity because their own associations, for most of the twentieth century, did not have as much authority in national matters.[11]

Nonetheless, we are well cautioned to remember that the PTA has neither sought to make radical change in schools and society, nor were its leaders—black or white—on the vanguard of liberalism. PTA leaders were not innovators but rather popularizers and promoters of others' ideas. Thus, the history of the PTA is less about noteworthy achievements and more about the day-to-day work it has carried out in countless communities in the north and south, and city and country. Following Darlene Rebecca Roth's observation that "Historians are disappointed when organizations do not make powerful political statements," I maintain that in the history of the PTA, common, everyday acts had a power and force of their own that have been overlooked.[12] The importance of the organization in public education is as much about the small, everyday acts of promoting study groups to educate parents, holding fundraisers to buy books and materials, and developing leaders within its ranks as it is about the major legislative reforms it has coordinated.[13] Yet I maintain that it is through these routine and ordinary acts that the PTA developed a strong organization and wielded power. That is, we should not view the minutiae of local PTA activity as separate and distinct from its broader civic role in shaping public education. At the local level, especially in the South for African American women, such acts were political, since they challenged white school leaders by influencing the curriculum and getting the resources that white school boards would not fund.[14] Therefore, the importance of the organization is revealed through its officers' and members' interactions in the interstices of its program goals and the mission of public education. It also allowed for rapid dissemination of information to members and the American public, the development of leaders within its ranks at each level of the organization, and the implementation of initiatives and programs around core principles that included healthful living and citizenship.

This study of the PTA, which explores a dimension of community-school relations, adds an institutional view from outside of schools but within communities in the hopes of revealing new insights about the role of civic organizations in popular education. The existing scholarship on the history of schools and communities consists generally of three overlapping lines of inquiry in interpreting the role of volunteers and citizens, organized and otherwise, each of which is useful in investigating the history of the PTA: gender, the conflict-cooperation continuum, and social capital. The first, gender, is one of the most common lenses and perhaps the most obvious. Since women made up the majority of school volunteers, this approach examines their efforts in light of various tropes, such as that of "new woman" or maternalism.[15] Employing them necessarily relies on the framework of separate spheres, which derives an understanding of separate and distinct arenas of activity for men (public, work) and women (private, home).[16] Therefore, much of the scholarship on women's clubs and parent-teacher associations argues that such groups gave white, middle-class women an acceptable public space in which to work.[17] For example, James L. Leloudis's study on the Woman's Association for the Betterment of Public Schools (WABPS) of North Carolina, a group which was formed in the early twentieth century and which later became the white PTA for that state, argues that volunteer work in schools gave bored, middle-class women an acceptable outlet for activity in the public sphere. Leloudis explains, "In performing that work, the women regained their lost self-esteem and perfected their traditional role in a public as well as private capacity." The WABPS took pains to reassure the public that there was no "new woman" attitude about their work, sought to distance themselves from the ideology of the new woman, and reminded the public that they were genteel Southern mothers.[18]

William J. Reese's research on grassroots efforts in school reform during the Progressive era makes a strong case for the importance of women volunteers in public education. He argues a point that has largely been overlooked in the history of education scholarship: that members of the General Federation of Women's Clubs and other women's associations influenced virtually every administrative, curricular, and social service reform in urban public schools in the early twentieth century. Reese uses the phrase "new woman" in reference to the clubwomen in his study and also calls them liberals. However, while the clubwomen in his study had a liberal political bent, the term does not adequately describe the ideological diversity of clubwomen undertaking similar work around the nation. Therefore, the historiography of the roles that women's organizations played in school reform efforts raises definitional issues regarding how to characterize the women members of the PTA. In seeking to categorize women school volunteers, historians have reached for readily available categories, which are not necessarily appropriate for a history of the PTA because the classifications are not able to span the geographical and temporal reaches of such a large organizational network. Moreover, since most of the terms connote degrees of political conservatism or liberalism, it is practically impossible to find one descriptor to capture a relatively broad range of beliefs. That is, what may be appropriate for a local case history or abbreviated time period, such as the Progressive era, does not hold when one considers that PTA women were part of larger translocal networks and that, in many instances, their work changed with circumstance and over time.[19]

Maternalism, or the belief that women's public work is based on their proclivity for care and nurturance, and that all women are united in their "common capacity for motherhood," is another frequently employed interpretation of women in the early PTA. Molly Ladd-Taylor uses the phrase "sentimental maternalists" to portray the founding leaders of the PTA, who were more apt to use the rhetoric of motherhood to argue for morality and social order than for democracy and justice. While the idea of sentimental motherhood certainly is useful in understanding the early leadership and program of the PTA, it is limited, again, because the movement to reform schools through volunteer efforts was so widespread and so appealing a notion, politically and socioeconomically, and because racially diverse women were involved in leading state and local units around the country. In fact, many PTA leaders outside of the inner circle of founding officers did frame their program and efforts in terms of justice and democracy. Finally, since maternalism as a framework became outdated after 1920, when women won the vote with the passage of the Nineteenth Amendment, it is inappropriate to use the term to describe PTA women through the mid-twentieth century.[20]

Race presents an additional complication for a study that includes black PTA workers, a group not typically considered by historians to be "new women" or maternalist in political bent. The lives of black women were vastly different from those of white women, even those of the middling classes, largely because of the need to combine waged with unwaged work, such as housekeeping and childrearing, as well as the emphasis on racial uplift that pervaded black women's lives. However, the presumption of greater economic and social independence has led Glenda Elizabeth Gilmore to argue that black college-educated women had indeed been "new women" since the days of Reconstruction, long before their white counterparts, just as their voluntary organizations predated white women's.[21] Ladd-Taylor reflects on maternalism in terms of the women of the National Association of Colored Women (NACW), arguing that even though they were involved in child welfare work and used the rhetoric of motherhood to justify their efforts, they cannot be considered maternalists, because they valued women's economic independence more than white women did. In this book, instead of applying existing constructs, I take a cue from Anne Meis Knupfer and choose a focus on the perspectives of black PTA workers from within their association that is grounded in their day-to-day activities and that seeks to acknowledge the interweaving of race, class, and gender. Again, my point is that given the relative diversity of PTA women, and the fact that this study spans seven decades, it is difficult, if not impossible, to utilize an existing trope from the research on gender and women's history to illuminate the political perspectives or frameworks within which PTA women worked. Nonetheless, the reader will find that some of the ideas discussed above can be found in my analysis of women's organized work in schools prior to 1920.[22]

In addition to using gender as an interpretive framework in the history of school volunteers, scholars have emphasized the struggle between professionals and laypersons, based on the premise that they are two distinct and opposing groups. This argument assumes that when the two interact, the result is either cooperation or conflict due to an imbalance of power and a struggle for control. The cooperation-conflict interpretation appears to be so obvious that we do not question its application. It necessarily hinges on the development of teaching as a profession and the bureaucratization of schools, as it presupposes a fissure between two institutions, home and school, and establishes a tension that must be resolved through the amity or enmity between them.[23]

Also, a tendency in the cooperation-conflict interpretation is to view schools as organizations in opposition to individuals, usually parents. One need not look further than the title of William W. Cutler's study, *Parents and Schools,* to note this imbalance. In his foundational study, Cutler argues that the relationship between teaching professionals and parent volunteers went from adversarial in the mid-nineteenth century to cooperative at the turn of the twentieth century and back again to adversarial from the mid-nineteenth to late twentieth centuries. Building on the work of David Tyack, he argues that the central reason for this tension is the bureaucratization of schools, which created a rift between home and school. However, while Tyack argues that bureaucratization drove parents and teachers apart, Cutler claims instead that bureaucratization and professionalization gave educators the skills to enlist parents as allies and to build them into the organizational framework of the school.[24]

This scholarship, by focusing on the potentially adversarial relationship between community members and education professionals, has created a dualism in the history of homes and schools that does not always hold. It is an appropriate interpretation, but a limited one. The cooperation-conflict line of inquiry overlooks the possibility of multiple constituencies, such as homes, schools, businesses, government, civic associations, all with a stake in public education. Also, this line of inquiry assumes that membership did not overlap and that the two groups—professional and citizen—are separate and distinct. As this study reveals, the leadership of the black PTA was composed almost entirely of teachers. African American teachers and school leaders built the NCCPT and directed it until the merger in 1970. Therefore, my analysis views the PTA as an organization unto itself as well as in relation to public education without placing the dichotomous relationship between school and home at the center. Moreover, in research on the segregated schools of the South in the early twentieth century, one rarely finds the cooperation-conflict interpretation, for good reason. In almost all of these cases, home and school—black teachers, parents, and citizens—were united by race work and the necessity of educating African American children in a racist and segregated society. Often these parties were united against white business leaders and school boards. Also, the fact that the black PTA at local, state, and national levels was led by black teachers changed the nature of PTA work, since it was typically viewed by the wider community as a professional association, or at the very least a hybrid that blended professional pursuits and volunteer efforts.[25]

Instead, the research on schools in the Jim Crow South has tended to employ social or cultural capital as an explanatory framework for citizens' efforts, meaning the benefits accrued to an individual or group through their networks or sets of relationships.[26] Because black schools in the South suffered materially for most of the twentieth century, the historiography of African American community-school relations draws heavily on social theory, in particular the theories of social and cultural capital, to reveal how segregated schools were built and supplied with resources donated by citizens. For example, V. P. Franklin explains that social capital within the black community helped develop banks, orphanages, settlement houses, and schools. He argues, "African Americans mobilized their collective resources to establish social and cultural institutions that would benefit not just individuals, but the entire group." Though the interpretive framework of social capital is not central, the idea of it is apparent in the research on case studies of black communities and schools, including Vanessa Siddle Walker's study of the Caswell County Training School and David Cecelski's treatment of Hyde County, North Carolina, during the Civil Rights movement. Both Walker and Cecelski uncover communities that supported schooling and education despite gross inequities in funding. These communities and others in the literature were rich in social and cultural capital.[27]

This study of the PTA, therefore, draws on the notion of social capital, especially its two forms. The first, bonding social capital, refers to members joining an organization because they are similar to one another, such as middle-class, white PTA women. Robert Putnam contrasts bonding with bridging social capital, which unites people across social and cultural divisions. For example, bridging capital is evidenced in the links that were formed across racial and class lines in the PTA, which united disparate members around a common goal or idea. In essence, bridging social capital, similar to Mark Granovetter's notion of the "strength of weak ties," makes for stronger associations and connections than bonding social capital because it links together a greater number of people. Therefore, bridging social capital helps explain the

PTA's ability to conduct such large-scale work across diverse communities and to be so successful for so long a period of time.[28]

Yet social capital does not entirely help me interpret the development of the PTA as an organization, because the concept is contingent on the idea of members trusting one another. An element of distrust pervaded the efforts of the segregated PTA. White PTA leaders did not trust that black PTA units in the South would remain true to the organization's principles, so they developed ways to monitor the NCCPT's activities over time. For example, although fundraising was a central feature of PTA work, white PTA leaders criticized black local units for their fundraising efforts, wondering aloud whether they detracted from the educational purposes of the organization. Likewise, black PTA leaders did not always trust that their best interests would be considered by white organizational leaders, yet over time many black PTA leaders became increasingly invested in the organization as a way to maintain control over the schooling and curriculum of black children. Motivated by distrust, African Americans in the PTA organized, amassed resources, and mobilized themselves through an organization that denied them full membership because that same organization gave them standing in the wider public and access to national educational and political leaders. Therefore, by considering social distrust in addition to social capital—which Skocpol argues is critical to understanding large-scale voluntary associations—I am able to look beyond networks of individuals to take a broader, institutional view that allows me to map the development of the PTA, placing up front questions about how members related to one another and for what purposes.[29]

White and black PTA branches, both federated associations with broad-based influential networks by the mid-twentieth century, employed various tactics to spread ideas and repertoires of skills among members to effect change in education. Viewing the PTA as an institution with a well-coordinated infrastructure reveals organizational leaders' efforts and accomplishments that do not emerge in individual case histories. PTA work was remarkably similar across the nation and constant across time, as a result of its organizational structure and bylaws. Yet local needs were met through the flexibility of this structure, which allowed for the organization's longevity. Central to this story is how black and white PTA workers carved out a means by which they could express themselves and their wishes for public education and faced the challenges of racism and segregation, and how they employed and interpreted PTA bylaws, structure, and programs to achieve various goals in the push to desegregate schools and the organization. In addition to recounting important ways the PTA shaped public education, I consider what is obscured by historians' interpretations to date and what other ways of looking might aid us in understanding the past of voluntary contributions to public education.

Diminishing as It Advanced

The PTA is so ubiquitous in the popular imagination that we often assume we know precisely what the organization stood for, who its members were, and what it sought to accomplish. While it is, of course, true that the organization focused on education and that its membership was largely composed of white, middle-class women, there is a subtext to the history of the PTA that has mostly gone unnoticed: the muted voices of those who wished to have a say in public life and education but who were marginalized in it. This book, therefore, is anchored by questions of race, difference, and equality as an investigation of the segregated policies and practices of the PTA drives the analysis. While the organization brought members together around certain core ideals—the belief in public education as the cornerstone of democracy, and the understanding that volunteers, citizens, and parents should play a role in schools and the shaping of the curriculum—it likewise offered a venue for racism, factionalism, and territorialism. Theoretically, the PTA allowed for its diverse membership to discuss and debate its hopes for the future through common projects and face-to-face meetings; such were the benefits of being part of a major national voluntary organization. Whereas the PTA could have given citizens what Evelyn Brooks Higginbotham calls a discursive arena, or a "social space of unifying and conflicting discourses," this potential was not realized, because of its completely separate federated structure and the infrequency of regular meetings between the two organizations. Therefore, the potential for the PTA to bring diverse members together around common issues was largely untapped, since the vast majority of local and state units were not integrated. Nevertheless, the separate PTA groups availed members a public place to carry on conversations about race and inequality, though these discussions were held within homogeneous groups.[30]

The PTA idea appealed to African American teachers and citizens, since it embodied principles and ideals that were not unique to any race, culture, gender, or socioeconomic class: the education of young people and their preparation for life in a democracy. The articulations of the segregated branch of the PTA, the National Congress of Colored Parents and Teachers (NCCPT), for a long time had been drowned out by the din of the larger, white, majority association. Founded as a parallel organization in 1926 for black members and with separate national, state, and local units, the Colored Congress, or black PTA, provided a forum for the wishes of African American educational leaders and citizens, mainly in the southern United States, in public education. We do not have a full picture of the history of the PTA until we consider the history of its segregated association and its relationship to the white organization.[31]

Proportionately smaller than the NCPT, but well known among and net-worked with black educational and political leaders and associations, the NCCPT gave its members a measure of control within school systems that sought to exclude or marginalize them. It allowed for the development of a black educational leadership that sustained itself over time and added an addi-tional network that united social, political, and educational leaders across the South to such organizations as the National Association of Colored Women (NACW), the National Association for Teachers in Colored Schools (NATCS), the Urban League, and the National Association for the Advancement of Col-ored Persons (NAACP). The fight for the desegregation of schools and the PTA by black members came at a steep price; in 1970 the two PTA branches desegregated, or merged, resulting in the loss of the black PTA's leaders, its membership base, and the control it had over the education of African Ameri-can youth. Black PTA leaders debated among themselves the price to be paid with desegregation, and ultimately, though not all were willing, they agreed to merge with the white organization. An organizational history of the NCCPT written by one of its members presages this fact in a foreboding note. Pub-lished in 1961, a decade before the last two state units were desegregated, its closing line reads, "So the National Congress of Colored Parents and Teachers marches on, diminishing as it advances."[32]

Reading the available documentation on the Colored Congress, which is sparse in comparison to the primary source materials on the white PTA, I was struck by the importance of the organization among black communities, the role it played in segregated schools, and its ability to bring together educa-tional leaders across great distances. As desegregation proceeded, black PTA records note the anxiety and concern that years of hard work would be lost, and its leaders called for the recording of its history and accomplishments. This was a failed effort, as little documentation remains of the organization. Therefore, this book seeks, in part, to remedy the situation by reclaiming the history of the NCCPT as I raise questions about the role of an organized, net-worked black citizenry in the lives of all schoolchildren. Through the process of reconstructing and interpreting this history, reading the extant papers of the NCCPT alongside NCPT documents offered a stunning revelation. While desegregation and equality in education were the central issues for the black PTA, they were barely mentioned in the voluminous white PTA collections I perused. Even though PTA founders built the organization's original platform on racial inclusivity, over time white members and leaders had the luxury of not attending to racial matters. At the same time, black PTA leaders used the organization to fight for racial equality and to build interracial bridges, a task that they only partly accomplished.

In the pages that follow, my narrative interweaves organizational develop-ment, the day-to-day activities of the PTA, and the association's racial policies and practices. I begin with an analysis of the development of the white PTA, the National Congress of Mothers (NCM), during the height of the women's club movement of the late nineteenth century. At this time, women's organizations began to focus intensely on improving public school systems around the country. Chapter 1 reveals how the federated Congress of Mothers was organized from the top down in a very short period of time as a result of its leaders' ability to build on existing networks, such as the General Federation of Women's Clubs. In addition to championing school reform efforts, the organization's leaders promoted the functional over liberal arts course of study by arguing that the rearing of children belonged in the school curriculum, but their hopes of remaking the school curriculum around parenting was never realized, because the interest of business and commerce won out as the curriculum came to favor vocationalism over parenting and home life. This chapter also shows how the PTA used its membership in the National Education Association's Department of Women's Organizations to create local- and state-level units around the country. While organized women at first stood on virtually equal ground with professional educational leaders, they were later relegated to a supporting role which, paradoxically, ended up strengthening the organization.

Chapter 2 traces the parallel efforts of black educators and clubwomen over the same time period, from the late 1890s to the mid-1920s, to establish a network of parent-teacher or home-school associations. I posit that the black club movement, as well as philanthropic initiatives to establish schools, resulted in the slow but steady rise of black home-school groups and school improvement societies. Unlike the white PTA, the black PTA was organized from the ground up by professional educators who provided leadership to black communities around the South. Four state organizations united in 1926 to create the National Congress of Colored Parents and Teachers, which relied on the white organization—by that time called the National Congress of Parents and Teachers—for materials and guidance.

Chapter 3 explores the work of the black and white PTA branches from the mid-1920s to the end of World War II, showing how the same bylaws and program were interpreted and implemented in each. The focus of this chapter is on the fundraising efforts of both congresses; I argue that what was supplemental for white units was essential for black. In other words, by the third decade of the twentieth century, white parent-teacher associations had the luxury of holding bake sales and other fundraisers for the nonessentials in schools. Since school taxes were disproportionately funneled to white schools, black PTA units focused on fundraising for the most basic of needs: to build schools and to buy books and other educational materials. For this, it was criticized by white PTA leaders who worried that such an overemphasis on money might be detrimental to the PTA program and to its focus on the moral and character education of young people. Also, I reveal how both branches of the PTA continued to concentrate on the school curriculum, in particular in promoting and helping carry out the Cardinal Principles of Education that originated with the National Education Association's Committee to Reorganize Secondary Education in 1918. Decades after public school educators embraced the seven Cardinal Principles, the PTA continued to organize its educational program around them.

Chapter 4 investigates the legislative and civic education initiatives of the segregated PTA and argues that the seeds for its unification were sown during the 1930s and 1940s as it focused on intercultural education and international understanding. As the white PTA came to wield much power legislatively, both branches benefited. Most importantly during these decades, as the organization began to embrace and promote the cause of the United Nations after World War II, its leaders were forced to face the segregationist practices of the organization. While the white PTA referred obliquely to race and inequality in the United States in its journals, the black PTA used the new programmatic focus to enlist members in the cause of racial equality in the PTA, and in schools and communities.

The last chapter explores the impact of the *Brown* decision on the segregated PTA. After the Supreme Court's decision on May 17, 1954, both congresses issued statements supporting the desegregation of schools and instructed members to do all they could to help educate communities and support education professionals. However, because the National Congress of Parents and Teachers deferred to its local and state units to determine the timeline and procedures for desegregation, it took nearly twenty years for the organization to unite. While the PTA units in the border states made the transition smoothly, the organizations—black and white—in the Deep South, following the pattern of school desegregation, held on until they were forced to comply by the National PTA leadership in 1970. With desegregation—or unification, as it was called—came the end of the Colored Congress, its strong leadership base in the black community, and the oversight it had of the education of black children. Also, membership among whites in the newly unified PTA dropped precipitously as a result.

The National PTA emerged from the women's club movement in the late nineteenth century as women began to organize in greater numbers to shape society through their activism. The PTA notion that organized parent and citizen volunteers can and should play a supportive role in schools was embraced by many, whether rural, urban, or suburban, rich or poor. It emerged as school improvement societies in the segregated schools of the American South in the early twentieth century and in the middle- and upper-middle-class neighborhoods of the 1950s in Upstate New York.[33] It manifested itself in the West through a series of organized citizens, and it became a site of activism in urban schools in the Northeast and Midwest in the second half of the twentieth century. It availed its members a voice in legislation, the power to shape local schools and curriculum, and an opportunity to socialize and build community. Few civic organizations can claim such a central place in American life, education, and culture. As it organized education for the better part of the twentieth century, its own challenges with segregation and difference resulted in a weakened federation and diminished power in schools and society. Since that time, there has been no centralized, united force of volunteers and citizens organizing on behalf of schooling, nor has there been an infrastructure to support the marginalized and voiceless. We should wonder what has been lost, what has been gained, and what role civil society can play in public education in the future.

CHAPTER 1

"No Hats to Be Worn"

Organizing the National Congress of Mothers

MANY OF the nearly two thousand women who converged on Washington, DC, that cold February day knew of the request. It had been well publicized a week before the first annual gathering of the National Congress of Mothers (NCM) on February 17, 1897, the gathering that would later result in the founding of the National PTA. Dr. Clara Bliss Finley, chair of the NCM Press Committee, forwarded the item to the major newspapers in the country: "hats off" was the unusual appeal of the NCM leaders. "I think that ceasing to be a nuisance to our neighbor is the place to begin," Finley explained. "Of course, the matter of removing hats is really left to the judgment of the wearer, but we will request that all who can will remove the nodding plumes and flower gardens while they are in the Congress."[1] It was a somewhat curious request to ask of the upper- and middle-class women delegates. "No Hats to Be Worn," proclaimed one headline in anticipation of the event. Yet, with the exception of the radical dress reformer Dr. Mary Walker, those who attended this assembly were not what we would call "bloomer women," though they did generally support certain reforms, such as the anti-corset movement, for health reasons.[2]

In the late nineteenth century, dress reform was by contrast a small matter, but it signaled the convulsing changes taking place on the American political, social, and economic landscape. No sector of life remained untouched. Urban centers flourished amid the pall of pollution, crime, and poverty. Millions of immigrants arrived on America's shores, many of them poor and in need of work and housing. Racial relations were at their nadir, as the gains won by the

Civil War and Reconstruction had been lost to growing laws and practices pertaining to racial segregation. In the 1890s myriad Jim Crow laws were codified, relegating African Americans to special sections in railcars and public buildings and to separate schools. The economy fluctuated wildly as the nation's leaders sought to bring the country through a series of depressions. There was a reason for the name "the Gilded Age," for it reflected the millions earned by captains of industry and also mocked the widespread poverty and destitution of the era.[3]

During this time, the lives of white, middle- and upper-class women were transformed, while their immigrant, rural, working-class, and racially and ethnically diverse sisters saw little improvement in their day-to-day lives. As the advancement of household technologies proceeded and domestic help became more affordable, even something as seemingly simple as indoor plumbing radically transformed the lives of privileged white women, since it reduced the effort needed for the most laborious and time-intensive household chores. As white women were left with more leisure time, they turned to self-improvement through study circles, which eventually led them out the front door into the public arena and community reform. Women formed clubs and associations across the country as they met together, worked together, and planned ways to remake society and to help the poor and underprivileged. From the 1870s through the 1890s, women's clubs spread quickly around the United States, following no discernible geographic pattern. Just as many organizations were created in California as in New England, and they were found equally in city, town, and rural setting. While many associations remained independent and local, many united to form national associations that linked women around the country.[4]

By the 1890s, the height of the women's club movement had arrived, as the number and variety of women's organizations had increased exponentially and they became a common feature on the American political and social landscape. This was an era of large-scale organizing, during which it was not uncommon for white, middle-class women to start, join, and direct groups into a variety of public works. Women's clubs offered, according to Sheila Rothman, female fellowship as they protected women's virtues in an acceptable structure while allowing for increased involvement in community affairs. Women's associations during this era were to be taken seriously, as they became "nationally organized and civically assertive."[5] While the largest associations had their origins in religious causes, such as the Young Woman's Christian Association (YWCA) and the Woman's Christian Temperance Union (WCTU), a significant few were organized on behalf of social reform and self-education.[6] By the 1890s the various causes became conflated into one broad-based agenda, as the leading women's organizations resisted being limited in scope. The WCTU,

founded in 1873, pioneered women's organized efforts in influencing community and legislative reforms, work that ended up having an impact on the
public schools. In the late nineteenth century, the organization had established
kindergartens, shaped the school curriculum, and attempted to reform the
public high school.[7] Through their efforts on behalf of public education, many
organizations sought to build bridges across difference, though these bridges
often were inadequately constructed and ephemeral.[8]

Thus the hat issue at the first Mothers' Congress was promoted as a symbolic
as well as literal gesture, one in which the white, upper-class society matrons
leading the charge sought to render a display of unity across class, religion,
and even race. The curiosity regarding the removal of hats was reported on
widely in the press while the Mothers' Congress sessions were being held over
three days in mid-February. One newspaper reported that founding president
Alice McLellan Birney took the lead at an early session and doffed her hat in
response to an anonymous note that circulated among the crowd requesting that she do so. As one newspaper reported it, "Her example was quickly
followed, and a flutter passed through the audience as hat pins were with-
drawn and hundreds of hats removed." The next day a newspaper reported in
a patronizing tone that "more hats and bonnets went off today . . . and with
better grace than yesterday, perhaps today the women were prepared—had
arranged their hair in anticipation of the request." In the days that followed,
however, newspapers presented conflicting reports on whether the women
indeed had removed their hats. Some explained that all stayed on, while others
described the "well-shaped heads of the women who are making such a lot of
history that is worth recording."[9]

It is not important to know whether indeed the women removed their hats,
but to consider the fact that the issue received such wide coverage in the press.
It did so because it reflected the public's fascination with the Mothers' Congress and inquisitiveness about what the women were attempting to accomplish. Some were concerned that the hats signaled a lowering of standards
and propriety, while others were not fooled by the society matrons' superficial
gesture. The Socialist Labor Party went on record as denouncing the efforts of
the NCM leaders. They charged, "The capitalist social system on which you
thrive stands in direct hostility to the home of the large majority of the people,
who constitute the working class, and its miasmas rise so high that it pollutes
even the gilded homes of your own class."[10]

The publicity stunt succeeded in getting the nation's attention as it reflected
the goals of the Congress. As one organizer explained, "The hats of an audience . . . may create antagonism, but intelligence is sympathetic and conta-
gious, and a hatless audience becomes at once human and responsive."[11] In
particular, the gesture symbolized the hopes of NCM leaders. First, it reflected

their maternalist ideology, that each woman had an important societal role to fulfill as a mother; it was a responsibility that was to be approached with seriousness and it was something for which women needed to be educated. At the core of NCM leaders' belief, mothering was a public endeavor, and all women should be instructed in the new scientific knowledge on parenting and childhood.[12] Furthermore, it showed that the Mothers' Congress leaders, at least in word if not in deed, were determined to go along with the appeal that differences be set aside for the duration of the Congress. That is, hats reflected one's social class position, and asking the women to remove their hats would, at least symbolically, put them on equal footing in order to carry out the work. In fact, Finley's request regarding hats was followed immediately by a pronouncement—liberal for its time, as Molly Ladd-Taylor argues—that received just as much attention in the press: "There will be no color line drawn." Thus, the two positions articulated at the first Mothers' Congress—the need for an educated motherhood and racial inclusivity—were considered complementary to those of the organization's founders.[13]

The maternalist ideology of the leaders of the National Congress of Mothers was the driving force for the organization; it held that motherhood was woman's most important role, and that with mothering came an unequivocal public obligation. Maternalism also held that women were united across difference, in particular across racial and ethnic divides, as a result of their capacity for motherhood, and that women's primary role in society was to raise "citizen-workers." The Congress of Mothers, while forward-thinking on the position of race, could not bring its practices in line with its pronouncements, as few black women joined the organization that resulted from the first meeting. Overall, as curious as it may have been to request those attending to remove their hats at this large public gathering, there was no mistake that despite its proclamations, the NCM did not seek to challenge accepted cultural definitions of woman's place. Thus, with this auspicious beginning, the organization made clear that it was not going to be at the vanguard of social change but would be a popularizer of existing ideas.[14]

The Congress of Mothers emerged from among the legions of women's organizations as it capitalized on both existing networks and the public's interest in shaping public schools. At the beginning of the twentieth century the last of the three major women's associations of the nineteenth century—the NCM, WCTU, and GFWC—were involved to varying degrees in public education, but by the mid-1920s, the PTA, as it had come to be called by that time, had begun to eclipse the other two organizations in its size, membership, and focus on public education.[15] The early PTA was both similar to and different from the other major women's organizations. It, like the WCTU and GFWC, was a large-scale federated association that was created by leaders' implementation of similar organizational strategies, and there tended to be much overlap in membership among these three and other women's organizations. However, the NCM platform was perceived by contemporaries as relatively narrow, with its focus on parent education and child welfare. As Anne Firor Scott has posited, "women's associations have been prolific builders of vital community institutions."[16] This chapter, therefore, explores the origins of home-school associations and the development of the PTA as a community institution that emerged from the women's club movement vis-à-vis the rise of popular education. The impetus to organize parents and community members came just as much, if not more, from outside of schools as an extension of the women's club movement and, therefore, it grew outward from cities in addition to gestating in rural areas. The origins of the PTA as an expression of civic engagement assured its success, not only by capitalizing on the club movement and the public's growing commitment to public education but also by using existing networks to build a membership base and to create an educational institution.[17]

"In the Home Lies the Only Solution"

As clubwomen found "their voices," or learned new skills and cultivated friendships, some cast a critical eye on their sisters. One such clubwoman, Alice McLellan Birney, remarked on the multitude of women's organizations at that time, noting their often exceptional attention to obscure and irrelevant matters: "The age in which we live is an age of 'movements'—it is a time of specialized work and of organized effort. Every conceivable interest, from the clothing of the Hottentot to the study of occultism, has been the subject of attention, of inquiry, and often of organization."[18] Birney viewed no topics as being as important as parenting and childrearing, so she set out to generate public sentiment and support for them. She was among a multitude of women during this era to join organizations and public work with abandon, and she, too, emerged as a leader from among the many undertaking similar work. Anne Firor Scott writes that leadership was a "key factor in the growth, development, and effectiveness" of women's associations and suggests it would be fruitful to find out who emerged as leaders during this period and how. What made them different? What led them to organize large-scale associations? One factor, according to Scott, is a "better than average education," although, as this overview of Birney's life reveals, social networks, life circumstances, and timing are additional factors to consider. In particular, her Southern upbringing and marriage into an abolitionist family shaped her views about race, which in turn influenced her vision for the Congress of Mothers. Nonetheless, Birney remains an enigma, in large part because of the absence of documentation on her motivation, actions, and thoughts. Much of what we know of her life story is told in sympathetic accounts by family members and friends in local newspapers and PTA in-house histories. Nonetheless, what can be pieced together tells enough about Birney to help us understand the founding of the Congress and its early years.[19]

Alice Josephine McLellan, the oldest of three girls, was born in Marietta, Georgia, a town northwest of Atlanta, on October 19, 1858, during a time of rapid change in the South. Birney's father, Leander McLellan, was a cotton farmer who was born in North Carolina, and her mother, Harriet Tatem— thirteen years her husband's junior—who would later play a supporting role in the early Congress of Mothers, was of English origin, her family having immigrated to the United States via St. Croix. Marietta before the Civil War was a thriving town with a reputation as an appealing place to live, and it was an important trading center because of its location and climate. Prior to the Civil War, Leander McLellan was a slave owner who ran a small business planting and selling cotton, a fact that is virtually unremarked on in Birney's many writings and the hagiographic portraits in PTA histories. She did not reveal this fact easily in her work with the NCM, but a biographical sketch written while she was president of the NCM explained that her father "owned only such slaves as were absolutely necessary to the conduct of his household."[20]

Similar to that of many other women's association leaders of the nineteenth century, Alice Birney's education shaped her thinking about her work in organizations. As was not uncommon across the South, her hometown faced no shortage of schools, giving white families in antebellum Marietta several options for the formal education of their sons and daughters. They could choose the coeducational Cobb Academy, which was founded in 1833, or the Kennesaw Female Seminary, which opened in 1845, to prepare young women for wifehood and motherhood. Young Alice received the bulk of her formal education after the Civil War, during a time when many Southern families educated their daughters to be teachers so they could support themselves. Certainly, however, like many young women of the South, Birney learned much informally from her mother's affiliation with the women's temperance and missionary societies of Marietta. As a result, she became used to seeing women in public roles through charity and volunteer work. However, Birney also learned what many Southern white women did, that her place was subordinate to men. As Anne Firor Scott explains, "Religious women were persuaded that the very qualities which made any human being a rich, interesting, assertive personality—a roving mind, spirit, ambition—were propensities to be curbed."[21]

Birney's formal education placed her and her family solidly in Marietta's middle class as she matriculated into Marietta Female College in 1874, which afforded her the label of a refined lady, or one who was "worthy of protection, admiration, and chivalrous attention."[22] Marietta Female College educated young women to be teachers and provided a free education for those who could not afford to pay full tuition. She studied the standard curriculum, which focused on drawing, painting, needlework, instrumental and vocal music, and languages. Each spring the college would hold exhibitions and entertainments, which became a part of the social life of the town. Thus Birney became steeped in the Southern vision of education for women for wifehood and motherhood, which included making close ties with other women, meeting potential husbands, and preparing for the starting of her own family.[23]

After leaving Marietta Female College, Birney traveled north to study at Mount Holyoke Seminary in the late 1870s. The trip north was not unusual for Birney to have made; Mount Holyoke was a popular choice for Southern residents, who favored the school's emphasis on teaching and missionary work. Founded in 1837 by Mary Lyon in Western Massachusetts, it was extending its reach beyond New England farmers' daughters to attracting middle-class women from around the country at the time Birney enrolled. At Mount Holyoke, Birney studied Latin, geometry, and algebra, a curriculum that was modeled on that of the male institutions of the period. The school likely appealed to the McLellans because of its emphasis on service to others and the useful education it provided; Birney would be able to support herself as a teacher if need be.[24]

As it turned out, Birney did have to support herself and her family for most of her young adulthood. After having completed one year of study at Mount Holyoke, she returned to the Marietta and, with a friend, opened a school in a small house. Two years later Birney met and married her first husband, attorney Alonzo White, of Charleston, South Carolina. The marriage was short-lived; White succumbed to pneumonia in 1881, leaving the twenty-two-year-old Birney expecting her first child. Birney moved back home to Marietta to raise her daughter, Alonsita, and helped support her mother after Leander's death in 1883. However, Birney made periodic sojourns north to try her hand at various ventures. After one year in New York City studying medicine, Birney could no longer afford the tuition, so she turned to a field that was called "advertising." During the mid- to late 1880s, Birney remained in New York and worked for an apparel company that promoted less-restrictive clothing for women on the premise that the popular styles of dress were dangerous to their health. She toured the South, promoting the notion that woman "could be lovely without a tiny waist and emphasiz[ing] the danger of tight lacing on the unborn child." Ever resourceful and needing to support herself, Birney also wrote for popular magazines on motherhood and dress reform during these years, honing her public voice. Birney's days of waged labor ended shortly thereafter. While visiting her mother in Marietta she met Theodore Weld Birney, an attorney from Chevy Chase, Maryland—the grandson of abolitionist James Gillespie Birney—who was staying at her mother's boarding house. The two married on December 6, 1892, and made a home in Chevy Chase, Maryland. Shortly thereafter, the pair added two more daughters to their family, Catherine and Lillian, born in 1894 and 1895 respectively.[25]

Alice Birney's life was grounded in the ideals of Southern gentility and woman's place. A persistent notion in the ideology of the Southern woman was the romanticization of motherhood as woman's highest role and her ability to influence future generations. This was a lesson Birney learned from her Southern upbringing, family, and formal education. Yet she challenged social convention as she lived by its dictates, a theme that would later echo in her founding of the Mothers' Congress. Birney's education afforded her a measure of independence because it enabled her to enter the workforce as a teacher and to take on other ventures. She did not toil in a factory, but wrote, traveled, and taught women about health and dress reform. Her marriage to Theodore Birney added another layer to her thinking about motherhood and women's place, as it added the necessary question of race. How could she marry into the Birney family and not be sympathetic to the cause of helping African Americans gain education and greater freedom and independence? Yet the belief in the equality of races was challenging for women like Birney, because it conflicted with their deeply held assumptions about the inability of some races to advance toward what they considered to be a more refined state of being. At the turn of the twentieth century, new ideas about race, womanhood, and social justice challenged Birney, and, like other middle-class women of this era, she sought to unite these notions into an organization that would work to ameliorate society's ills.

Advancing the Weal of Women

Until the late 1890s, when the major women's federations were organized, many local women's clubs were not generally aware that there were others like them. As women moved around the United States, however, they started new clubs and associations and learned that there were other groups with similar interests. Sorosis, a New York City professional women's club, was initiated by Jane Cunningham Croly in 1869. Barred from the New York Press Club the year before because she was a woman, Croly was determined to give working women in New York a venue of their own to develop professional contacts. At an early organizational meeting, she and her colleagues were surprised to find out that one member had belonged to the Minerva Women's Club in Indiana, because they mistakenly thought that they were the first in organizing a new movement. As the years wore on, Sorosis members learned of many other women's clubs as they came to realize there was a critical mass of others like themselves.

For the twenty-first anniversary of Sorosis, Croly called a convention of women's clubs which women from nearly one hundred clubs around the nation attended. The agenda for the convention included "the enunciation of the woman's club idea and its point of departure from the society . . . and the influences exerted upon communities in which they exist." The authors of the call set to work on drafting a constitution and electing officers for their General Federation, which was organized at the convention in 1890 to unite the many local women's study and service clubs around the country. With the goal of bringing together under one umbrella white women's clubs that were undertaking social, educational, and economic improvement projects, the General Federation of Women's Clubs (GFWC) quickly established itself as a major national force in community reform. By 1892 the GFWC had made a formal commitment to the cause of municipal housekeeping, or as one leader put it, the position that "housekeeping does not begin at the front door and end at the back door, but rather begins in the street, includes the back alley and all the vacant lots around." Municipal housekeeping became the *raison d'être* of women's clubs during the Progressive era; it held that woman was the center of the home and also the shaper of the "moral tone" of the community. In other words, women's idea of domestic responsibility led them from their households out into the community.[26]

Men and women who took on large-scale organizing employed similar techniques, such as letter-writing campaigns and circuit riding—traveling from town to town to give speeches—to create national associations and enlist members.[27] Shortly after the founding of the GFWC, the National Congress of Mothers was organized using the same strategies. In 1895, just after the birth of her youngest daughter, Birney traveled alone to Chautauqua, New York, the popular adult education center in the western part of the state. That summer a group of kindergarten educators had convened to discuss the importance of education for motherhood. Birney later claimed that she first generated support for her Congress of Mothers idea while at Chautauqua. After returning to Chevy Chase, she was "convinced that some workable plan for educating mothers could be found and developed." That fall she spoke at a General Federation of Women's Clubs meeting in Atlanta, after which she sent circulars to educators and philanthropists seeking their opinion about whether a congress for mothers as a way to promote education for parenthood was of interest to them. However, Birney realized she could not carry the idea further without financial support. Relying on her social ties and the network of kindergarten educators she met at Chautauqua, Birney gained an introduction to the philanthropist who would become a cofounder of the NCM, Phoebe Apperson Hearst, who contributed $15,000 to the first gathering of the Mothers' Congress.[28]

The daughter of a Missouri farmer, Hearst had been a teacher at a village school in Franklin County, Missouri, before her marriage in 1862 to the mining magnate and senator from California, George Hearst. Their only child, William Randolph Hearst, was born the following year. By the time she met Alice Birney in the mid-1890s, the widowed Hearst was a well-known philanthropist who subsidized various educational ventures, almost all of them related to her interest in the kindergarten. Her many undertakings included helping found the Columbian Kindergarten Association (1893), funding a training school for kindergarten teachers (1897), and opening the National Cathedral School for girls (1900). When Hearst met Birney in 1896 and agreed to back the NCM, she was supporting three free kindergartens in Washington, DC, two of them for African American children. Hearst stood out among the legions of upper-middle and middle-class white clubwomen because she had an extraordinary measure of clout as a result of her deep pockets and extensive social capital. Thus she was viewed among women organizers as someone who could help others realize their goals. If one enlisted the interest and aid of Phoebe Hearst, one could consider her project well on its way to success. After Hearst's help was secured, Birney effused, "I am confident she is doing more good in the world today than any other one individual. . . . [Y]ou cannot wonder that I rejoice that she stands before the world as godmother for this plan for a National Congress of Mothers."[29]

Like many civic association organizers of this era, Birney and Hearst tapped into their networks to call together a group of like-minded women to convene the first Congress of Mothers. While Birney called on family members, Hearst turned to the female relatives of President Grover Cleveland's cabinet members. Hence the founding group became known in PTA lore as the "Cabinet Ladies" (see figure 1.1). They included the wives of Vice President Adlai Stevenson, Postmaster General William L. Wilson, Secretary of the Treasury John Carlisle, Attorney General Judson Harmon, and Secretary of War Daniel Lamont. Although Hearst and Birney shared a common bond through their humble upbringings—both were from rural areas and had been trained as teachers—this is where their similarities ended. Hearst was reserved and solemn, rarely speaking publicly on any issue, even the Mothers' Congress. Birney, though described as shy, was the ideological leader of the Congress and was prone to waxing sentimental on motherhood in her speeches and writings. Whereas Hearst lent her support to a variety of initiatives that captured her interest, Birney was a one-organization woman; all her energies for the rest

FIGURE 1.1

The "Cabinet Ladies," or first Board of Managers of the National Congress of Mothers, 1896. Alice Birney is in the front row, third from left. Phoebe Hearst is seated to her left. (*Source:* Photo reprinted with permission and courtesy of National PTA)

of her life would be devoted to the Congress of Mothers and to furthering its principles.[30]

The small group of organizers began to meet regularly at Hearst's Washington home through 1896, which became the Congress headquarters. Birney was the dreamer, Hearst the doer. Birney assured Hearst, the organization's sole financial backer, that her money was being well invested: "There is no question in my mind as to our financial position *after* the public is thoroughly cognizant of the nature and scope of our work, as it will be after our first national meeting." The team of about a dozen women worked through 1896, planning for the February 1897 Congress of Mothers. They sent circulars and spoke to women's association gatherings, relying on the convenient and expansive network of the General Federation of Women's Clubs. By the mid-1890s, the GFWC had experienced a surge in membership under the leadership of Ellen Henrotin, who doubled the number of state units in the organization. In 1898 the GFWC reported membership at approximately 60,000 women and a well-organized national network of 35 state units.[31]

Beyond being visible in newspapers around the country, publicizing the Mothers' Congress through GFWC members assured a successful turnout at the first convention. Emma J. Masters, a GFWC member from Illinois, responded to the call with enthusiasm, noting how the idea would appeal to a multitude of women:

> My plan for bringing this matter before the Women of Illinois would be to utilize the numberless State and Village organizations. It seems to me that a Mothers' Congress is a sort of fulfillment of the Mother's Meetings of the W.C.T.U. And certainly the Woman's Suffrage Association would not delay taking part where there is to be such an opportunity for presenting that which they seek; then our Clubs big and little are always ready to push anything that will advance the weal of women.

Another GFWC leader, Janet Richards, addressed the delegates at the Biennial Convention of Women's Clubs in Louisville, Kentucky, on May 28, 1896, and announced "a formal statement of the objects and organization of the new society and an urgent invitation to the women of the convention to attend the first Congress of Mothers." Sensing that GFWC delegates perceived a rival in the NCM, Richards assured the crowd that the Congress had the backing of the organization's president, Ellen Henrotin. Yet even though club leaders viewed all organizational work as a way to forge links among women around common interests and projects, Henrotin remained concerned about what she perceived as the NCM's narrow focus on motherhood and child welfare. She cautioned Hearst, "Specialization . . . gives a one-sided and unnatural view of life and in no way do such organizations develop the capable and best women or comprehensive life." Henrotin did, however, agree to continue to help NCM organizers by promoting the Mothers' Congress to her members.[32]

In general, Henrotin may not have seen a competitor in the NCM, both because of what she viewed as its narrow agenda and because Birney had conceptualized it as a one-time meeting of mothers, not as a rival organization. Beyond that, Birney envisioned a national clearinghouse based in Washington, DC, that would circulate information on parenting and child development to local mothers' and women's clubs. She believed that local mothers' groups— such as those organized by kindergarten educators and the WCTU—had value as sources of information and support for women and that linking them together would unite these groups around the common focus of motherhood, rather than the broad-based agenda of the GFWC. The NCM idea proved to be a rousing success, in part because of the public relations campaign the Congress leaders launched, but also because it promoted one of the central tenets of the kindergarten movement: prevention, and not reform, as the means to a better society. The idea appealed to citizens of various political stripes.[33]

Approximately two thousand women attended the first National Congress of Mothers on February 17, 1897, which was more than ten times the number its organizers expected. The public relations campaign had the intended effect. Not only were Congress organizers able to capitalize on their own name recognition; their declarations on the removal of hats and being racially inclusive had caused enough of a stir to attract the attention of the earnest as well as the curious. Furthermore, it was not difficult to enlist the press, because by this time William Randolph Hearst was a well-known newspaper tycoon who had just extended his newspaper empire to the West Coast with the purchase of the *New York Journal* newspaper chain. In December 1896, two months before the Congress, Phoebe Hearst had sponsored a publicity event at the Waldorf Hotel in New York City that was well covered in the society pages, with prominent coverage in, of course, the *New York Journal.* Ten women, including Birney, her sister-in-law, Helen T. Birney, and some of the Cabinet Ladies, hosted a reception that was free and open to the public. The *Journal* reported that the NCM focus was "the children, but they wish to reach them through the hearts and lives of the mothers." Another New York paper announced the Congress's goals of eliminating "evils in the pre-sent methods of schools" and the NCM organizers' hopes in bringing about a closer relationship between school and home. Without a word regarding nepotism, Birney later remarked that the press "stood valiantly by the cause from the very beginning."[34]

NCM officers had also mailed circulars to prominent men and women in communities around the country, including almost seven hundred letters to clergymen. The leaders had received confirmations from the majority of them, as the Congress of Mothers became the topic of a multitude of sermons that year. NCM officers also distributed information written by experts on advances in child development and parenting. By promoting books by educa-tors, medical doctors, and those in the newly developing social science fields— such as psychology and anthropology—the NCM tapped an available market, finding a niche in forward-thinking, white, middle-class women who wanted the latest materials on childrearing. Such women were engaged in what Julia Grant calls "intensive parenting," in which they focused on the emotional and physical development of their children.[35]

As the Congress headquarters was flooded with correspondence from middle-class white women asking for reading materials and information on how to start mothers' clubs, organizers affirmed their endeavors and remarked, "The responses which have already come from the women's clubs and societ-ies in various parts of the country, prove that hundreds have been waiting for some such movement." Successful public relations campaigns, however, can sometimes garner unwanted attention. NCM leaders also were inundated with requests for monetary assistance after the first round of circulars was mailed. These requests came from individual women—not clubs—who sought the financial aid of the society women. After deliberating on the role of the Congress in responding to such requests, the Board agreed that it could not "aid even a few of these applicants." The assumption of the wider public that the NCM was there to help monetarily was an understandable one; women's associations since the eighteenth century had been organized to provide such assistance. Plus, the leadership of a well-known philanthropist likely contributed to the assumption that the Mothers' Congress would help individuals materially. Despite the sometimes negative attention and publicity they drew, the organizational strategies of Mothers' Congress organizers were successful in laying the foundation for a new institution. As a result of the success of the first convention, the NCM became an organization instead of an annual meeting, as Alice Birney had originally envisioned.[36]

"A Race Full of Birthrights"

At the turn of the twentieth century amid concerns about immigration and health, and along with the push for universal public education, the Congress of Mothers offered a forum for women who wanted to join an association that emphasized their roles as mothers and nurturers first and who wished to improve the lives of other people's children. Thus, the Congress of Mothers' "three-fold" program—parent education, home-school cooperation, and child welfare—struck a chord with Americans of various political leanings. Theodore Roosevelt served on the Advisory Council until his death in 1919, promoting the NCM as an antidote to society's ills in its valuing of women in their maternal roles and an antidote to the fears over "race suicide," though he did endorse the idea of men joining the Congress.[37] On the other end of the political spectrum, social reformer Florence Kelley also played a role in the early Congress, agreeing to serve as the Chair of the Committee on Child Labor in 1902. Kelley viewed the NCM as a vehicle for her work in child labor legislation, though her relationship with the Congress was short-lived.[38]

The original Declaration of Principles reads, in part, "The objects of this Association shall be to promote conference on the part of parents concerning questions most vital to the welfare of their children, the manifest interests of the home, and in general the elevation of mankind . . . which will make for enlightened parenthood and for a race full of birthrights."[39] Steven L. Schlossman thus characterizes the Congress of Mothers as embracing the "new racism," which had less to do with overt acts of discrimination and more with eugenics, the movement that held that race determined one's intellectual capacities and that the purpose of social reform was to encourage breeding among the racially fit and to discourage the unfit from procreating. However,

Congress of Mothers leaders were not blatant eugenicists but rather maternalists who believed that all women were mothers first. Therefore, Congress
organizers maintained that African American children and mothers had a
chance at racial advancement if they just heeded the advice of experts whose
ideas were promoted through NCM meetings and publications.[40]

For Birney and the NCM leaders, racial and ethnic inclusion were key
dimensions of the organization's program in the effort to create a better society through parent education and child welfare. Therefore, topics on race and
ethnicity were included on the program in early years, exploring such themes
as parenting styles in the "Hebrew Home," presented by the noted clubwoman
Rebekah Kohut. Local units just forming during these years found it challenging to put such ideals into practice because of the challenges of crossing the
imagined but intractable boundaries of ethnicity and class. In other words,
there were few if any means by which women from different walks of life
could interact socially, given what the NCM perceived as the commonalities of
motherhood. The Lockport, New York, Mothers' Club pondered the request—
the details of which are not specified in the minutes—of a mothers' club from
the "Italian district." After some deliberation, the members decided, "As the
club differed some in their opinions and as nothing definite was presented the
subject was left for some other meeting." The uneasiness in working across
ethnic boundaries challenged the members and the matter was not returned
to, or was not recorded in future minutes.[41]

In keeping with the emphasis on racial inclusion, African American leaders were included in early NCM conference programs, giving a platform to
prominent educators and activists such as W. E. B. Du Bois, Frances Watkins
Harper, and Mary Church Terrell. However, the emphasis on racial equality was a distant second to topics such as motherhood, kindergartens and
day nurseries, and child study. Furthermore, Birney was an enigmatic leader.
She was the child of a former slave owner who married into an abolitionist
family; as she assumed an inclusive posture she also espoused the ideals of
racial determination. She was fond of quoting Frenchman Edmond Demolins'
treatise, *Anglo-Saxon Supremacy*, on the causes of the superiority of English-
speaking peoples, framing these superior traits as the ideal to which women
of all races should aspire. Birney viewed his theory through her maternalist
lens, claiming that although he "proves at some length that the supremacy of
the Anglo-Saxon is due to his love of home . . . [t]he trait is not peculiar to
this race, but it is developed in it to a marked degree." Such statements reveal
the complexity of thinking during this era and caution present-day readers to
refrain from facile characterizations about the racial beliefs held by people in
the past. As Glenda Gilmore argues in her discussion of the WCTU, one cannot call such women racist, because we know little about their actual practices
and, furthermore, racism is not a static phenomenon.[42]

Simplistic assumptions about gender ideology are also challenged upon a close read of NCM documents. In perusing the speeches and topics in conference proceedings, it is easy to come away with the impression that Mothers' Congress leaders felt that woman's place was in the home raising children, though this pronouncement did not match the reality of the public and active lives the women led. On the matter of woman's place, an incident at a Congress meeting reveals the intricacies of organizers' thinking as well as the limits of their willingness to challenge societal expectations. Dr. Oscar Chrisman, a professor of "paidology"—or child study—at the Kansas State Normal School, gave a talk at the 1900 meeting of the NCM. Not one to underestimate his own talents, Chrisman presented the importance of his work to the delegates, highlighting women's emotionality against men's rationality. Emphasizing the separate spheres trope, he explained that the reason universities were not crowded with women was that universities had "little or nothing to offer the average woman," as she was best suited to the care of children. This may have gone over well enough, but once Chrisman declared that men reason and never love and that they were capable only of "sex-attraction," the women seethed. One delegate recalled, "He might as well have tossed a live snake or box of mice into the auditorium for all the excitement he created." Faced with gender expectations stretched to the proportions of caricature, NCM delegates were forced to reconsider their beliefs about women's roles. The delegates responded to Chrisman that they believed men needed to share in child-rearing duties and that both sexes should be educated for parenthood. Amid the time allotted for questions, one of the few male delegates, Thomas Smith of Harlan, Iowa, was given the floor. Smith challenged Chrisman and argued for the higher education of women and asserted that a woman could be intelligent, educated, and a fine homemaker, thereby earning the support of the audience. Chrisman, however, was given the final word and responded summarily, "the discussion has proven exactly what I said to you[:] . . . a man reasoned and a woman intuitioned. . . . I wanted to get you to talk and I have." The discussion carried over to the Board of Managers meeting following the conference, at which Birney refused to challenge Chrisman's authority. She explained, "Dr. Chrisman was our guest, and if he held opinions not in accord with our opinions we could still be courteous and kind and discuss them with toleration and wisdom."[43]

Because Birney's main goal was the viability of the Congress of Mothers, she sought to avoid controversy. Also, Chrisman was an expert in Birney's eyes and was not to be challenged. It was the reason not only for her willingness to accept Oscar Chrisman's point of view but also for her refusal to let the Congress endorse suffrage for women. At this time, members of suffrage organizations were far outnumbered by clubwomen, many of whom did not feel the need to fight for women to enter the realm of formal politics. Club-

women believed their feminine—read moral—influence, after all, was better served outside the confines of what her contemporaries perceived as the
sullied male preserve known as the ballot box. Nonetheless, the WCTU had
supported suffrage for years, and the GFWC rallied around the cause in 1914.
When the formidable Susan B. Anthony asked Birney if the NCM could put
its significant weight behind the fight for suffrage, Birney refused, claiming
it was too divisive an issue. "We are a congress of mothers," she explained,
representing "all the mothers of the nation, and could we afford to champion
a cause which all the mothers of the land do not advocate?" However, since
Birney's presidency was short-lived (1897–1902) and because of the federated
structure, which allowed for local interests to drive local agendas, clubs at the
local level did pursue suffrage at the dawn of the twentieth century.[44]

Commenting on another major issue of the day, NCM leaders criticized
higher education for women, claiming that it steered women's lives away from
traditional domestic roles and left educated women unprepared for "the realis-
tic life choices available to their sex." Ironically, the Mount Holyoke–educated
Birney argued that a more appropriate education for women included the
scientific study of all she would need to know in her role as mother. In 1897
she remarked, "The higher branches of book learning are well enough for the
girl or woman who has the inclination or time for them, but they should be
secondary in her education to the knowledge which shall fit her for motherhood." She continued this line of thinking in later years, explaining, "I believe
in higher education for women . . . but I claim that it is . . . unjust to place it
before . . . [woman's] maternal instinct." In general, however, Birney was single-
minded in her pursuit to put motherhood first in what she called women's
highest calling. Other Congress organizers and those who followed bought
into this late-nineteenth-century belief to a lesser extent, since many of them
had attended college and placed their public, or organizational, work alongside their parenting obligations.[45]

Education for parenthood was so important to Birney and the NCM's early
leaders that they championed a school curriculum remade to serve this goal.
By the dawn of the twentieth century, with the development of experimental
psychology and the rise of secondary education for the masses, schools revised
the humanistic or liberal arts curriculum to address more functional goals.
The new psychology influenced educators' thinking about curriculum and
instruction, as a greater focus was put on the individual child, curriculum was
organized around practical ends, and citizenship became one of the primary
goals of education. While the main emphasis was on replacing the humanities
with tracks of learning that would prepare workers for an industrial society,
parent and homelife education were promoted by the women of the Mothers'
Congress.[46]

Therefore, the NCM embraced the new education, which emphasized the individual child and "an end to excessive memorization, recitation, and testing." Instead, the new education emphasized kindergartens, vocational education, and nature study, and was necessarily a moral education.[47] Women's and mothers' club members read the works of English philosopher Herbert Spencer, American psychologist G. Stanley Hall, and German kindergarten innovator Friedrich Froebel and sought to bring their works and ideas to the schools to support parent education. In Spencer's best-known work among clubwomen, written in the mid-nineteenth century, he applied Darwinian thought to the development of knowledge and social relationships. His 1859 essay "What Knowledge is of Most Worth?" triggered a revolution in thinking about the school curriculum as it challenged the idea of a liberal arts education. Spencer's notions about the functional goals of school curriculum first made waves in his native England, after which they entered American educational parlance in the late nineteenth century. By the early twentieth century, Spencer's functional criteria for the development of curriculum sparked a major revolution because they did not follow selecting the "great cultural resources of Western culture," but instead focused on life experience and usefulness as the basis for determining what was worth knowing, and therefore teaching. His doctrine remade the American school curriculum by placing the sciences in a more prominent position in the secondary school curriculum, positioning curriculum around the development of the individual, and altering thinking about curriculum as a means to an end.[48]

Of Spencer's five criteria, the one that placed a value on child rearing as a central life activity resonated with Alice Birney and other white, middle-class clubwomen. Birney was especially fond of mentioning Spencer's influence on her thinking and reiterated his point that the education of women should eschew the ornamental in order to prepare them for future roles as wives and mothers. In 1905 she gave a speech in which she reminded her audience of Spencer's book *Education,* claiming, "If you think child-study through other mediums than your own limited experience a theory, read that book; it will change your conviction as no argument of mine could ever do." As a result of her belief in Spencer's doctrine, Birney became an acolyte of the noted psychologist G. Stanley Hall, who around the time of the founding of the Mothers' Congress pressed for a curriculum influenced by Spencer's notion of natural law and for the education of mothers.[49]

Hall is well known for creating the field of child study, which he first expounded on in an 1882 speech to the National Education Association. The focus of Hall's child study program was that physical development and health were the proper foundation of mental and moral development. He believed health should be the primary factor in determining educational policy, since he feared that an early emphasis on intellectual education would be detrimental to the health of children and young people. Hall viewed child study as a means by which educators could determine how to teach children and organize curriculum. As one historian explained, Hall wished to use "behavioral-science knowledge to create a science of pedagogy." Though he abandoned the child-study idea in 1885, Hall reclaimed it in the early 1890s when it was embraced by the growing association of women's national organizations who favored it, in particular, the Congress of Mothers. Clubwomen had followed Hall's lead in interpreting the scientific psychology as a pedagogical enterprise, and Hall shrewdly capitalized on their zeal, exploiting it to further his career.[50]

The ideas of Spencer and Hall, and likewise the new practical emphases in the school curriculum, were thus spread to the American public in large part through the vast networks of women's associations. Hall's ideas also were promoted through the NCM's suggested reading lists for mothers, and he was a featured speaker at the early annual meetings. On occasion, he made the rounds to local clubs, where he may have faced his toughest critics. One member of the Lockport [New York] Mothers' Club recalled, "We had G. Stanley Hall [as a speaker] once and were quite disappointed for alas he was more interesting to read than to hear." Nonetheless, clubwomen took up his cause with great energy and announced, "more women than men sympathize with the new education and are endeavoring to introduce art and utility into the fossil of public education. It is therefore particularly appropriate that the kindergarten and manual and artistic training should be placed in their hands." To Hall, a practical education was by definition gender-specific and the education of women should be geared to "motherhood and homelife." Hall responded to this interest by announcing that he saw "large promise" in both education and science through their child study circles, and he called child study the "woman's science," a point relished by Birney and the other leaders of the NCM. Thus the goal of motherhood was likewise a suitable objective for the new functional curriculum that was designed to serve students' future lives. In a speech on organized motherhood in 1900, Alice Birney spoke on behalf of the nation's middle-class parents, claiming that they "have regarded their children *first of all as future mothers and fathers,* next as citizens, and they are demanding that public educational systems adopt their standards of values in the adjustment of curricula."[51]

Therefore, organization and efficiency were the guiding tools of motherhood and delineated not only the kind of education that girls and young women were to receive but also where it was to take place. These ideas did not originate with the NCM; they were borrowed from the GFWC, at the founding of which, in 1892, first president Charlotte Hawkins Brown commented on the importance of mother education but suggested that it belonged in local clubs rather than in the humanistic curriculum of the schools. "Girls find good elementary instruction in schools, but only practice, such as clubs give can make that instruction available in the battle of life." By 1900 the NCM had embraced the principles of a functional curriculum and sought to position schools as the proper places for parent education. Congress leaders argued that the ennui suffered by college women after graduation was reason enough for preparation for child rearing and other family duties. Birney claimed there was a "serious menace in any education which at the close of a four-year period sends a girl to her home discontented with her environment; unkindly critical of her parents and former associates; longing for a career; [and] impatient with the interruptions inseparable from family life."[52]

Alice Birney had conceived of the idea of a Congress of Mothers and developed its platform, but her sentimental rhetoric and single-minded emphasis on motherhood as woman's highest calling were outdated among newly emerging ideas about woman's place and role in society and the home at the dawn of the twentieth century. As a result, interpersonal differences challenged Mothers' Congress leaders, as they might any other rapidly ascending organization. Even though the Congress's first year was successful, many of the original leadership group dispersed, leaving Birney and the Congress of Mothers searching for replacements. Clara Bliss Finley, the outspoken press chairperson who acted also as treasurer and recording secretary as needed, left after an acrimonious dispute with Birney over her leadership style. In her letter of resignation, Finley "predicted failure for the Congress under the direction of the existing administration," referring to Alice Birney, since Hearst had cut ties with the organization in 1898. Such an upset in leadership in the early years of an organization's existence can present significant challenges to its direction and viability. For example, in reference to the continuity in leadership of the WCTU under Frances Willard, Ruth Bordin writes that it "insured efficient implementation of program goals, a rank and file that knew its leaders and frequently had some personal contact with them, and a national visibility that a constantly changing leadership could never have achieved." Yet the NCM weathered the upset, as middle-class women replaced the "Cabinet Ladies" and redefined the Congress slightly to suit newer purposes and interests. The new leadership group was well versed in advocacy and community reform work and represented different regions of the country, rather than being concentrated on the East Coast, which set the foundation for the PTA's institutional infrastructure, making it truly national. Inasmuch as organization and efficiency described NCM leaders' view of motherhood, it also reflected the way they approached building an association.[53]

"From Center to Circumference"

At Hearst's suggestion, NCM leaders adopted a constitution and mapped out the organization's federated structure after the first gathering in 1897. Immediately, several states—New York being the first—organized Congress units. The constitution recognized state and territory unit representatives and required them to meet with the Board of Directors before and after each annual meeting and throughout the year at the president's discretion. The constitution also outlined rules for delegates, committees, basis of representation, affiliation, dues, certificates, elections, amendments, organizers, and other official business that would guide the association for the next century, with slight modifications added over time. PTA members came to rely on these bylaws, turning to them on matters of principle and policy, because they afforded much stability to the organization's infrastructure.[54]

Alice Birney remained affiliated with the NCM and promoted its platform from 1902, when she stepped down as its president, until her death in 1907. Speaking at a 1904 Congress meeting, she had little changed her sentimental maternalist rhetoric as she used terms like "mother-heart" and "mother-spirit" in reference to women's work in education. She was a nineteenth-century women's organization leader, and her maudlin waxings on motherhood and its purity sounded outdated next to the more businesslike speeches of her successor, Hannah Kent Schoff, who brought stability to the organization. Schoff led the organization from 1902 to 1920, becoming the longest-serving PTA president, and was responsible for crafting the program of the association for the twentieth century, with the public schools as its centerpiece. If under Alice Birney the early PTA developed its ideological moorings, it was under the second president that the organization took action on these ideals and established itself as an American institution.[55]

Born in 1853 near Philadelphia, Schoff was the oldest of five children and the daughter of a woolen manufacturer and a teacher. She married Frederic Schoff, an engineer from Massachusetts, in 1873, and the couple had seven children. In 1897 she attended the National Congress of Mothers as a delegate from the New Century Club of Philadelphia. Within two years, Schoff's leadership capabilities were recognized when a vacancy occurred in the office of vice president of the National Congress of Mothers and she was offered the position. At the same time, she was a key figure in organizing the Pennsylvania Congress of Mothers in 1899, and led the fight to establish juvenile courts in that state in 1901. After she assumed the presidency of the Congress of Mothers in 1902, she developed its program in several key directions: the schools, the development of juvenile courts, and child labor legislation.[56] Schoff knew well the commitment made by the GFWC in 1897 to concentrate its energies on the public schools. One of her first acts as president was to compose a letter to all superintendents in the state asking them to "bring the literature and the work of the Congress to the attention of all teachers in your district, and [to] ask them to call a mothers' or parents' meeting in every school of your district, and organize a meeting of mothers, which may convene monthly with the teachers." In 1897 GFWC President Henrotin had announced that the Federation would "exert their influence to secure needed legislation, good school boards, good superintendents, skilled teachers, improved sanitary conditions of schoolhouses, and should endeavor, above all, to co-operate with the school authorities." The effort resulted in a revised program of the organization and the name change in 1908 to the National Congress of Mothers and Parent-Teacher Associations. That same year it joined forces with other white women's associations to lead the Department of Women's Organizations in the National Education Association.[57]

Under Schoff's leadership the PTA grew exponentially from the top down, as local and state units took root around the United States. Membership data are virtually nonexistent for the first ten years of the association, with an estimated total of one thousand in 1897 and the next figure recorded in 1910 at approximately twenty thousand members. State-by-state membership data are not recorded on any consistent basis for another ten years after this. By 1918, the National Congress of Mothers and Parent-Teacher Associations stood at 98,000, only to double just two years later, Schoff's last year as NCM-PTA president. Yet the National Congress of Mothers and Parent-Teacher Associations could not develop its institutional infrastructure without the help of other networks and organizations. Even though the association had begun by first creating a national-level office, it took nearly three decades for the majority of its state units to organize. During this time, the NCM-PTA relied on other women's organizations and the clout and power of a major professional education organization, the National Education Association (NEA), to establish its network and expand.[58]

Building on William J. Reese's argument that every major curricular and administrative reform of the Progressive era was accomplished by women's associations, this section reveals the national coordination and direction of such efforts, showing that they were more widely directed by a national leadership group than previously contended.[59] Their accomplishments were so notable that historian Mary Ritter Beard sought to catalog them in her 1915 book, *Women's Work in Municipalities*. Beard organized her discussion into four categories: political activity, curricular innovation, structural innovations, and physical concerns. She noted that through parent-teacher associations "women participate on equal terms with men, where they do not direct the aims and activities themselves."[60] Overall, women's organization members sought to bring about greater attention to health in the school environment, to impose greater efficiency in the schools and curricula, and to ensure that the school curriculum met the goals of moral education. In these vast efforts to reform schools, women's organizations did not intend to perpetuate long-term contributions to public education. As in their social welfare reform work, they sought to enact reforms that they hoped to hand over to school authorities and boards of education to run. In many cases they did, but as the NCM-PTA grew as an institution, it directed many initiatives beyond the Progressive era.[61]

As urban schools were centralized under the purview of school boards, and school districts were consolidated in rural areas to make the best use of available funds, educational leaders worked to wrest control of local schools by instituting bureaucratic systems that would organize schooling and the curriculum. The only national coordination of such an expansive effort by professionals could come from the NEA, and the organization was working toward that end by convening a series of curriculum committees from the 1890s through late 1910s. However, the NEA, while able to prepare policy directives, did not have the communication and action networks of major women's organizations in terms of being able to rapidly circulate ideas and enlist citizens in supporting them. A parallel can be found in the state-building campaigns of women reformers of the early twentieth century. As Theda Skocpol argues, "Especially from 1900 to the mid-1920s, federations of women's voluntary associations enjoyed political leverage within U.S. federalism that was entirely unavailable to higher-educated reformist professionals—except when the latter cooperated with the voluntary federations on terms influenced by the federations' own outlooks and organizational structures." Likewise, women's voluntary organizations shaped public education during the Progressive era through their well-coordinated networks and political strength, a strength that overpowered, for a short time, that of organized education professionals. Their accomplishments were evidenced in the curricular changes and structural improvements they supported with respect to schooling, health, and social service initiatives.[62]

With the decision to become integrally involved in school reform work at the turn of the twentieth century, women volunteers of the GFWC, early PTA, and other organizations wished to form an alliance with the NEA. Representatives of the GFWC, the leading women's voluntary organization undertaking school reform in the 1890s, began to attend NEA annual meetings and, on occasion, to speak at the gatherings of the Kindergarten Department of the organization. Founded in 1857 as a professional association dedicated to advocacy and research, the NEA was at that time a debating society run by elite male scholars and school administrators. Although women teachers in general were marginalized within the association, women volunteers were, for a time, able to carve out a niche in which they could share ideas with other organized women and have the ear of professional educators. The alliance between club-women and the professionals of the NEA lasted only a little more than two decades, after which the fissure between school volunteers and education pro-fessionals became permanent and fixed. During that time, however, two major goals were accomplished: clubwomen were able to coordinate national school reform efforts with the backing of teachers and school administrators, and the leaders of the PTA, unlike those of the other women's organizations, made use of the opportunity to more fully establish the federation.[63]

Beginning in 1893 volunteers of women's organizations earned a place on the NEA agenda, attending and presenting at the meetings of the Kin-dergarten Department. At subsequent annual meetings, women's club lead-ers discussed child study circles and the spread of the kindergarten idea, and showcased the vast accomplishments of their associations in public schools. In 1897 speaker Mary Codding Bourland, an educator from Pontiac, Illinois, showcased the founding of the National Congress of Mothers as an example of women's widespread interest in public education. As women's voluntary associations generated momentum in school reform work in the early twenti-eth century, their leaders had become less content to give the occasional talk at annual NEA meetings. After over a decade of being guests, and recognizing that their efforts were integral to the shaping of public schools, the leaders of the major women's voluntary organizations aspired to a more permanent place in the NEA. In 1907 Ellen Abbott, the chair of the Education Depart-ment of the GFWC, and the representatives of six other major women's associations—the NCM-PTA, the Association of Collegiate Alumnae, the Daughters of the American Revolution, the WCTU, the National Council of Jewish Women, and the Southern Association of College Women—met with NEA officers at the Board of Directors meeting. Convinced that "by meeting each year with the National Education Association, these national societies of women may co-operate more successfully with each other and with the educators of the country in bringing the home and the school in more help-ful relation," NEA representatives petitioned for the women volunteers to be given their own department. The motion passed, the Department of Women's Organizations (DWO) was formed, and clubwomen began preparations for the 1908 annual meeting in Cleveland, Ohio.[64]

At the time the Department of Women's Organizations was created, NEA membership was just over five thousand. This figure, which grew slowly in subsequent years, was eclipsed by the membership of women volunteers, which stood at nearly 300,000. In 1908 speaker Mrs. O. Shepard Barnum observed the power that was found in numbers by reminding members that the Depart-ment could coordinate vast networks of women rapidly. She argued that the clubwomen represented in the Department wielded power through "their standing committees [, which] receive[d] impulse and instruction quickly and systematically from center to circumference." Such communication and action networks were not possible among professional educators at this time.[65]

Through the DWO, volunteer and professional women as well as professional men were united around a common cause and had access to a forum for their ideas. It was not unusual to have women's club leaders as officers of the Department working alongside professional women who worked in colleges, normal schools, and classrooms, making the relationship symbiotic between the two groups. Also, given that volunteer work provided a training ground for nonprofessional women, officers in voluntary associations came to hone their leadership and organizational skills to a greater extent through their participation. The Dean of the Women's Department at the State Agricultural College in Fort Collins Colorado, Helen Grenfell, highlighted the importance of women's associations in educational work, explaining that the "woman of the future" has been "taught through association in mutual interests the value of united effort and thru [sic] wise direction the true needs of all children." Thus, the new Department offered both fellowship and leadership training to those with a vested interest in public education.[66]

Subsequently, the NCM-PTA was vital to the running of the Department of Women's Organizations, as President Schoff served as its first vice president—until elections were held—along with Laura Drake Gill, the president of the Association of Collegiate Alumnae, and Mrs. Philip N. Moore, a trustee of Vassar College from St. Louis. State-level NCM-PTA leaders such as Cora Bright, from Illinois, were integrally involved with the DWO, serving on the nominating committee of the first group of officers. At the 1908 NEA meeting and at succeeding meetings, three officers were elected to run the department: a president, vice president, and secretary. In the fourteen years the DWO existed, leadership included a balanced representation of professional and volunteer women, as did the list of speakers at annual meetings. The Department's officers created a structure whereby representatives of the national women's organizations would plan together with the three officers the work for the coming year and would work to coordinate local and state women's club activities through the DWO.[67]

U.S. Commissioner of Education Elmer Ellsworth Brown addressed the DWO at the 1908 NEA meeting and offered his support to the organization's newest department. He reflected on the losses to education that came with the professionalization of teaching, remarking that as schooling increasingly became a function of the state it relied less on benevolent societies and voluntary organizations. He believed the DWO was trying to recapture the "shadow land," as he called it, between professional and community responsibility, "where some of the most vital questions of today are found." Brown, however, made it clear that teachers and other education professionals had the last word on school matters: "Not a book should be placed in the school library nor a picture on the schoolroom wall . . . unless it have the approval of the teaching force within the school." However, the women's organization leaders saw things a bit differently. Recognizing that education was "a state affair," they believed their position within civil society afforded them an opportunity to improve curriculum, standards, and resources nationally. At their first gathering they resolved to work for compulsory education laws around the country, support teacher preparation and increased pay, help provide adequate school facilities, and promote a curriculum that provided "training for the hand, as well as for the head, and definite instruction in ethics and civics."[68]

In the beginning, tensions were evident between the power of women's civic associations and professionals' desire to maintain control over education. At the annual meeting of the NEA in 1909, Department of Women's Organizations president Laura Drake Gill reminded her audience, "The only real danger in this method is the chance of having the name of the National Education Association involved in some unwise state activity," but she reassured her audience that since the work was organized by knowledgeable and experienced officers of the Department, that would not likely happen. Gill was also happy to report that year that there was "no friction with school officers" as the women carried out their work. Gill reflected the wider belief of women volunteers that they had a special capacity to carry out the work of school reform, in particular because men's civic associations were not as well coordinated and established as women's.[69]

For the first two years the DWO coordinated the national educational reform efforts of the Department's member organizations, reports of which were detailed at each annual NEA meeting. Department president Gill presented the long list of accomplishments of the twenty-five states with fully organized committees, through which women's associations directed health, structural, and curricular reforms in public schools. She detailed how women's organizations agitated for new or renovated school buildings and curricula, many of which were focused on manual and industrial training; and how they beautified and improved school grounds and established kindergartens and day nurseries for working mothers. They set up playgrounds and ran vacation schools to keep children occupied during the summer months; they conducted medical inspections of children at schools and supported education around civics and ethics; they worked to make white schools in the South attractive and comfortable. Speakers representing various regions detailed the work on the coasts and in the heartland, in the upper Midwest, and the Southwest.

In 1908, reflecting clubwomen's influence on curriculum, Mrs. O. Shepard Barnum, of the Cumnock School in Los Angeles, pointed up the new demands on society that necessitated a move from the three R's to the three H's (training of the head, hand, and heart), the three C's (character, conduct, and citizenship), and the three B's ("the supplying of body, brains, and bringing-up"). Barnum thereby revealed the three-pronged and overlapping interests of women's organizations: the functional—or practical—school curriculum, health, and civic education. The functional curriculum had a moral dimension for women's club leaders in that it held the possibility to teach young citizens the proper morals by emphasizing parenthood over future employment. Clubwomen's health reform efforts had the most significant impact on the school curriculum, including health inspections, better-ventilated schools, and school lunches. A multitude of women's clubs put into place drinking fountains, school nurses, and playgrounds, since hygiene was of particular concern to limit the spread of disease. Like those of many women's clubs around the nation, these curricular reforms involved updating or even installing school plumbing. For example, many women's clubs accomplished what one club in Illinois reported: that it had introduced "bubble fountains and proper toilets for boys" in the early 1900s.[70]

In 1910 the DWO became the Department of School Patrons (DSP) in an effort to be more inclusive in its membership. Moreover, since the goal of organized educational work was "effective citizenship"—of young people in schools as well as the members of the voluntary organizations—it necessitated the inclusion of men. By this time, the NEA had come to support vocational education as differentiated instruction, something the clubwomen of the new department promoted. There was a noticeable change in the way meetings were run after this point, as the role of speaker was reserved for men and women professional educators, supplemented with the lengthy reports of the DSP officers, the leaders of women's voluntary organizations. The rhetorical shift did not effect an actual transformation regarding the name change, however, as the DSP continued to be run by volunteer and professional women and continued to represent several major national women's associations.[71]

The NCM-PTA continued to be central to the running of the Department of School Patrons. Cora Bright of Illinois—an officer with the National PTA—was its secretary. The DSP's leaders had, by this time, honed their ability to communicate with and coordinate the activities of the state-level organizations of the representative women's associations. At each annual meeting, the president gave an overview of the work of the DSP state-by-state, and each time the report became longer, even though some state committees did not submit reports. In Little Rock, Arkansas, women's organizations published articles on the educational needs of the state that they then circulated through the newspapers. In California, organized women worked for teachers' pensions, school bond issues, and the right for school boards to select superintendents. In Iowa, women's clubs started school gardens, organized parent-teacher associations, and "Introduced some industrial work in twenty-four schools." In New Jersey, women volunteers surveyed legislative matters regarding education, child labor, and juvenile court procedures. The work was well coordinated and efficient, since it was staffed by a representation of women volunteers from around the country who were invested in school reform work and who believed in the cause of public education to shape future citizens. Much of these efforts, however, required organized women's input on and support of financial issues. Economic conditions were a main reason women should support manual training, according to speaker Helen Grenfell, since it met "the needs of the majority."[72]

NEA leaders acknowledged the power of women volunteers in 1910 when the president of the association, Ella Flagg Young, approached the Department of School Patrons for help with considering how the network of organized women could be put to work on school financing. Young, an experienced teacher and administrator who held a doctorate from the University of Chicago, was serving as the superintendent of Chicago's public schools at the time. She was known for her support of teachers having a greater role in educational and administrative decisions, and she believed deeply in democratic decision making.[73] Given this, Young supported the efforts of teachers and organized women. Perhaps she took to heart DSP president Mrs. O. Shepard Barnum's comment the previous year that educational reform from the top was "painfully slow" and that the Department of School Patrons was the best means by which educational reform would pass from the NEA "mountain top to the valley and the plains."[74] Responding to Young's request, the DSP created a school revenue committee with NCM-PTA leader Helen Hefferan serving as its president. Within a year's time, the committee prepared a survey to gauge the public's involvement with school funding. Then, the DSP mailed the survey to school superintendents to get their input on how school revenue operated and how it was distributed in their states. The committee on school revenue prepared a summary and handbook report that was distributed at the 1911 annual meeting.[75]

Almost immediately, the women's efforts were met with success. Illinois clubwomen, along with the State Teachers' Association, successfully waged a campaign to quadruple annual school appropriations. They were able to accomplish this feat by urging all parent-teacher associations and women's clubs in the state to write their legislators and the Committee on Appropriations. Volunteer and professional united by taking the matter to the House and Senate committees in that state. The successful campaign was held up as exemplary at that year's DSP meeting, as Hefferan suggested other states take up similar work. The State Superintendent of Public Instruction in Illinois, Francis G. Blair, rallied around the DSP's efforts and supported a campaign "to create sentiment among school patrons, taxpayers, and lawmakers."[76]

During this time, white women's organized efforts to improve the nation's schools reached their apex. The Department of School Patrons had expanded by organizing two committees to coordinate its work, school revenue and health, in 1913, and added a committee on rural schools the following year. Minnesota's report from 1911 is reflective of efforts around the country:

> The individual drinking-cup, sanitary soap, and sanitary towels have appeared in our schools during this year. The temperature of our schoolrooms, which used to be kept dangerously high in the cold Minnesota winters, has been lowered, and fresh air from window and doors substituted for the air supposed to be made pure by ventilating systems. The medical inspector and school nurse are now a part of our school system. Playgrounds are multiplying. . . . The school census has been taken by members of women's clubs and normal students in training. The truant, the backward child, the sick child have been discovered and relief has been undertaken. The social assistance rendered in quiet fashion by the best women in the community to young adolescent boys and girls without social opportunity, has been the result of circulars sent out through the clubs.[77]

Women's organized efforts showed no sign of abating during the years of great activity among school professionals and volunteers in regard to public education and the curriculum. Moreover, true to their goals of institutionalizing reforms, clubwomen around the nation built in their obsolescence as they turned to new projects. DSP reports document these successes, such as the vacation schools that were begun in Chicago in the 1890s by the woman's club and turned over in 1911 to the board of education. And, in Minnesota in 1910, the medical inspector and nurse initiated by the NCM-PTA were taken over by the school system to maintain. The work continued through 1916 as the clinics started by the NCM-PTA in California were assumed by the schools. School meals, offered as early as the 1890s, expanded to the extent that by 1913, three dozen cities had meal services, each one having been initiated by clubwomen through the DSP. In general, by the time the United States entered World War I in 1917, schools took over the meal service, and at this time over one hundred cities had meals for working- and lower-class children. Even as municipalities took on the role of financing the meals, women volunteers continued to help administer them. With nurses, health checkups, lunches, and other innovations initiated by nonprofessional women and managed by school districts, the purpose and function of schools was shaped.[78]

By 1915 the DSP decided the state-by-state accomplishments should include discussions of the particular national organization that carried out the reform, because it made more sense to use the networks already in place within each separate organization than to create additional administrative layers in the DSP. The PTA in Delaware held lectures and demonstrations on nursing and domestic science; the Council of Jewish Women in Kentucky "completely metamorphosed" a rural school; and the GFWC in Maine improved health conditions in and through the schools. Given this, the reports became length-ier, for each state-by-state account now included the accomplishments of the women's organizations for each state. The reports consumed so much time during NEA sessions that DSP president Mrs. O. Shepard Barnum remarked in 1912, "It has proved impossible this year to incorporate or even to indicate in this summary all the many and full reports received." She did attempt to give an overview, nonetheless, but she also directed those attending to read the GFWC Education Department reports for the biennial period 1910–12.[79]

As the DSP provided the means to coordinate national efforts in educa-tional reforms, it legitimized women's volunteer work in schools through their networks. As long as clubwomen worked with and through the NEA, accusa-tions that they were meddlers were few and far between and were more the result of local clashes between volunteer and professional. In many instances, professional and volunteer dovetailed their efforts. Local networks, mimicking the relationship of women's national organizations to the NEA, were often sub-sumed under state departments of education. Such was the case in Kentucky, when in 1911 the state's school improvement leagues—the typical name for parent-teacher associations in the South—were placed under the control of the Kentucky State Department of Education. A clubwoman was then hired to organize and supervise the leagues as a paid officer. In this instance, as in others around the South, the school improvement league representative was funded in part by the Southern Education Board.[80]

In addition to the lengthy reports on the accomplishments of women vol-unteers, another important development was noted at NEA annual meetings: the need for parent-teacher associations in all communities. NCM-PTA lead-ers, therefore, used their position in the DSP to build the organization by establishing local units around the country. While undertaking the work of the coordinated women's associations, they encouraged the founding of new local clubs among a variety of women, including women with grown children and immigrant women. In other words, as the NCM-PTA enacted reforms through the NEA Department, it worked to ensure the stability of its own organization by gaining affiliated local and state units. In 1909 a speaker at the Department of School Patrons meeting, Mrs. Henry J. Hersey of the Colorado Congress of Parents and Teachers, explained that the NCM-PTA was coordinating the efforts of local units in thirty-two states, even though the organization had only half that number of affiliated state units. By 1915 the campaign to build the NCM-PTA through the NEA Department of School Patrons had become so successful that the organization claimed thirty-three state units. As a result, it withdrew for a time from membership in the DSP. In 1915 no NCM-PTA leader served as a DSP officer, a first since the department was organized in 1907. Beginning in 1916 NCM-PTA representation was dropped from the minutes of Department meetings, even though the work of reforming schools and curricula was still being carried out by the organization and the DSP.[81]

The NCM-PTA did not rejoin the DSP until 1918, the year after the United States entered World War I. It was an act of patriotism, since at this time the schools took on the work of national defense and preparedness. Furthermore, given the fact that the U.S. Congress had organized women's organizations under the Woman's Committee of the Council of National Defense, the PTA would have been brought into the fold anyway. One speaker remarked on the importance of organized women in the war effort, outlining that "Many additional school activities must be undertaken on a large scale as preparedness measures." These activities were the same as before—school gardens, physical education, vacation schools, the support of vocational education—but had the added urgency of helping the nation during the war. Again, DSP leaders reiterated the importance of their networks and reminded school professionals of their ability to spread ideas and to mobilize human and material resources. One speaker went so far as to point out that she had "heard no mention of ways and means for securing adequate funds for patriotic work except here in the Department of School Patrons." Clubwomen maintained that between the research training of the members of the Association for Collegiate Alumnae and the Southern Association of College Women and the far-reaching networks of the NCM-PTA, GFWC, and Council of Jewish Women, the nation's war needs could be met.[82]

After the war, the Department of School Patrons changed radically as the school's relationship to the home changed. Many of the changes brought about by clubwomen's Progressive-era reforms were either institutionalized in schools or disappeared, such as the school as social center. Moreover, the war brought an end to Progressive-era reform fervor. From that point on, only professional educators served as speakers at annual meetings of the DSP. Volunteer women were given less autonomy, and by 1920 only one officer was chosen to head the Department of School Patrons. Within two years the NEA would decide to discontinue the DSP. At this time, the PTA had a membership of over 400,000, while the GFWC had approximately 420,000 members. Even though the NEA had grown exponentially, from 8,400 members in 1917 to 118,000 members in 1922, it was still markedly smaller than the major women's associations. A rhetorical shift connoted a change in relationship between volunteer and professional, as the focus became cooperation between home and school. No longer were women's club leaders championing their organizations' far-reaching powers; instead speakers referred to the role of organized women in helping professional educators. Also gone were the lengthy reports of organized women's efforts in securing health, curricular, and financial reforms in education.[83]

In a final act of breaking with women volunteers, the NEA in 1922 disbanded the Department of School Patrons.[84] The women's associations that composed the Department continued nonetheless and even collaborated through other groups, such as the Woman's Joint Congressional Committee, which was created to institutionalize women's lobbying activities.[85] Several factors accounted for the changed relationship between organized women volunteers and professional educators. In large part, America after the war was a different place. Also, with the passage of the Nineteenth Amendment in 1920, women's lives changed drastically, as did their reform work; such gender-segregated activities had lost their appeal. Women having won the vote, their efforts in voluntary organizations were less urgent as additional outlets for political work became available to them, even though a female voting bloc did not materialize as expected. The maternalist line of reasoning that fueled municipal housekeeping became outdated as an ideological framework as more politically radical women turned to other justifications for their work in the public arena. Sheila Rothman claims that white, middle-class women became disillusioned with social reform in the post–World War I period, as a result of an emphasis on romantic marriage over motherhood as a uniting ideology and the fact that the reforms of the Progressive era did not "enhance opportunities for women in structural ways."[86] Finally, municipal and state governments did exactly what organized women wanted them to do: they assumed the work that the women had begun, thereby institutionalizing it into the school curriculum and administrative structure.

However, the end had not come to women's community organizing on behalf of public education; on the contrary, this was just the beginning. This work paralleled the rise of activity among civic voluntary organizations through the 1960s.[87] After Hannah Kent Schoff stepped down in 1920, women's voluntary activism in public education became less intrusive in school affairs and was subsumed under the direction of the NCM-PTA. Schoff saw her association grow from eight state units and a little over a thousand members in 1902 to thirty-seven state affiliates and 189,202 members by the time she left office in 1920. She helped remake the organization from a small, national body to a thriving federation with a solid footing in public education. In the mid-1920s, President Margaretta Willis Reeve (1923–28) directed the association to defer to the professional authority of school administrators and to embrace the language of cooperation. As a reflection of this transformation, the organization became the National Congress of Parents and Teachers, or NCPT, in 1924. By the mid-1920s the association had three-quarters of a million members, and just five years later, by 1930, 1.5 million members. It had, by then, surpassed the GFWC's 800,000 members.[88]

"This work above all others has seemed to me best worth doing. I started out as part of a little army—I march now with a great and growing one," recalled Cora C. Bright, the Illinois organizer who had been active in the Department of School Patrons. Legions of women organizers like Bright took up their work with a zeal that was unrivaled in voluntary organizations dedicated to the cause of public education. Women such as Bright read the books recommended by the NCPT and hence became well versed in the latest thinking on education. They traveled their states and regions, presenting to school administrators and normal school graduates the plea for a parent-teacher association in every school. For Bright and tens of thousands of organized white women, the early twentieth century was a time of building the schools through their associational alliances, while at the same time these alliances established an educational institution. The very public ascent of the National Congress of Mothers, along with the GFWC's commitment to public education, was responsible for the groundswell of interest among women's associations in public education in the 1890s. The Mothers' Congress aided the GFWC in making schooling a priority for women's organizations. Parent-teacher groups and mothers' clubs were organized again and again in towns, cities, and rural areas around the country in the early decades of the twentieth century. Many of them affiliated with a national organization, usually the GFWC or PTA, while in many instances women held multiple memberships.[89]

By attending national meetings, clubwomen learned about the latest research and practice from experts, often other women. Muncy argues that because of male administrators, women teachers could not cultivate full professional autonomy. Therefore, they united with other women. Clubwomen and women teachers returned home from conventions and formed home-school organizations and created school departments within their existing women's or mothers' clubs, often to apply new educational theories, establish kindergartens, set up playgrounds, and help raise money for new school buildings. Women who could not attend national and regional meetings were informed by reading lists and periodicals shared at their regular meetings by those who had made the journey. The web of relations was tightly woven as the ideology, leadership, and goals of the major women's associations overlapped.[90]

As the educational activities of the GFWC and other women's associations dwindled through the 1920s, the PTA emerged as the major educational organization in the nation. It had established its infrastructure by uniting with other women's organizations and by using the opportunity it had as an affiliate of the NEA to create its own local and state units. The PTA thereby set a solid foundation that subsequently assured its continuation as a voluntary organization linked with the public schools after the other women's organizations left this work behind. Perhaps most importantly, the PTA retained a working relationship with the NEA after the demise of the DSP, but it was a relationship in which the women's organization had to remain in its place. Margaretta Willis Reeve appeared on the NEA program during her administration, articulating the role of the PTA and its relationship to education professionals, and emphasizing the common refrain of cooperation between home and school. The proximity of the two headquarters supported an ongoing working relationship, since the PTA in 1920 sold the Washington, DC, headquarters it had purchased in 1918 and rented an office in the NEA building until 1938.[91]

However, another, perhaps more subtle transformation had taken place in the PTA from 1897 to 1924. What originated as an association that would not discriminate based on race became, by the 1920s, an organization that barred black associations from its membership in practice. Faced with the contradiction of its commitment to democratic principles through public education and on behalf of children and families, the PTA helped found a segregated association for its growing black membership. Therefore, the 1920s would prove to be a pivotal time for the National PTA, as its segregated counterpart, the National Congress of Colored Parents and Teachers, was organized. The founding of a black PTA was not carried out entirely by white leaders, because a local-level, grassroots movement to organize parent-teacher associations in segregated schools had begun to take place around the South beginning in the 1890s.

CHAPTER 2

"To Work More Effectively and Gain Better Leadership Experience"

The Founding of the National Congress of Colored Parents and Teachers

IN HER address at the National Congress of Mothers' first meeting in 1897, activist and writer Frances Ellen Watkins Harper appealed to the elite white women to support education for African Americans.

> I do not ask any special favor for the colored mother. . . . But I do ask you to give what we cannot touch ·with our hands, the ideal things that can not be measured with a line nor weighed in a balance. . . . Trample, if you will, on our bodies, but do not crush out self-respect from our souls. If you want us to act as women, treat us as women.

Citing thirty years of emancipation from slavery and the paltry gains made in the schooling of freedpeople, Harper implored her audience to provide for the education of the young black women working as domestic servants in their homes. She argued, "A young girl trained as a kindergarten pupil might be of great value to a young mother as a useful assistant in the work of child-rearing." Harper was a powerful presence, a seventy-one-year-old writer and leader who had dedicated her life to temperance and other moral issues from the postbellum years into the twentieth century. Harper's speech was a rare attempt by a black woman to address the racism of whites in a public forum, but any suggestion of reproach was palliated by the acceptance given her by the Mothers' Congress. She was viewed by PTA leaders as nonthreatening and sympathetic to the ideals of the association: child welfare and parent educa-tion. Her presence was intended to reinforce the NCM's position that it would be open "to all mankind and to all womankind, regardless of race, color, or condition." Newspapers reported the next day that Harper's "address was liberally applauded."[1]

Another reason Frances Harper was the perfect choice to speak at the PTA's first gathering is that she was a member of the National Association of Colored Women (NACW), which was organized in 1896 by black clubwomen who were barred from membership in the General Federation of Women's Clubs (GFWC). As I demonstrate in the previous chapter, the PTA relied on an existing network of women's clubs and associations to establish a national organization. The ability to tap into this network—or multiple networks—of women enabled white PTA leaders to disseminate their ideas rapidly and efficiently in order to build a membership base, but the problem of how to enlist black women remained. Despite the racially inclusive policy that was pronounced at the founding meeting of the Mothers' Congress, the elite white Board of Managers could not ever, in the context of the Jim Crow era, conceive of working side-by-side with black women. Moreover, attempts at being racially inclusive were thwarted by the practice of segregation within the organization over time. The Supreme Court's decision in *Plessy v. Ferguson* solidified the segregation of the races in 1896, and Jim Crow laws were firmly codified that decade. By the early 1920s the white PTA began to deny membership to any local club that was affiliated with a segregated school. The organization, for the first several decades of its existence, attempted to manage black women through available networks and eventually succeeded in helping coordinate the founding of a segregated black association with a parallel structure of local, state, and national units. In large part, the PTA accomplished this by working with the leadership of the National Association of Colored Women (NACW).[2]

With or without white oversight, however, an analogous and independent movement to organize black parent-teacher associations emerged in the 1890s in the American South. During the Progressive era educated black women—working within a long tradition of clubs and benevolent societies since the early nineteenth century—began to establish parent-teacher groups and school improvement societies. Black women's organizations predated those of white women, as they were the first to organize on behalf of self- and community improvement in the 1830s. Given that African Americans led the campaign for public education during Reconstruction, community-school groups in the late nineteenth century were a natural evolution of such events. These efforts at promoting education and building schools were part of a collective consciousness of African Americans who believed that their status depended on their relationship with the larger group.[3]

When the NACW was founded in 1896, it began to unite the work of local-level school improvement groups with a network of black women leaders, becoming a nationally coordinated effort to support schools and to undertake reform work through a federated organization. After having been barred from membership in the GFWC, middle-class black women organized the NACW and, like the Congress of Mothers, proclaimed, "we are not drawing the color line." Given that the original purposes of the NACW were "to elevate and dignify colored American womanhood" and to "foster 'moral, mental, and material progress,'" the organization's leaders placed a special emphasis on education.[4] The NACW's focus on education was reflective of the interests of the majority of its founding members who were teachers, but also reveals how black clubwomen were raised and educated with a sense of mutual obligation among other clubwomen, their families, and the wider community.[5]

In this chapter I investigate the origins of the black PTA, the National Congress of Colored Parents and Teachers (NCCPT), and reveal how the federation developed from the ground up, in contrast to the white PTA. Its genesis can be located in at least several different movements for black education in the South in the late nineteenth and early twentieth centuries, two of which developed translocal networks of parent-teacher associations. One major force was the club organizing of the NACW, and another was a group of teachers, the Jeanes supervising teachers, funded by white philanthropists, who worked across the South to establish rural schools. These two major efforts were supported by the white PTA leadership, who encouraged black women to organize a separate association but did not work alongside them. However, black women's volunteer efforts in schools were just as widely networked as white women's through churches and voluntary associations, though these networks were not always visible to the wider public. Also, black women's club organizing was deeply committed to racial uplift. The charge to create parent-teacher associations was that of black teachers who, by virtue of their race and profession, had a lengthy list of responsibilities that extended beyond the school walls and out into the communities in which they worked.[6]

Thus the differences between black and white clubwomen's approaches to school reform work were grounded in their contrasting ideologies of womanhood and motherhood. As I demonstrate in the previous chapter, white women extended motherhood from their own homes out to municipalities in order to exert moral influence over their own and other people's children. The distinction with black women's mothering is that while it, too, sought to exert moral influence on others, it had the additional purpose of protecting black children in a racist world. As Paula Giddings argues, for African American women "the home [and its ideological extension to the community] was not so much a refuge from the outside world as a bulwark to secure one's passage through it." Even more so than white women, middle-class black clubwomen made the home the center of social reform as they fought to challenge the stereotype of the black woman as immoral. It was this stereotype of the black woman that Frances Harper challenged at the first Mothers' Congress when she asked that black women be treated as *women* first, emphasizing the unity women shared around gender rather than the chasm between them called race.[7]

Molly Ladd-Taylor's assertion that "maternalist politics were necessarily racial politics" is evidenced in the white PTA's claims that it would not discriminate, because all women were mothers first, a condition that in theory united them across racial and ethnic barriers. However, the social and political climate at the turn of the twentieth century necessarily held that women of color would not be treated as equals. While black women activists drew on the language of motherhood, they cannot be considered maternalists, because they generally rejected the notion that all women were intended for motherhood. Instead, black clubwomen believed that they should not be forced into traditional roles, and they often spoke out on this in club publications, even challenging the limited expectations of them by black men. Black women led starkly different lives with regard to labor, employment, child rearing, and waged and unwaged labor, and these differences shaped their work in schools and communities.[8] Nevertheless, clubwomen such as Frances Harper used the language of maternalism to appeal to the National Congress of Mothers and other white women's groups. Another major difference between the social reform work of black and white clubwomen was that they had different attitudes toward the poor. White women were more likely to differentiate the worthy from the unworthy poor, while black women's views of class and poverty favored environmental factors, not birth or previous experience. In fact, black clubwomen often bridged class barriers by taking up issues that affected the poor, working mothers, and tenant farmers. Race and prejudice united black women across these differences, and this contrasting perspective gave black clubwomen a different approach to working with lower-class women and children, which carried over to community-school organizing in the South.[9]

During the first three decades of its existence, the PTA struggled with the challenge of remaining true to its inclusive policy in a racist and segregated society. At the 1901 annual meeting in Des Moines, white PTA leaders announced that "every mother identified with the Congress, rich or poor, black or white, is welcomed to attend this reception, her tiny badge of pink and blue being her credential of admission."[10] Yet, despite these pronouncements, local units remained segregated with few exceptions, and these examples were reflective of working relationships, tradition, and Jim Crow laws in communities around the country.[11] Beyond the South, a handful of white clubs included black members but still practiced the custom of segregation at their meetings. The state PTA units for Ohio and Tennessee, for example, seated

African American members at separate banquet tables and in segregated sections of gathering spaces during state and regional conventions. Only rarely did black and white clubs join together. The leaders of the Annie Murray Club, for instance, the only African American women's club in Des Moines, occasionally joined efforts with the white Iowa Congress of Mothers.[12] A half-century later, PTA historians Harry and Bonaro Overstreet defended the PTA's segregationist practices, claiming societal pressures thwarted organizers' efforts to be inclusive: "the Congress did not operate in a social vacuum; it operated in a society that, at certain times and in certain places, has drawn racial lines." However, segregation did not always come from white resistance. In many instances, black PTA members did not wish to work alongside white women, because they wished to manage the education of African American children.[13]

James D. Anderson argues that rural blacks built a network of segregated schools in the South between 1900 and 1935 with their own resources since they received little to no help from state and local governments. Concomitantly, a black teaching force was trained during these years, with the largest growth occurring between 1920 and 1930. Therefore, it is no coincidence that the development of the National Congress of Colored Parents and Teachers marched alongside the advancement of black schooling and the development of a black teaching cadre in the South. As various school improvement societies and parent-teacher associations became increasingly linked to one another within and across state lines, forming part of the institutional infrastructure of segregated schools, schoolhouses were built and curricula put into place by teachers and volunteers.[14]

After three decades of local work on behalf of public education, the National Congress of Colored Parents and Teachers was organized in 1926 by black teachers, clubwomen, and school leaders. The existing scholarship has overlooked the role of widespread voluntary groups of African Americans in carrying out this task; in fact, a growing network of black parent-teacher associations was integral to the development of a school system for African Americans in the South and unified by a political agenda to promote education for black children and a liberal arts curriculum. In contrast to white clubwomen's extensive school reform efforts, which supported the state in controlling the lives of schoolchildren, black clubwomen's reform efforts did not have the same political influence. In other words, black women's efforts often operated in opposition to state control and other forces that sought to direct black education and to implement the Hampton-Tuskegee, or industrial, model of curriculum. Nonetheless, the struggles over the school curriculum in segregated schools are not easily parsed between liberal arts and industrial education. Homemakers' clubs, an important philanthropic initiative that taught agricultural skills to rural African Americans, and that supported the development of the black PTA, were generally embraced by black communities in the South.

The existence and types of parent-teacher organizations in the segregated schools of the South challenge the central interpretation in the research on the history of the relationship between parents and schools. The cooperation-conflict dualism was virtually nonexistent in the early years of PTA organizing in segregated schools because black teachers enlisted community members in the endeavor to build schools. Moreover, these same educators organized and led local parent-teacher associations and school improvement societies, so the friction between professional and lay constituencies was muted for the first several decades of the twentieth century. The typical tensions between white parents and teachers during this era arose out of different approaches to child rearing and conflicting opinions over who had responsibility for education. However, this friction did not exist for segregated schools, because black educators and parents were united—usually in opposition to white citizens and school board members—in securing educational opportunities for youth, and black teachers were respected as community leaders. Not only were black educators and community leaders often working at odds with whites; they were also beholden to them: virtually all black educators, from rural teachers to college presidents, were appointed by whites during this era. Thus, the most salient difference among African American citizens in the drive to build schools and organize curricula was socioeconomic class, which was most evident in the relationship between black clubwomen and teachers and the community members they enlisted to build a system of schools.[15]

The Origins of Black School-Community Groups

The post-Reconstruction era, also called the time of the New South, saw a regression in the rights of African Americans and their subjugation under white supremacy. Historian C. Vann Woodward remarks that during this period the per-capita wealth of the South lagged significantly behind that of the North. The distribution of health, education, and a comfortable standard of living was uneven between the South and the rest of the country and even within the South itself. Inequities were perhaps most pronounced in the schools for black children. Blacks in rural areas, unlike the working classes elsewhere in America, received little support for schooling from state and local governments. Although the lack of funds and the need for child labor allowed for a shorter school year, education consistently remained a priority in black communities in the South. After having been denied access to literacy and education because of slavery, the freedpeoples saw education as both an expression of freedom and a way to guard themselves against deception and manipulation. Through decades of oppression following Reconstruction, Southern African Americans rallied around the need to provide education for their young in the hopes that it would lead to release from oppressive conditions as well as to economic stability and security. Political leaders as well as clubwomen viewed education as the means to racial equality and the development of African Americans' full potential. Nonetheless, despite this valuing of education there remained, by the end of the nineteenth century, too few schools in the South; two-thirds of the school-aged population did not have access to free, public education.[16]

Many whites in the South were opposed to education for African Americans out of fear that with it would come their greater political and economic power. Even among those whites who supported education a tension existed; while education would make African Americans better citizens and workers, it held the potential to educate them out of their places in the socioeconomic and racial hierarchies. Sociologist Hortense Powdermaker, conducting a study of a town in Mississippi in the 1930s, documented a commonly held belief among white Southerners on the inadequacy of either position: "If you educate the [Negroes], you ruin the South; if you don't educate them, you ruin it too."[17]

Overall, the development of schools in the South—for blacks and whites—lagged behind the rest of the nation. It was not until the first three decades of the twentieth century that school systems were developed, although the resources allotted to segregated schools were paltry. African Americans carried the burden of double taxation for public schools, wherein their funds went primarily to white schools, after which they dug deeper into nearly empty pockets to pay for schools for their own children. In addition to monetary contributions, community members and teachers provided labor and materials to improve schools and educational resources. These efforts sought to support and sustain schools that were too few in number according to black educational and political leaders. Furthermore, the separate schools for African Americans suffered in virtually every way, with the exception of community spirit. School terms were shorter, educational resources and materials were outdated or, worse yet, scarce, and physical plants suffered for proper ventilation and lighting.[18]

In addition to the drive for education from within black communities, white philanthropists contributed to the development of a system of segregated schools. In 1900 the creation of the General Education Board (GEB) and Southern Educational Board (SEB) created a virtual monopoly over the development of segregated schools in the South. The GEB, a consortium of philanthropists, and the SEB, composed of Southern white male educators, were created to fund and oversee the development of schools and the implementation of a curriculum for African Americans in the South. While the SEB focused on studying and disseminating industrial education for blacks, the GEB was its funding machine. Originally set up by John D. Rockefeller, Sr., in 1901 with an endowment of $1 million in 1902, the GEB's purse grew to a staggering $53 million by 1909 with supplementary funding. By 1929 Rockefeller had contributed over $129 million to the Board, which was used to establish rural one-room schools, county training schools, and urban public high schools around the South.[19]

Northern philanthropists and other white educational leaders resolved that if education was to come to the black community in the South, it would emphasize an industrial curriculum and prepare African Americans for manual labor. Therefore, schools funded by white philanthropists were supposed to have an industrial curriculum, but Anderson argues that this rarely was the case, as black community members resisted the industrial model being imposed on them and as segregated schools embraced liberal arts curricula that included black history. Likewise, many black women's clubs studied African American literature and history, which they sought to bring to segregated schools. The shaping of the school curriculum also was aided by the nascent networks of black professional educators, who shared notions about teaching black history and the liberal arts. Oftentimes, however, vocational and liberal arts education were not either-or but both-and propositions for educators and citizens who wished to give their children every opportunity for success.[20]

In characterizing the curriculum debates in black education of this era, historians frequently draw on the opposing stances of Booker T. Washington and W. E. B. Du Bois. Yet, in practice, these polar views were often melded together. Washington, a former slave and a principal at Tuskegee Institute, was perhaps the most well-known African American public figure at the turn of the twentieth century. He viewed education in manual labor for work as the precursor to economic stability and advancement, a position that white philanthropists and business leaders embraced. Harvard-educated scholar and sociologist W. E. B. Du Bois favored education in the liberal arts for the "talented tenth," or teachers, who would then lead the rest of the race. Each philosophy took root in educational institutions during the period in a variety of ways, and often the two were combined. Institutions emphasizing the liberal arts almost always included some measure of vocational education, while schools such as Tuskegee, even though their emphasis was on manual training at least until the 1920s, incorporated the liberal arts, but with vocational ends in mind.[21]

With the development of segregated schools in scattered local areas in the South came the rise of black school-community groups beginning in the

1890s, primarily as a result of the efforts of teachers and other educational leaders. These endeavors often relied on the support of black professional and voluntary associations, such as the local and state branches of the National Association for Colored Women and the National Association for Teachers in Colored Schools. Another push for the development of black parent-teacher associations came from white philanthropy, which channeled money through the GEB to support segregated schools. In most instances, the teachers of those schools organized school improvement societies and other types of parent-teacher groups. Therefore, white philanthropists and school administrators unwittingly aided in the establishment of networks of parent-teacher associations across the South by funding black teachers' efforts in building schools, thereby strengthening their networks.[22]

"In Union Is Strength": The National Association of Colored Women

One of the major factors that supported the development of the black parent-teacher movement in the late nineteenth century was the founding of the National Association of Colored Women. With education at the center of its program, the NACW also offered a national network to support the spread of ideas and coordinate the efforts of local-level clubs. The NACW emerged as a federated association shortly after the creation of the GFWC (1890) but just before the PTA (1897) and, like them, experienced a significant increase in membership in its first three decades. However, by the 1920s the PTA's membership far surpassed that of the GFWC and NACW (see figure 2.1). As might be expected, the leadership and membership of the two white associations overlapped a great deal, while there was virtually no crossover between white and black association membership. Nonetheless, the leaders of each of these three organizations spoke on occasion at the annual meetings of the other two. Even though the leaders of the major women's organizations worked along the same lines in the Progressive spirit for a better society, racial relations and tensions between and among women club leaders played out on a national stage.

In July 1895, Josephine St. Pierre Ruffin, a community leader and clubwoman, convened a meeting in Boston to organize the Afro-American Federation of Colored Women. A year later, the organization joined forces with the Colored Women's League of Washington, DC, to create a new entity, the NACW. Activist and educator Mary Church Terrell became its first president. The founding leaders of the association wanted, in part, to carry out what they called "human service work," independent of white women's associations and the Baptist church, through which many middle-class black women were

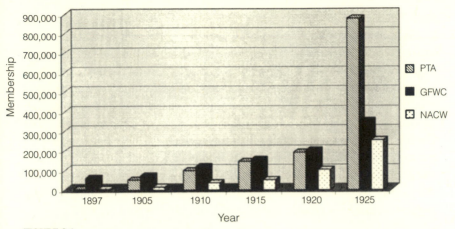

FIGURE 2.1

Comparison of PTA membership data, 1897–1925. (*Sources:* PTA and GFWC data from Civic Engagement Project, Harvard University, under the direction of Theda Skocpol and Marshall Ganz, in author's possession; NACW data from Elizabeth Lindsay Davis, *Lifting as We Climb*, xvii)

linked. This would free them from the attempts at subordination by men in the Baptist convention, even though during this period black Baptist women continued to work through the convention, broadening its public division and making it, as Evelyn Brooks Higginbotham argues, "the most powerful institution of racial self-help in the African American community."[23]

Even though black clubwomen founded the NACW as a reaction to having been barred from the GFWC, the organization was not an emulation of the white women's club movement, nor did black women's reform efforts draw on the same motivations as white women. Black women had been raised by families and in communities that taught them to use their education in socially responsible ways; unlike white women they were prepared for lives of activism. In addition to municipal housekeeping, their activism focused on strategies of resistance to assaults on black men, women, and children. Chicagoan Fannie Barrier Williams outlined the central difference between white and black women's clubs at the time by explaining, "The club movement among colored women reaches into the sub-condition of the entire race. . . . [It is] the struggle of an enlightened conscience against the whole brood of social miseries, born out of the stress and pain of a hated past." The leaders of the NACW were an exceptional group of college-educated black women who spread middle-class values among the masses as they generated financial support for community institutions and their educational and social service programs. In addition to working for others, and unlike white women community reformers, black women were also working for themselves. Knowing that they were judged by whites who made little distinction between lower- and middle-class blacks,

African American clubwomen knew that in order to gain respect, they needed to improve the economic and social conditions of the entire race. Unfortunately, however, they were sometimes elitist in their work with blacks of lower socioeconomic status, which at times widened the gaps between the classes.[24]

While a sense of *noblesse oblige* in working with the less fortunate gave white and black clubwomen a common bond, the similarities stopped there. The leadership group of black clubwomen stands in contrast to the all-white Congress of Mothers leadership of this time, which was not viewed as radical, or even liberal. They were conservative white women without much recognition in the public eye, except for their being related to well-known men. On their own, or affiliated with the organization, the leadership cadre of white women did not achieve the kind of public recognition that the leaders of the National Congress of Colored Parents and Teachers did. Black PTA leaders were activist women who were used to being in the public eye, for better and for worse. At the very least, the key similarity between the leadership groups of the two branches of the PTA is that they had the approval of male leaders across the political spectrum.

What little crossover there was between the two organizations took place at national, and sometimes state, meetings. At least several NACW leaders served as token representatives of their race at the early annual meetings of the PTA, such as Frances Harper, introduced at the beginning of this chapter, community leader and educator Mary Church Terrell, and kindergarten reformer Anna J. Murray. Attempting to remain true to the inclusive policy of the Mothers' Congress, white PTA leaders invited them as fellow clubwomen and representatives of their race at the rate of about one notable black speaker each year. Harper, Terrell, and Murray agreed to address the white delegates because it was an opportunity to further racial goals by enlisting potential allies. Moreover, each one seized the opportunity to promote her particular agenda.

Mary Eliza Church Terrell, a graduate of Oberlin College, was a suffragist and teacher from Memphis. She later taught at the M Street School in Washington, DC, and served on the District of Columbia Board of Education from 1895 to 1901 and then again from 1906 to 1911, the first black woman to do so. Terrell gave an official welcome from the National Association of Colored Women at the third annual Congress of Mothers in 1899 and used her time on the platform to address racial inequality. She began, "[we] are putting forth every possible effort to discharge our duty [as NACW members] worthily. Into the homes of our people we go preaching the gospel of cleanliness, and morality, cultivation of the mind and the dignity of labor." After having reassured her audience of black women's intentions, she admonished them, "did it ever occur to you, Mothers of the Congress how difficult a thing it is for colored women to inspire their children with hope or offer them an incentive for their best endeavor under the existing conditions of things in this country?" Terrell's call for the equal treatment of children of all races was based on her argument of motherhood uniting all women across racial lines, a central tenet of the NCM leaders' maternalist belief. Therefore, Terrell's message likely came across not as abrasive but as worthy of compassion and support.[25]

A kindergarten educator from Washington, DC, Anna Murray, took the same tack in her talk on "Mothers' Clubs Among Colored Women" at the 1900 meeting of the PTA, by addressing the delegates as compatriots. Murray recognized a fundraising opportunity even though she had been advised by NCM officers not to solicit donations. In her presentation she alluded to the rapid ascension of the NCM organization, stating that she could not bring comparable "reports of systematic organization [of the NACW]. . . . We are too young . . . to have accomplished as much as has been brought here from the different states by the more fortunate women." Revealing black women's appreciation of the inclusive policy of the Mothers' Congress, she noted that the women of the NACW looked favorably on the founding mission of the PTA: "It appealed to us because, as Americans—not as colored women—we believed it struck at the very root fibres of our national character." Murray's time on the podium at the Mothers' Congress was spent kowtowing to the NCM delegates and allying herself, at least in public, with Booker T. Washington's approach to racial relations. Echoing his metaphor, she announced to the crowd that black clubwomen decided "to allow each one to let down her bucket where she could do the most good."[26]

Murray spoke to the parallel work of black women's clubs by detailing the work of the early years of the NACW in regard to education, which focused on initiating mothers' meetings, establishing day nurseries and kindergartens, and opening homes for orphaned children. With each example she showed how a dedicated organizer brought women of a community together and taught them about the work that was to be undertaken, all of which led to the spread of local associations and their eventual coalescing into state units. She shared the examples of Margaret Murray Washington, who developed a network in Alabama, and Laura Titus, who carried out similar work in Virginia, where she had enlisted twenty-five clubs in a new state organization. Prior to her speech, NCM officers had instructed her not to ask for donations for her efforts in establishing more kindergartens for African American children in the District of Columbia, explaining, "those who wished to learn more of [your] special work could seek information from [you] in person." Murray ignored their request and, after she had spent some time establishing the common bonds between white and black clubwomen, spoke in detail about the work of the kindergartens in meeting special "race needs" by teaching character education. She concluded with an announcement that the kindergartens were in dire need of funding and appealed to the white delegates' patriotism and dedication to the principles of freedom in supporting her venture.[27]

Terrell, Murray, and Harper played into the sentiments of the leaders of the Mothers' Congress to obtain a wider public support for their message about race and education. Like many others at the turn of the twentieth century, they recognized the magnitude of the growing association and its influence on public life, so they were willing to appear on the annual meeting programs with other leading public figures. In addition to emphasizing motherhood as a shared bond, African American educational leaders used the PTA's declaration of inclusivity to attempt to forge racial understandings. None of the remarks offended the delegates and leaders of the Mothers' Congress since the black speakers positioned themselves as subordinate to whites, and NCM leaders satisfied their wishes to reach across the racial divide. However, black clubwomen realized that their words fell on deaf ears as they saw clearly the PTA's tokenism, observing that the "WHITE organization had shown little or no interest in NEGRO children although they were sworn to work for child welfare."[28]

It would be facile to characterize these and other black speakers at the white PTA annual meetings as either accommodationist or liberalist, along the lines of Washington and Du Bois. Such categorizations are overly simplistic, do not fully capture black women's hopes in addressing white audiences, and do not account for individuals' changing viewpoints over time. For instance, while Frances Harper's rhetorical tactics in 1897 seemed to echo the accommodating racial politics of Booker T. Washington, she was, in fact, a supporter of liberal arts education for blacks along the lines of W. E. B. Du Bois' "talented tenth." Also, while Mary Church Terrell was far less reserved than Harper in her speech just two years later, her politics at the time favored accommodationism before she moved further to the left as early as 1905. No matter what their beliefs, Terrell and other leaders were not going to let the PTA's policy on race stand without comment. In her address to the PTA, Terrell challenged the organization to remain true to its commitment to being inclusive by raising their own children by the same principles: "May I not ask you then, that when you teach your children the lofty principles this Congress represents, you will make a special effort to train them to be just and broad enough to judge men and women by their intrinsic merit, rather than by the adventitious circumstances of race, or color or creed?" The NCM's inclusive policy gave black women club leaders a modicum of hope that equality in education and of opportunity might be attempted, if not accomplished.[29]

Other than the occasional black speaker at annual meetings and the few instances of integrated PTA gatherings discussed above, little transpired in terms of improved race relations in women's clubs and parent-teacher associations at the turn of the twentieth century. By 1902, in an effort to appease its racist clubs, the GFWC took a firmer stance on segregation in its ranks and announced publicly that it would not include any black women's clubs in its membership. This presented a problem for the PTA, since it was founded on the principle of racial inclusion at the same time it sought to build on the existing network of GFWC local units. As a result, calls for interracial coalitions in the PTA fell silent after 1902, because organizational leaders did not want to jeopardize their partnership with the GFWC. The alliance grew even stronger in the first two decades of the twentieth century as the PTA, GFWC, and other white women's organizations banded together in the Department of Women's Organizations of the National Educational Association to dovetail forces around school reform activities.[30]

However, a small but growing number of black organizations continued to seek membership in the PTA at the local and state levels, challenging leaders with how to include them given variances among state and local laws and practices, particularly in the South. Regional differences tended to dictate local practice. In Delaware black and white clubs generally worked together, while in Indiana and Illinois black members had limited roles in the local units. African American members could join, but did not typically hold leadership positions. In the West, given that the black population was small, there were very few organized black associations. Therefore, black members attended Congress conventions and meetings in Washington and California. The South was an entirely different matter; black and white clubwomen almost never met together. For white PTA leaders who were interested in building racial bridges in the South, the only appropriate way to organize black women was to help create segregated associations, rather than coordinate integrated clubs. To do otherwise would not only be inappropriate; it would risk alienating white members.[31]

After the white PTA's first decade, its leaders expressed an interest in forging a stronger connection with black clubwomen, so they attempted to organize them in ways the GFWC would have found challenging to its politically and regionally diverse membership. In 1908 the PTA endeavored to organize a black national parent-teacher association and gave officer Helen T. Birney, sister-in-law of Alice Birney, the charge of identifying a black clubwoman "who would take the initiative in forming a congress of colored mothers." Helen Birney was deeply involved with both the National Congress leadership and the District of Columbia Congress of Mothers, having served as its president for eleven years. She was known among her peers as an efficient and business-like leader. Because black club leaders distrusted the women of the NCM, they consequently refused the overture and stated their intention to continue to work through the NACW network, explaining, "A colored woman would do a better job organizing the colored mothers of the country." The effort was viewed as a failure by PTA leaders, since no black national organization resulted. However, the white PTA's efforts did help galvanize the development of local-level parent-teacher associations in segregated schools since it offered a model for organizing the communities around the newly forming schools. Most of the work in segregated schools, therefore, found guidance not from the women of the PTA or GFWC but, as black educational and business leaders had wished, through the NACW.[32]

By coordinating extensive work in education at the local level, the NACW served a function that would later be assumed by local and state black PTA units and eventually the National Congress of Colored Parents and Teachers. From its inception in 1896, the organization had maintained a commitment to education and by 1904 created departments for mothers' clubs, kindergartens, and domestic science. Each of the departments, twelve in all, was to carry out its work under an appointed leader and to support the goal of "making a conscientious and untiring effort for race elevation."[33] The educational work of the NACW in its first thirty years challenged the Social Darwinist belief of the turn of the twentieth century that the races progress in an evolutionary manner. Black clubwomen, in considering the progress of civilization as related to their own "perfect womanhood," sought to show that they, too, could reach a higher level of civilization and, ultimately, achieve social equality with whites. NACW leaders and members acknowledged this common assumption of the times, conceding, "no people could reach perfection in sixty years," as their work focused on illiterate parents, mothers who were ignorant and who therefore bred "criminal types," parents without respect for law and order, children without proper recreation, and children who received "no aesthetic training."[34]

In addition to these broader interests in advancing the race, the efforts of local-level women's clubs, black parent-teacher associations, and school improvement societies served local needs and interests. As they did so, the development of the NACW as a federation generally followed the same pattern; women's clubs and parent-teacher associations emerged in local settings, forged state units, and joined the national organization once they achieved a certain measure of success and stability in membership. For example, in Henderson, Kentucky, the Peerless Club was organized in 1904 to "help in the charitable, civic, and religious work of the community." Having enjoyed many successes in its work, in 1908 it joined the state unit, the Kentucky Federation of Colored Women's Clubs, which two years later affiliated with the NACW. Since the Peerless Club had carried out school improvement efforts beginning with its first meeting in 1904, a separate parent-teacher association grew out of the work, as the Douglass Street PTA was organized formally in 1910. It equipped playgrounds for local schools, purchased a high school for African American students, and fed and clothed needy children in the community. The two organizations—the women's club and the parent-teacher association— worked together to improve the community and educational, economic, and social conditions for blacks. The Peerless Club president, Eugenia A. Mundy, reported the group's accomplishments to the NACW: "We have contributed to the tuberculosis hospital, to the child health clinics, to the N.A.A.C.P., and to the Douglass High School Parent-Teacher Association toward the purchase of the first building which was used until the present year." Another central interest for black leaders at this time, civic education and voting, captured the interest of the Douglass Street PTA, which paid for a citizenship course at the high school.[35]

In 1916 women in Wilmington, Delaware, joined the State Federation of Black Women's Clubs in order to carry out their work more efficiently. Through the 1920s they established schools for African American youth and, like clubwomen around the state, successfully lobbied for the passage of a bill to appropriate funding for industrial schools for girls. They also successfully petitioned the City Board of Education for a black nurse for the Wilmington Public Schools. As one club president put it, "The legislative Department is very active and exercises all efforts to see all bills are passed for the protection of women and girls in our racial group." In the early decades of the twentieth century, the Jacksonville, Florida, unit of the NACW engaged in typical women's club work by establishing playgrounds, improving school plants, and placing nurses in the colored schools. More formal curricular endeavors also interested the work of local women's clubs, including civic education, as discussed above, and homemaking and farming skills. These extensive efforts challenge the understanding that black schools fought against an industrial curriculum in favor of the liberal arts (see figure 2.2).[36]

Many women's clubs and parent-teacher associations in segregated schools supported homemaking and other practical curricular activities along with a humanistic course of study to give black youth essential skills for their health and survival during the lean years of the early twentieth century. In a retrospective written in 1932, one member of an NACW-affiliated club noted that her group had been among the first to organize canning clubs among black citizens, that at its peak it had over 46 members, and that its president worked with "white friends" to enlist a "Colored County Canning Demonstrator." Securing the canning demonstrator was significant because it virtually ensured that the network would expand; the charge of the demonstrator was to organize new clubs in her region. The emphasis on homemaking and other practical skills supported the efforts of white philanthropists and the U.S.

FIGURE 2.2

Elementary school band at a Rosenwald school in Stone Mountain, Georgia, n.d. Women's clubs and school improvement associations supplied instruments for music instruction in schools. (*Source:* Photo reprinted with permission from Narvie J. Harris and Dee Taylor, *African-American Education in DeKalb County,* Arcadia Publishing, 1999; http://www.arcadiapublishing.com)

government. Therefore, the commitment by black clubwomen to homemaking education intersected with philanthropic and governmental initiatives to help establish home-school associations and a network of citizens and professionals across the South. As the NACW locals were gradually building a national network, homemakers' clubs were organized with increasing frequency after 1910, part of the growing interest in developing industrial and agricultural education for African Americans in rural areas.[37]

Therefore, the multiple networks of black clubs and associations were not, during this time, very far from white intervention. Many white educational leaders saw the network of the NACW and other groups as means to organize segregated schools and to further the goals of agricultural education. In a November 1913 report, the white State Supervisor of Negro Schools for Kentucky, F. C. Button, noted "three matters of large import to the colored people" in his state to organize black education: the Kentucky Educational Association for Colored Teachers, the Women's Clubs, and the government's farm demonstration project. He remarked on the Educational Association's growing membership and decision to permanently locate itself in Louisville, which offered a couple of advantages. It afforded the association reduced railroad rates and, since it planned to meet the same time as the white association, "they will be able to secure many of the best white speakers for their meetings." White speakers, of course, could promote the industrial and agricultural curriculum and maintain at least a modicum of oversight of the building of black schools. The second network, the NACW's Kentucky branch, representing 102 local clubs, was viewed by Button as a vehicle for education work as well. He reported, "I spoke to them concerning the rural schools and we shall have the influence, which is very large, of this Federation back of us in the work of the colored rural schools."[38]

Button noted correctly the significance of the third effort, the farm demonstration project, that he was expected to help coordinate and report on to the GEB. In the 1910s the GEB disbursed funds to help support agricultural and horticultural training for blacks and had two benefits, according to the U.S. government. First, it would advantage the nation by developing farming skills among and providing food for a rural, poor population. Congress rationalized that the effort would "awaken . . . a more lively, immediate interest in the industrial development of the country generally, and [. . .] change specifically the agricultural condition throughout the land." Next, political and educational leaders believed it provided moral education to a population that needed it, "so as to change and check the present alarming tendency towards city life and excitement." The education of black citizens took place in organized groups, called Homemakers' Clubs, which were managed by white educational leaders who in turn enlisted the help of black teachers. It was a complex endeavor that, although it had the oversight of white educational leaders, was run by black educators who took ownership of the clubs and developed a network of school improvement associations across the South by the late 1910s.[39]

"I Esteem It a Favor to Myself and My Race": The Homemakers' Club Initiative

The GEB and its partner, the SEB, were responsible for funding the separate schools of the South and coordinating the implementation of a curriculum that emphasized industrial training for African Americans. The Rosenwald Schools paid for by the GEB essentially became the system of schools for African Americans in rural areas in the first three decades of the twentieth century, during what Anderson calls the "second crusade for universal common schooling," the first being the efforts of the Reconstruction era. By 1932 nearly five thousand Rosenwald schools had been built with white philanthropic money and black labor, time, and capital. Two of the GEB's other funding initiatives, the Jeanes Supervising Industrial Teachers and Homemakers' Clubs, contributed to the organization of a nascent network of local parent-teacher associations and school improvement societies that later helped form the foundation for the National Congress of Colored Parents and Teachers. The local units of the NACW and the teachers affiliated with the National Association for Teachers in Colored Schools—which had a low membership but was spread across fifteen Southern states at the time—also contributed to this foundation. Therefore, the parent-teacher groups of the newly built schools were not completely disconnected local groups as is often portrayed in the scholarship, but were linked through associational alliances to existing voluntary networks.[40]

In 1908, the General Education Board began to disburse the funds for the Jeanes Supervising Industrial Teachers, previously called the Negro Rural School Fund, which hired black educators to travel around the rural areas of the South, not only to enlist volunteers in building schools but also to promote industrial education and community involvement in the schools. Within two years there were 129 Jeanes teachers across thirteen Southern states, and the majority of them had been trained at Hampton and Tuskegee, which stressed industrial education. Jeanes teachers interpreted their role broadly, both as teachers and as community builders. As one historian put it, "No absolute rules were laid down for Jeanes Supervisors." Their efforts in remote regions resulted in the unintended consequence of a network that promoted lay involvement in the newly constructed separate schools and helped rally community members around education. Most importantly, the Jeanes teachers did not just call on individual parents and citizens; they worked with local teachers in organizing them into home-school groups. As a result, Jeanes teachers honed their own leadership skills, as well as those of rural teachers and community members.[41]

The GEB also strongly supported the creation of citizens' organizations once it assumed responsibility for the Homemakers' Clubs. The clubs had been started by the United States Department of Agriculture through the Office of Farmers' Cooperative Demonstration Work around 1912. At that time the U.S. government initiated Homemakers' Clubs in Kentucky and Virginia, and in Arkansas the following year. In 1914 the Smith-Lever Bill was passed, providing federal money for extension services and agricultural education for the improvement of rural life among blacks and whites. Agricultural education, through initiatives like Smith-Lever, in part sought to preserve the virtues of agrarian life in a rapidly changing industrial and social order in the early twentieth century. The Smith-Lever Act, then, was additional ammunition for philanthropic efforts that promoted industrial education as the most appropriate to prepare African Americans for a subordinate role in the Southern economy and society. At that time, the federal government found it expeditious to hand off the Homemakers' Clubs to the GEB, since they dovetailed with the Board's other projects.[42]

In 1914 the GEB began to send appropriations to Southern state departments of education to hire Homemakers' Club agents—the majority of whom were black women teachers—to travel around the state and establish clubs to teach young men, women, and their mothers farming and food preservation techniques. The state supervisors of Negro education acted as liaisons between the teachers and the GEB and oversaw the project. During the first year the GEB funded them, Homemakers' Clubs formed in six states: Alabama, Arkansas, Georgia, Kentucky, North Carolina, and Virginia. The clubs varied according to region, relying on local needs to determine their foci. For example, they were called "corn clubs," "canning clubs," and "pig clubs," depending on local agricultural and farming emphases. Homemakers' Club agents received specialized training in canning and preserving foods so that they could teach citizens these skills. In many of the participating Southern states the agents attended the well-known Tuskegee summer institutes, which stressed housekeeping, sanitation, and canning. While the club agents sometimes covered their own expenses for these institutes, the GEB paid their tuition in most instances, seeing it as a worthwhile investment.[43]

Homemakers' Clubs among the black population in the South were intended to extend the school day's focus on industrial arts by offering home economics for girls and their mothers and agricultural education for boys.

The idea was similar to the vacation schools in Northern urban areas that occupied young people's free time. Using the club model was an efficient way—according to those directing the program—to organize blacks around common educational goals. It also afforded a way to easily link the movement with other African American organizations in order to promote the model of industrial education. For instance, J. A. Presson, the white state supervisor of Negro schools in Arkansas, directed the Jeanes teachers to exhibit the clubs' wares at meetings of the National Association for Teachers in Colored Schools. Moreover, club work took care of the problem of how to occupy black children during the summer months of a too-short school year; it also enlisted the children's parents in learning about agriculture. Club work emphasized practical education, mirroring the zeitgeist of curriculum reform in the early twentieth century and revealing attitudes toward the intellectual capacity of blacks. For six years the GEB funded Homemakers' Clubs throughout the South, encouraging them to teach rural African Americans to preserve produce, raise livestock, and harvest staple crops such as corn. Club members displayed their products and often sold them to raise money for local schools.[44]

The idea to use the Jeanes teachers as Homemakers' Club agents was first proposed in 1913 by the Arkansas State Supervisor of Negro Education, Leo M. Favrot, as the GEB was assuming responsibility for the clubs. Favrot submitted a "Plan for Broadening the Spheres an[d] Increasing the Utility of the County Industrial Teacher" to the GEB in which he suggested that "Jeanes Fund teachers desiring to do so be made collaborators in farm demonstration, for the purposes of organizing boys' and girls' agricultural clubs." Enlisting the Jeanes teachers helped the school supervisors who were overburdened with work responsibilities, but it also helped the teachers. Being hired as Homemakers' Clubs agents gave the Jeanes teachers summer employment, which allowed them to earn year-round salaries. In most cases it paid them for work they were already doing anyway, since organizing local citizens into clubs predated the initiative.[45]

The Virginia State Supervisor for Negro Schools, Jackson Davis, reported on the vast organizing of Homemakers' Clubs being carried out in the eastern part of the state. In October and November of 1912 he spent about half his time in the office and the rest in the field visiting, among other things, YMCA meetings; attending a "Colored teachers' meeting in Ruthville"; and attending exhibits of the girls' canning clubs in the commonwealth. He reported, "Most of the mothers have also taken up the work and learned to can more kinds of vegetables." About fifteen mothers "testified" at the meeting that they had saved more canned goods than "ever before" and that they had "better things to eat during the winter months."[46] Revealing the challenges of his job in the following month's report, Davis wrote again of his travels and explained,

"It was encouraging to note the progress which these schools [of Henrico County] have made within the last few years, but we found in two school communities considerable prejudice still remaining on the part of the colored patrons against industrial work in the schools." At that time, given Davis's many duties, he appointed Jeanes supervisor Virginia Randolph to "look after his Negro schools" because he did not have time to do so. The trend, in which Jeanes teachers were given increasing responsibility to relieve the load of state educational supervisors, was common among Southern states. With each new responsibility, the Jeanes teachers further developed their leadership and organizational skills.[47]

Jackson Davis was among those white workers promoting parent-teacher collaboration associations and gatherings by encouraging the segregated schools to hold Patrons' Day events. He reported to the GEB in 1912, "I have also used every effort to have Patrons' Day, November 1st observed in the colored schools. I have had very heavy correspondence and have sent out a good deal of literature in connection with this work. I think the day was generally observed with excellent results." Arkansas' J. A. Presson instructed his Jeanes teachers on how to conduct their work: "Industrial classes for both boys and girls should be organized in each school. . . . It is expected that the county industrial teacher, in cooperation with the local teacher, organize and maintain an active school improvement Association in connection with each school. Probably no better way will be found for securing the interest and cooperation of the patrons." As always, the industrial education of youth involved enlisting parents, as white educators worked to teach entire communities the virtues of agricultural education through the clubs. As George Godard, the State Supervisor of Georgia's Negro Schools, explained to his agents, "Get the consent and secure the cooperation of the parents of these members. You can do very little without their help."[48]

Despite the emphasis on agricultural education, the Jeanes teachers embraced the Homemakers' Clubs initiative. They also supported the involvement of parents and citizens as a result of the values they learned at home and in schools; they shared strategies and ideas for doing so at the various institutes and meetings they attended. Jeanes supervisor Virginia Randolph explained, "We used labor donated by parents to make repairs and improvements on school buildings and grounds. I am very proud of the Home Improvement Societies I was able to organize."[49] Ardenah Marcus, a State Industrial Teacher in Georgia, did the same thing during her travels across the state each month as she encouraged the formation of patrons' clubs.[50] In general, the agents followed the stated purpose of the Homemakers' Clubs and taught African American girls, boys, and mothers how to preserve food, raise farm animals, and carry out other homemaking duties, all with the intended goal of improving the quality of life for African Americans. While industrial education was generally a tough sell to black communities, this was not always the case. Black teachers helped develop and sustain a network of citizens interested in education and schooling across their respective states, and they taught much-needed skills to the masses. Moreover, club work around agriculture lessened some of the class distinctions that were found in women's club reform work because of the emphasis on agricultural production and sustainability for all.

As with the rest of their reform work, the Homemakers' Club Agents themselves viewed the clubs as important to racial uplift and the development of community. As Stephanie J. Shaw argues in her book on black professional women, their efforts were "not simply acts of charity[;] . . . they were a matter of developing the infrastructure of the community and community itself." Even under the watchful eyes of white supervisors, the agents enacted a form of community-building among the counties they visited as they encouraged African Americans to clean up homes and schools by whitewashing and tidying them, and to work for the common good through food preservation and other activities. Moreover, this emphasis on cleanliness in segregated schools was connected to the teachers' aims to encourage character development both within the school population and in the community in general. Most importantly, they did not just tell citizens what to do; they established Patrons' Clubs and School Improvement Leagues and enlisted local teachers and citizens to lead them since they traveled throughout the year and were not always there to lead each meeting. In Alabama a rural supervisor explained how the Homemakers' Clubs were run in his region: "In some communities a local teacher or competent mother agreed to act as president of the club and give weekly lessons during the season under the general supervision of the agent. In others, the instruction was given entirely by the agent and the club met only when the agent made her visits." Therefore, an important part of community-building was the establishment of networks of citizens and professionals, linked through club ties and teachers' associations.[51]

The club agents displayed much ownership of the initiative, viewing it as an extension of their classroom work. The rural teacher thus was "teaching all the time." One agent in Alabama in 1915 revealed her commitment to Homemakers' Clubs by claiming, "I esteem it a favor to myself and my race." The enthusiasm of E. Birdie Taylor of Kentucky is evidenced through her eagerness to get to work, even though the club agents did not typically begin until mid-May: "I would like to begin the club work if possible, the first of March in order to have all the children well started before school is out. I would like to have all the members plant seed early in boxes or hot beds." The agents traveled far and wide to enlist citizens in the educational efforts of the Homemakers' Club, but as discussed above, the boundaries of this work were fluid. Lula

M. Thomas, an agent in Montgomery County, Alabama, reported that she had used two days in August of 1915 to attend Sunday school and a "Woman's Missionary Convention." She also traveled around the county, attending school improvement society meetings, discussing "school improvement work with them and urg[ing] them to fix up their schoolhouses."[52]

Often, as in the case of Virginia Randolph, Jeanes supervisors rose to leadership positions to assist the state supervisors in overseeing the Homemakers' Club agents. Medora Reed of Arkansas took on work of exhausting proportions, which included organizing local home-school associations, leading canning clubs, traveling vast distances, and preparing reports for the Negro School Supervisors. One spring, Reed spent only five days in the office preparing reports; the rest were spent going to meetings and demonstrations. An entry for mid-March notes, "As the agent in Mississippi County was new, I spent almost the entire week with her, trying to give the needed instructions as to the beginning of her work."[53] Another entry for April reveals the multifaceted nature of her work and the centrality of organizing community members:

> This week was spent with the agent in Mississippi County. As she was new in the county, her work was principally organizing. We found all schools and communities eager for the work and even ready to begin work. The schools at Osceola and Holt have some equipment for a kitchen and very effective work can be done there. At Joiner, the clubs were organized and after an explanation of the work, they were very much interested in poultry. The women are very eager to learn to can vegetables and promise to plant to that effect. This is a large county, with a fine field for the work. Saturday was office day.

By 1917, even though the Homemakers' Club initiative was not successful in terms of the proportion of rural blacks it enlisted, each of the Southern states had devoted workers like Reed, who traveled the state organizing Homemakers' Clubs and establishing a nascent network of home-school associations that they then left in the hands of local teachers to manage.[54]

In 1917 the U.S. Congress combined Smith-Lever with a major industrial education initiative to form the Smith-Hughes Act, which offered federal monies to the states for vocational education. With this move, vocational education was planted firmly in the public schools and was funded generously by the federal government. As Herbert Kliebard argues, "Congress found it expedient to link the needs of industry and agriculture under the general aegis of the national interest." With the passage of Smith-Hughes, funding for Homemakers' Clubs was removed from the administration of the GEB, thereby ending the short-lived philanthropic support for the clubs as of July 1, 1919. In 1919, the last year of the GEB's support, eleven states in the South had established

Homemakers' Club networks: Alabama, Arkansas, Georgia, Kentucky, Louisiana, Maryland, Mississippi, North Carolina, South Carolina, Tennessee, and
Virginia. The appropriations that year ranged from a low of $1,375 for Mary-
land to a high of $7,800 for Virginia. Whereas the GEB was the sole source
of funding for the Clubs in 1914, by 1919 appropriations were supplemented
with other state and local funds, which was the express hope of the GEB. The
result was less attention to the specific needs of blacks in terms of what whites
thought of as industrial education, as Smith-Hughes broadened its scope to
encompass the entire nation. Nonetheless, important groundwork had been
carried out during that time in developing a network of school leaders who
organized community members around the goals of education, racial uplift,
and community-building. By this time, the clubs were standing on their own
as some began to be linked to the network of black parent-teacher associations
that were emerging in Georgia, Alabama, and elsewhere.[55]

Although the Homemakers' Clubs did not accomplish the far-reaching
goals set for them by policymakers and the GEB, what did result was greater
momentum around community-school organizing in segregated schools and
an even stronger network of associations organized under the Jeanes Industrial
Teachers, which continued until the 1960s. Since the Jeanes network remained
intact through the middle decades of the twentieth century and Homemakers'
Clubs were transformed into home-school organizations, black PTA organizers had a more solid foundation on which to build. The Homemakers' Club
initiative, coordinated primarily by Jeanes teachers, thus can be given the
credit for the widespread promotion and establishment of community clubs
of various types, parent-teacher associations, and school improvement societies, and the Negro Rural Supervisors and other educational administrators
recognized this.[56]

In some instances, Jeanes teachers who worked on behalf of the Homemakers' Clubs went on to leadership roles in the NCCPT.[57] For example,
Annie W. Holland was hired as one of the first Homemakers' Club agents
in North Carolina and rapidly rose through the ranks to become a leader of
agents. She was discharged with the duty of training agents in homemaking
tasks and organizing community members. N. C. Newbold recognized her
capabilities, writing, "Mrs. Holland has been visiting some of the new supervisors and helping them organize and promote the Home-Makers' Club work in
ten counties." Holland worked in this leadership role for the duration of the
GEB initiative, from 1914 to 1919, and remained the highest-paid agent in the
state. Her work as a Homemakers' Club agent gave her leadership training that
served her in her later role as first president and founder of the North Carolina
Congress of Colored Parents and Teachers in 1927. Her efforts, and those of
other Jeanes teachers, were mirrored in urban areas by clubwomen and teachers who organized parent-teacher associations.[58]

Organizing the National Congress of Colored Parents and Teachers

In the first three decades of the twentieth century, the pace of organizing parent-teacher associations and school improvement societies increased as a result of various grassroots efforts. In some instances, middle-class black clubwomen worked in the cities and aided rural areas and schools. In others, Jeanes supervising teachers organized Patrons' and Homemakers' clubs for the betterment of schools and communities, and these associations were further supported by white educational administrators. Through in-service workshops, teacher training, and membership in state education associations and the NACW, black teachers began to learn about similar efforts in other regions and discovered they were not alone in the effort to organize citizens. Thus the founding of the black PTA was the result of a confluence of grassroots forces in rural and urban areas and from black as well as white leaders.

If the National Congress of Colored Parents and Teachers can be said to have originated in any one location, it would be Atlanta, under the leadership of clubwoman Selena Sloan Butler. Butler was educated at Spelman and active locally and nationally in civic and educational reform throughout the first half of the twentieth century. In 1897 she wrote to her alumnae magazine, *The Spelman Messenger,* and revealed her support of black advancement and education: "study the past and current history of your race and with pride tell it to your pupils in the classroom or to your children as you sit around the fireside. If you do not do this, who will?" Butler's associational ties were vast; she was a representative of the Atlanta Woman's Club at the organizational meeting of the NACW, organized a chapter of the Eastern Star in Atlanta, and served on the board of the Phillis Wheatley Young Women's Christian Association. The alumnae publication remarked on her accomplishments, "Temperance, health, Sunday School, and church work, free kindergarten, social purity, parent-teacher clubs, in fact, every kind of movement for the betterment of her race [has been] worthy to receive her encouragement and aid."[59]

Married to one of Atlanta's first black doctors, Butler had worked as a kindergarten teacher before serving as preceptor at Florida State College at Tallahassee. She was known by Mothers' Congress leaders because she was one of the NACW members contacted by Helen Birney of the NCM in 1908 to organize a black national PTA. Butler refused their offer, having decided at that time to continue to work at the local level in the Atlanta area. Her resistance was reflective of black club leaders' distrust of white clubwomen, inasmuch as it shows the suspicion of the wider black community in the South, which had turned increasingly inward from the 1880s to the 1920s, refusing white help from the networks of civil society or the federal government. Moreover, Butler likely considered the task too challenging at that juncture. Given that the majority of African Americans in the South lived in rural areas and the establishment of schools and school systems were still being undertaken, Butler had virtually no foundation on which to build a segregated PTA. Instead, the networks with which Butler worked, such as the YWCA and NACW, were already providing the support that the Congress of Mothers would offer, but in black associations and with black leadership. In short, Butler and other community leaders had nothing to gain by joining the white PTA in 1908.[60]

Butler and other black Atlantans were, at that time, much more focused on the crisis that had arisen in the city's educational system during a time of racial unrest and educational inequity. At the turn of the twentieth century, black residents began fighting for equitable funding in education and adequate school facilities. Starting in 1908, with over 90 percent of them living in poverty, 4,500 children were closed out of the city's public schools. For the next several years, black children attended half-time, as segregated schools were used for double sessions. In March 1911 Butler organized a parent-teacher association for African Americans at the Yonge Street School, with the help of principal Olive Taylor, in order to rally community members around the issue (see figure 2.3). Taylor's invitation to parents was well received, and at the first meeting they established a parent-teacher association and elected Butler as president. Neighbors took note of the successes of the new parent-teacher association. For instance, a 1913 report of schools compiled by black settlement workers of the Atlanta Neighborhood Union found "unhealthful conditions existing in all of our public schools except Yonge Street School." As the Yonge Street PTA continued to meet during the school year, Butler and her associates reached out and helped nearby Atlanta schools organize their own associations. Clubs spread so rapidly that by the next school year Butler created the Parent-Teacher Council of Atlanta to coordinate the efforts of the local groups.[61]

Selena Butler continued to lead local efforts around the greater Atlanta region until 1919, when she called a statewide meeting of parent-teacher associations. Held at the War Camp Community Center in Atlanta, the first state meeting drew the attention of white Georgia PTA president J. E. Andrews, who contributed ten dollars to the fledgling organization. Butler again was elected president and led the black local units in starting school libraries and health programs, instituting school lunches and playgrounds, and holding leadership workshops. She was not alone. Similar work was being carried out in other Southern states such as Alabama, Texas, and Delaware by a cadre of educated black women that mirrored the ground-up organizational development pattern in Georgia. Grassroots organizing led to the gradual building of a nascent infrastructure as organizers linked their local units to regional or state councils with the support of established associations, such as the NACW, YWCA, and Urban League.[62]

FIGURE 2.3

The Yonge Street Parent-Teacher Association (date unknown). (*Source:* Photo reprinted with permission and courtesy of National PTA)

As in other Southern states, there were gross inequities in funding between Alabama's black and white schools. Also, while the school term in the state for blacks was under 100 days in the 1910s, it was 142 days for whites. Double taxation was a way of life for the state's African Americans. Organized women worked diligently in many counties, purchasing the land for school buildings, often with donations that matched the GEB's funds for Rosenwald Schools.[63] Parent-teacher organizing in the state began in Selma, Alabama, under the leadership of schoolteacher and clubwoman M. A. Dillard, who was a representative of the Woman's Mutual Improvement Club at the NACW organizational meeting convened by Josephine Ruffin in Boston in 1895. In 1914 she served as the president of the Alabama State Mothers' League, which ten years later changed its name to the Alabama State [Black] PTA.[64] The origins of the black PTA in Alabama reflect larger trends across the South; the association was driven, in large part, by educators. The State Mothers' League—the name was chosen so it would not be confused with the white Alabama Congress of Parents and Teachers—held its inaugural meeting at State Teachers College in Montgomery. Dillard was elected its first president, and her energies in those early years were focused on getting parents interested in PTA work and providing the leadership training to parents and teachers necessary to sustain the movement. White and black educational leaders at the state level helped guide the new association, including J. S. Lambert, a state Rosenwald worker; H. Councill Trenholm, the president of Alabama State Teachers College; John W. Abercrombie, the state superintendent of education; and Mary Foster, a state supervisor. Foster operated as a field secretary for the newly formed organization, adding the duty without compensation to her travels around the state. Lambert, Trenholm, and Abercrombie were well-known political and educational leaders in Alabama at this time, so their involvement with the founding of a statewide black PTA lent visibility to the venture.[65]

Black PTA organizers, however, did not always need or get the support of state educational administrators. In Fort Worth, Texas, schoolteacher W. S. Benton organized a mothers' club in her home around 1908. Encouraged by local principals, she helped establish mothers' clubs for each public school in Fort Worth in the 1910s; these were eventually subsumed under a city-wide PTA council. Having been encouraged by her successes, and swept up in the fervor that characterized parent-teacher organizing, Benton took her skills on the road and organized parent-teacher associations in Dallas, Mineral Wells, LaRue, Clarendon, and Port Arthur, covering hundreds of miles in doing so. The perils of travel for African Americans during this era cannot be underestimated, as few hotels opened their doors to them and many railcars were segregated. The specter of racism added to the burden of treks into rural areas with underdeveloped transportation systems, as black women leaders often felt humiliated when dealing with Jim Crow laws around the South. Such challenges continued into the twentieth century. For example, in the 1930s NCCPT President Sarah F. Brown faced many obstacles in her travels because she often journeyed at night by train in order to attend the next day's meetings. Many times she was met by horse and buggy and "had to ride over the poor and uncomfortable roads in order to visit the organized unit or to organize new units."[66]

All black PTA state units began as segregated associations, with the exception of Delaware. That state, where PTA work began fairly early on, presents a unique case of an integrated network that later segregated itself. As discussed earlier in this chapter, Delaware had an active network of women's clubs that did much work on behalf of education. The women's clubs of the federated National Association of Colored Women started parent-teacher associations, since much of their work focused on education, and these associations began to work with the white Congress of Parents and Teachers in that state. The white state PTA in Delaware was officially organized in 1911, the year it joined the National Congress of Parents and Teachers. From the beginning, many of the local units were integrated, and they remained so for nearly a decade, after which black PTA workers began to voice their concern over their lack of representation with the state Board of Managers. In the 1910s the lone black representative was J. Graham Scott, principal of Banneker Junior High, who served as "first vice-president in charge of Negro activities." As black members became increasingly interested in managing their own affairs, they decided to leave the white PTA in 1920 and create their own organization, as they explained it, to "work more effectively and gain better leadership experience." Nonetheless, they continued to work cooperatively with the white units in the 1920s; they were the only civic organization in the state to do so.[67]

African American teachers' organizations also helped advance the network of parent-teacher associations. For example, in Henderson, Kentucky, the parent-teacher association of Alves Street and Douglass High Schools was organized in 1910 to establish playgrounds, provide books for school libraries, and build a new high school. During this time, the local black parent-teacher associations of Kentucky were welcomed at the annual meetings of the Kentucky Teachers and Education Association (KT&EA) until 1917, when their attendance became too large and made the meetings unwieldy. Therefore, the KT&EA relegated nonteachers to a separate department, which consequently became the Kentucky [Black] PTA in 1921. Time and again black educators took the lead in organizing PTA units. In nearby West Virginia, Dr. W. W. Sanders founded a school improvement society in Premier to serve the one-room schoolhouse he was in charge of in 1911. Three years later he became the first black State Supervisor of Negro Schools in the country. This position afforded him the opportunity, among other things, to catalyze the creation of local-level parent-teacher associations around the state, which eventually culminated in the founding of the West Virginia [Black] PTA in 1923. The West Virginia black PTA attempted to join the white PTA but was denied membership, because by that time the National Congress of Parents and Teachers had begun the practice of not accepting into state or national membership any black parent-teacher associations from segregated school systems. In just two decades the National Congress of Parents and Teachers had reneged on its promise to be inclusive, thus creating the impetus for a segregated branch.[68]

The pace of organizing black parent-teacher associations gained momentum by the early 1920s as Selena Butler and many other black activists and educational leaders carried out the process of building schools and communities as they sought to reform them. Butler's organizing of a state black parent-teacher association drew the attention of the black community of Georgia, as well as the attention of the white Georgia Congress of Parents and Teachers. In some instances the parent-teacher association was organized before the school was built in order to gather resources. One local group in Mississippi in the early 1920s focused on their "immediate problem . . . [which] was to get something resembling a school."[69] Even though the black state PTA in Georgia represented approximately one hundred local associations in 1923, with strong representation in Atlanta, it faced a crisis that it could not totally avert. The educational situation in Atlanta had deteriorated further, with schools running on triple sessions and a board of education continuing its overt discrimination of African American schools and students. As the white PTA was growing stronger in its national influence and ability to shape schools and the curriculum, it was at this juncture that Butler decided to organize the National Congress of Colored Parents and Teachers, almost twenty years after she was first approached by white PTA representatives. In correspondence with white PTA president Margaretta Willis Reeve, Butler expressed her desire that they adopt the YWCA model by having separate state and local units but one national leadership. Reeve refused, however, and insisted on two separate national offices, out of fear of alienating white PTA members.[70]

With the support and encouragement of white PTA leaders, as well as those of the National Urban League and National Association of Teachers in Colored Schools (NACTS), Butler issued a call to the other black state associations to send delegates to Georgia's sixth annual convention in 1926. Of these, three accepted the invitation: Alabama, Delaware, and Florida. The call explained that the new organization would "offer opportunities for its members to develop their abilities to an extent not otherwise possible" and was endorsed by the white PTA president, A. H. Reeve, and chair of the Committee on Extension of Parent-Teacher Associations among Colored People,

F. W. McAllister. At the Liberty Baptist Church in Atlanta, on May 7, 1926, the Colored Congress was created as a segregated federation to the National Congress of Parents and Teachers. A long list of officers was elected, with representatives from the four original member states. In addition to seven vice presidents to handle the different departments (e.g., health, public welfare, home service), the NCCPT elected a historian to record the organization's accomplishments.[71]

In accordance with NCPT policy, a white PTA member was appointed to chair its "Committee of Extension among Colored People." PTA member Mrs. Fred Wessels assumed the role of liaison to the NCCPT. She immediately surveyed the white state PTA units on the existence of and need for separate black PTA organizations. In her first report to the National PTA leadership she justified the establishment of an entirely separate federation: "Equality of races, is not an amalgamation of races, as so many negroes seem to think, therefore it is logical for them to form their own associations for the development and progress of their race, thus becoming originators, and not merely imitators." Inasmuch as NCPT leaders wanted to include black members on behalf of child welfare and parent education, they were not up to the challenge of creating an integrated association. Therefore, they helped create a separate and unequal organization that, at least in the beginning, depended on the leadership and contributions of the white association. White and black PTA leaders at the national level drew up bylaws outlining that a state could create a Colored PTA branch if it had fifteen associations with a membership of 300 persons, thereby allowing the NCCPT to extend its network beyond the *de jure* segregation in the Southern United States.[72]

However, black PTA leaders viewed the reach of the Colored Congress differently. Selena Butler made it clear to the new members that the organization was only to "function in those states where separate schools for the races were maintained."[73] She did not want to encourage the spread of segregation elsewhere:

> Where there are no separate schools for the races I would not advise organizing a separate Association for Colored Patrons. There has been too much separate working already where it was not necessary. The colored women should join the P.-T.A. of the school of which they are patrons and throw their best efforts and unselfish cooperation with the Association of the school. . . . In those sections where separate schools are maintained because of TRADITION, the Colored schools must have their own P.-T.A.'s.[74]

The four states—Georgia, Alabama, Delaware, and Florida—representing approximately 3,000 members in 300 units, were the first to join the NCCPT.

This was small in comparison to the white PTA, but Butler assured her counterparts in the NCPT that it would not take long to establish a membership base.[75] She was elected the organization's first president and, referring to the wider reach that an affiliation with the PTA would have, explained that the Colored Congress would "give leadership among [its] members as well as develop deeper interest in the work and thereby accomplish better and larger results." Butler believed her organization would unite the efforts at organizing home-school associations around the South, in which African American teachers and parents were working to resolve complex local problems and to develop individual children and the community in the process.[76]

The ground-up development of the black PTA allowed for a gradual building of an institutional infrastructure that relied on the strength and leadership of existing African American organizations. The women's club movement, Homemakers' Club initiative, and endeavors of black teachers converged to set the foundation for the NCCPT. These networks could have stood on their own to serve segregated schools, but they did not. Not only did they link with one another; they affiliated with the National PTA. In the 1920s, after decades of working separately, Butler and other black educational and community leaders found it propitious to join forces with the white PTA for several reasons. Black educators during the early twentieth century were all too aware of racial hostility and the threat it posed to the tenuous nature of the development of schools and school systems for African American children. Moreover, blacks in the South were voiceless in improving public schooling through existing educational policies, so their influence had only indirect channels through which to go. By the 1920s, however, black educational and civic leaders recognized the growing strength and influence of the white PTA and viewed it as an indirect avenue for race work.[77]

As the National PTA ceased to work through the NEA Department of School Patrons and began to develop its membership base through the 1920s, it assumed responsibility for aiding in the support of public schools. During this time its membership increased exponentially. Developing a segregated branch with separate national, state, and local units presented its own set of challenges, not the least of which was communication and the continuity of programs and policies. With associational ties came distrust and confusion over how to coordinate the efforts of a segregated federation, while difference and diversity allowed for a fuller extension of the Congress into communities that otherwise would not have access to its network and programs. Through the middle decades of the twentieth century, the NCPT struggled with its relationship to the NCCPT as both PTA branches worked toward the same goals but with different emphases.

CHAPTER 3

"For Convenience of a Better Education and Training for My People"

Organizational Growth and Stability

"YOU CAN'T teach a child if he doesn't come to school. He can't come to school if he doesn't have any shoes—he doesn't have any clothes on his back." These were the thoughts of newly trained Jeanes teacher Narvie Jordan Harris, when she decided to organize a parent-teacher council in DeKalb County, Georgia, in 1945. After looking over the conditions of the region and visiting homes, she noted extreme poverty and the lack of educational opportunities as two major challenges in the lives of African Americans. First she tried working with parents individually, but she found it was not effective. So she met with her principals to form a support network for the schools in her purview:

> So that's when I got with my principals, and I said . . . "I would like for you to send [teachers], and when possible, you come." I had principals to come [*sic*], "and we are going to work with these parents to try to improve them." . . . My office was in a funeral home, upstairs. And there was a chapel as you came in the door. So people say that one day Mrs. Harris was having a meeting in there and there was a body in there the next day. But the body didn't ever bother me, and I didn't bother them, one way or the other. We would make a joke about it. But that is where we were headquartered and where we met. And it was through them that we tried to do something—well, we did. We didn't try; we did.

After having initiated the parent-teacher movement in her region, in the post–World War II years Harris went on to unite the seventeen schools for African

Americans in DeKalb County, twelve of which were in churches and lodge halls. These schools became the DeKalb County Council of Colored Parents and Teachers.[1]

Born around 1917, Harris was raised in Atlanta, the second of seven children of James and Anna Jordan. James Jordan was the only black man to own a department store in the city and he, like his wife, was active in church and civic organizations. In 1948 James Jordan fought for the integration of Atlanta's police force. In addition to the lessons of fighting for racial equality, Harris recalled another important dictum her parents taught her: "Education is the answer. You don't get anywhere if you are illiterate." Along with her siblings, Harris attended Booker T. Washington High School—the only high school for blacks in Atlanta at that time—and graduated in 1934. She then majored in home economics with a minor in education at Clark College, where she also earned a master's degree. After a short stint in the public schools of Henry and Calhoun counties, Narvie Harris was hired as one of the first six Jeanes teachers in DeKalb County, a position she held from 1944 to 1968. It was as a Jeanes teacher that she led the development of a PTA network in her region (see figure 3.1). Harris served as Atlanta PTA district president from 1953 to 1959 and later was elected to the office of the president of the Georgia Congress of Colored Parents and Teachers (1966–71), seeing the organization through its most crucial episode, the desegregation of the organization in that state and across the nation.[2]

Harris was the typical black PTA leader in the South in the mid-twentieth century. The majority were teachers, and many were Jeanes supervisors, who took it upon themselves to organize in the schools and communities in which they worked. They usually acquired their inclination to organize from their families and the education they received at historically black colleges and universities. Harris recalled that while at Clark she learned to acquaint herself with agencies that would support her work, such as the Red Cross and police and fire departments. As a student she was required to undertake a community study to meet the requirements for supervision, so she surveyed the health conditions at the Avondale Colored Elementary and High School in DeKalb. This type of training would later serve black PTA leaders such as Harris in their work, both by teaching them skills in community organizing and by helping them maintain close contact with a network of graduates. Furthermore, black history and culture were emphasized at places such as Clark University, as racial uplift was stressed throughout the academic curriculum.[3]

Harris, like some other regional PTA leaders, was not completely aware of the efforts to organize parent-teacher associations going on across the South or the founding of the National Congress of Colored Parents and Teachers. Therefore, the impetus to organize came not necessarily from her knowledge

FIGURE 3.1

Jeanes teacher and PTA organizer Narvie Harris (center) in her office above Cox Funeral Home, 1945. The teachers on either side of her are Isoline Sherard (left) and Marion Wells (right). (*Source:* Photo reprinted with permission from Narvie J. Harris and Dee Taylor, *African-American Education in DeKalb County,* Arcadia Publishing, 1999; http://www.arcadiapublishing.com)

of the organization but out of necessity in the workplace and community. As she explained, "Now, I had been doing things [other parent-teacher associations] did, but I told you I was not aware when I organized—I did it for convenience of a better education and training for my people. . . . I was in isolation as far as PTA was concerned."[4] Moreover, her training as a Jeanes teacher placed her in the center of a web of relations; workers around the state "would know the Jeanes supervisor if they didn't know anybody else." As Harris explains, the Jeanes supervisors were the liaisons among citizens, schools and groups, agencies, and organizations such as the Urban League and United Way. Despite Harris's not being aware of—or paying much attention to—the national-level development of the PTA, the association was growing and expanding. However, it did not take long for Harris to rise through the ranks to become a well-known PTA leader in the state of Georgia.[5]

Twenty years before Harris organized PTA units in her region, white PTA president Margaretta Willis Reeve attempted to clarify the organization's program to its members and to stem the tide of PTA workers overstepping their boundaries in school matters. Her words, that the PTA was "*not* a crusade to reform the schools. . . . [nor was it] a federation of clubs, in which each club develops its peculiar interest according to its fancy," contradicted virtually everything members believed about the organization. This comment was made in 1924, just after the organization dropped the words "Congress of Mothers" from its name to become the National Congress of Parents and Teachers, or NCPT, and ceased to be a department in the National Education Association. As the other women's organizations faded into the background and took up work in other arenas, the NCPT took one giant step forward in terms of developing its organizational network and enlisting members in helping support the public schools. At this juncture, Reeve tried in vain to bring members into line with a streamlined focus and programs, but members' resistance to these changes resulted in a stronger, more expansive organization.[6]

After the Progressive era, the PTA leadership sought to distinguish itself from women's organizations by defining for itself rhetorically a more supportive role in public education, one that deferred to the expertise of professional educators. It instituted a bylaw—one that challenged PTA officers and members for years to come—that instructed members not to seek to direct the administration of schools or influence education policy. However, it was practically impossible to change the activities of local units and redirect women volunteers into other pursuits. For local-level members, the PTA offered a means by which they could attend to more pressing matters of school funding and curriculum development. Therefore, in practice, the PTA sought to strike a balance between directing member units to adhere to bylaws and policies and allowing for local concerns to determine local interests, and nowhere was this more evident than in the Colored Congress branches. From the time of the founding of the NCCPT to World War II, local units tailored the PTA program to the immediate needs of communities as both branches of the organization grew stronger and continued to have wide appeal to different constituencies.[7]

The Progressive-era school reform efforts had ended by the mid-1920s. However, in the decades that followed, black and white women volunteers took up the cause of PTA work with even greater zeal, often to the consternation of education professionals. Even though national-level PTA leaders were not successful in directing members away from meddling in local schools, they did accomplish an important feat in organizational stability: they were able to standardize organizing procedures and programs in order to maintain continuity across state and local units around the country. From the mid-1920s until World War II, the organization focused on building a stronger membership base, fundraising, and shaping the school curriculum while it struggled to define the relationship between its black and white branches. PTA leaders at the state and local levels were well networked and willing to donate much time on behalf of the organization and education. The majority of white PTA leaders were married women who did not work outside the home, which left them time for volunteer work. Most black PTA leaders, in contrast, were educators who assumed PTA activities as part of their professional responsibilities. What the two groups had in common was their commitment and multiple memberships in civic associations, and these affiliations aided them in their work by affording them a large measure of social capital to assist them in carrying out PTA activities.

The ability of local-level PTA members to make change in education is evidenced in the threat they posed to school administrators, who wished to contain and direct their energy and activities. White PTA women challenged the authority of male school administrators with their ability to organize volunteers, raise money for schools, and shape the school curriculum and schools as institutions. For white school leaders, fundraising was especially challenging and thus was a double-edged sword; it provided needed funds to local schools but threatened the emerging structures of school funding and administrative control in the 1920s and 1930s. In segregated schools, fundraising took on a greater sense of urgency because it was a necessity; without it there would be no schools and no books and materials. Likewise, white school administrators thought PTA workers too involved in curricular decisions. These tensions around the school curriculum were not as evident in black parent-teacher associations, since local units were often led by teachers.

Black and white PTA workers, however, successfully promoted practical-oriented developments in the curriculum, in particular the Cardinal Principles of the Committee on the Reorganization of Secondary Education (1918), which emphasized health, citizenship, and the strengthening of family life. The PTA adopted the Cardinal Principles in 1929, which guided organizational programs at least until the 1960s, long after educational leaders had rejected them. Called life-adjustment curriculum in the 1930s and 1940s, the Cardinal Principles Report was the codification of the early-twentieth-century curriculum shift that created tensions between proponents of the liberal arts and more practical courses of study, such as business math, business English, and home economics. While the National PTA for decades organized its program around the principles of life adjustment, white, middle-class PTA leaders made sure their own children were educated in the liberal arts. Just as the leaders of the NCM embraced Spencer's functional criteria for the development of curriculum, PTA leaders of the twentieth century refused to give up on the idea of schooling for the masses as preparation for home and family life. In contrast, local-level black PTA units did not make much of a distinction between liberal arts and the functional curriculum, since black teachers viewed both as critical for the future success of young African Americans.[8]

From the 1920s through the mid-1940s, a tenuous relationship existed between the two branches of the PTA as white leaders acted in an advisory capacity to the black organization, reflecting an unequal balance of power. This imbalance was there from the start, since the creation of the black PTA in 1926 was aided by the white association. Adeline Wessels, chair of the Committee-at-Large on Extension among Colored People at the time, assisted founding president Selena Sloan Butler and the NCCPT as needed. Some state units enlisted extension workers on special committees as well. In the late 1920s, Texas, North Carolina, Florida, South Carolina, Georgia, California, and Oklahoma benefited from such committees. In some cases, the Extension among Colored People committees prepared the bylaws for the black state associations, instructed them on PTA protocol, and distributed PTA literature to them. Even though the white association worked with the black branch, its work could be described as assistance from a distance. White PTA leaders would attend the occasional state-level meeting of the Colored Congress, or correspond with black leaders, but they generally did not partake in the day-to-day work of local units in segregated schools.[9]

In the two PTA branches, individual leaders had to contend with their racial beliefs and prejudices as each had to filter assumptions about the other through the association's espoused ideals and programs. In some cases, especially at the local level in the South, whites and blacks suffered for lack of resources, a fact that united them despite their differences. As Narvie Harris observed, "we had the cooperation of the whites, way back in the forties. And I thought that was significant.... They want to eat; they want to be warm. They get cold. All of us want education for our children. So there was a lot of commonality—even though we did not meet together, when we approached them, they were struggling as well as the blacks." Yet, in terms of the state and national PTA leadership, in many instances the threat posed by white women to school leaders was, in turn, the same threat they sensed in their relationship with the black association. One major concern of white officers, having over-looked the sheer necessity of fundraising, was black workers' extensive atten-tion to it. Until the World War II years, black parent-teacher associations and school improvement societies devoted almost all their energy to fundraising in order to get black schools much-needed buildings, supplies, transportation, and programs. Fundraising did not raise the issue of challenging professionals within black communities, because citizens and teachers were generally united in bringing resources and educational programs to local schools. One com-munity member recalled that the relationship was not perfect but that parents and teachers were in agreement because "all they did was for the betterment of the children." However, the efforts of black educators and local PTA leaders did often create conflict with white school boards and administrators.[10]

This chapter analyzes the work of local and state units from 1924 to 1945, tracing organizational growth and stability through the Depression to the end of World War II. During these decades, the PTA emerged as a major voluntary organization yet struggled with its own growing pains as a segregated associa-tion. Some confusion resulted after the Colored Congress was organized, as PTA leaders struggled with the place of African Americans in the organization and as black members and organizers sought to maintain control over the education of their children while reaping the benefits of membership in the federation. During these years, the PTA became firmly segregated, as the Col-ored Congress made the transition to independence, for the most part, from white oversight and assistance. In what follows, I compare and contrast the work of the two PTA branches, considering the centrality of race work for the black association alongside the virtual silence of race in the work of the white PTA. In particular, both PTA branches focused primarily on fundraising and curricular issues in schools while developing a network of leaders to perpetu-ate the organization and its activities. The successes they met in local schools and in developing a strong organizational infrastructure were not paralleled in the relationship between the black and white branches.

Ease, Quick Results, and Economy

Even though they were part of the same organization, the two branches of the PTA followed different paths to development. The white PTA, founded in 1897, was organized from the top down by elite society matrons; it was a national organization from the start, after which state and local units were added. Conversely, the black PTA grew from the bottom up, beginning with local clubs and school improvement associations that coalesced into state units, after which a national leadership team was elected. Both organizations depended on existing networks of women's voluntary and education professional associations for their development, and both later broke away from them once the PTA infrastructure was established. The membership of the white PTA had increased almost tenfold in a decade; in 1910 there were 20,013 members, which grew to 189,212 in 1920. By 1926 the white PTA had units at the state level in all existing U.S. states, the majority of which had been formed between 1905 and 1923 (see figure 3.2). International affiliations were made in 1958 with the recognition of the European Congress of Parents and Teachers and as late as 1991 with the Pacific Congress.

During the mid-twentieth century, membership rose exponentially for the white PTA, as women flocked to join the federated parent-teacher association. By 1930 the NCPT had approximately 1.5 million members, which was about 1.3 percent of the total U.S. population. The organization's growth through the mid-1950s was fueled in large part by women leaders who dedicated themselves to lead, serve, and promote PTA policy, as well as by the public's perceived need for the institution (see figure 3.3).[11]

Local-level black and white PTA meetings were remarkably similar around the country, owing to the association's standardized program and policies, which were circulated to members through official publications. Yet, despite the expectation of national-level leaders that local units adhere to the framework of ideas and suggestions given them, tremendous flexibility existed in state, regional, and local parent-teacher associations, which allowed for members to sustain their interest. This organizational structure—standardization with built-in flexibility—accounted for the steady growth and longevity of the PTA. In a circular titled "Why Belong to the State and National?" the PTA leadership spelled out the benefits of the association, under the headings *courage, safety, ease, quick results,* and *economy.* In addition to connecting members at the local level to "all the most important child welfare sources in the country," membership in the National PTA prevented a local unit from just "muddling through" by expediting their specific agenda items not only through the considerable organizational network but also through its cooperating organizations, such as the American Legion, the Boy Scouts of America, and the YWCA. The importance of a well-organized array of PTA workers was an argument that would sustain the organization through the desegregation years.[12]

National-level NCPT leaders scripted the start-up meetings at the local level with such documents as "How to Organize." The initial gatherings were

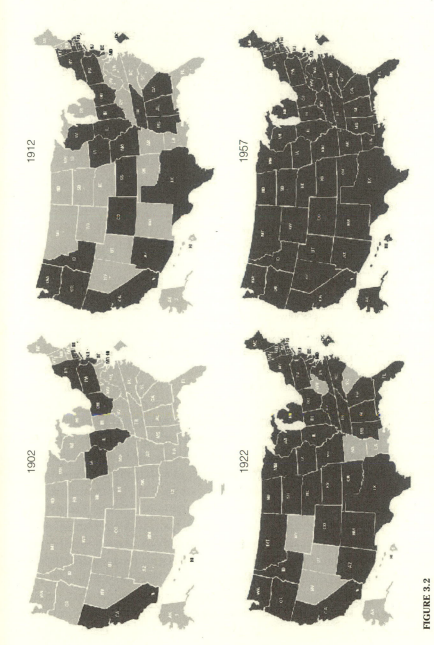

1902

1912

1922

1957

FIGURE 3.2

State units of the NCPT, 1902, 1912, 1922, and 1957. (*Source:* CEP data, in possession of the author)

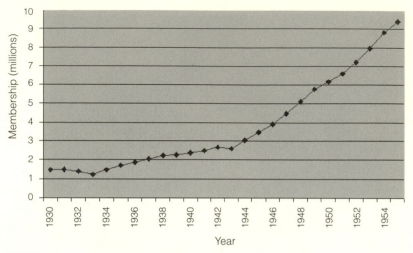

FIGURE 3.3

NCPT membership, 1930–55. (*Source:* CEP data, in possession of the author)

to be adequately advertised to community members, and it was suggested that the first meeting include community singing, a short address on "Why a PTA," the adoption of bylaws and nomination of officers, and, after other organizational business, the requisite "Social Hour" to give members a chance to become acquainted with one another. No detail was overlooked, even something as innocuous as singing at meetings. Community singing was defended by the NCPT as "the most effective means of opening a program. If well conducted, it makes for a spirit of fellowship and informality, and it draws the audience from its little groups of two and three conversing together into a unit ready for group thought and action." PTA literature was even made available to help guide subsequent gatherings, which included convening the executive and organization committees. Once local units were organized, the national office sent them an outline on how to run meetings, which included instructions to begin on time, how to incorporate entertainment as well as business matters, and the importance of ending on time. It was highly recommended, and therefore happened quite frequently, that each meeting end with a hospitality hour during which it was suggested that members visit classrooms, view school exhibits, play games, and even partake in folk dancing.[13]

Therefore, the typical PTA program for white and black units in the mid-twentieth century was part social hour, part business meeting. The social hour became a central feature, as it was an integral part of the cultural and community-building work of women volunteers. Meetings included a well-ordered lineup of singing, praying, readings by or listening to speakers, and ongoing reports of committees on legislation, publicity, and membership, among other matters. Tree plantings were a major feature of PTA gatherings, and were usually carried out annually. Since the oak tree became the official symbol of the National Congress of Parents and Teachers in 1922, local and state units around the country planted them to honor PTA founders and to remind themselves and the community of their strength in numbers. Local units were directed to adhere to the monthly themes that covered membership, Founders Day, and other elements of an educational program, all while allowing for local issues and needs to be addressed in the face-to-face meetings of the PTA forum. Therefore, the PTA meeting not only served as a social space but also offered a civic space within which members could share their hopes for public education and a better America. One of the primary organizational goals was to develop leaders in communities and to give them the skills and means to solve local problems and undertake school reform work.[14]

The example of the white John's Island, South Carolina, PTA illustrates the origins and early years of a developing local PTA unit. In the South, even though the women's club movement lagged ten to twenty years behind the North, South Carolina clubwomen quickly caught up. The South Carolina Federation of Women's Clubs (SCFWC) was organized in 1898, and within a year it had twenty-six clubs and over a thousand members. The Julian Mitchell School formed the first parent-teacher association in the state in 1912, although, of course, women's clubs and school improvement societies undertaking similar work already existed. By the early 1920s the SCFWC had over 4,000 members, and the South Carolina Congress of Parents and Teachers brought approximately 1,800 members into its fold at its founding meeting in 1921. The PTA became so popular in the state that by 1932, the South Carolina Congress of Parents and Teachers had won an award for being second in the nation in percentage of membership.[15]

Organized in 1924, the John's Island PTA held its meetings the first Friday of every month at four o'clock in the afternoon to allow as many parents to attend as possible. Fourteen members attended its first gathering on March 7, 1924. At that meeting the membership committee reported "six letters written, 9 homes visited, resulting in securing five new members, bringing the total membership to date, 14." The association agreed to discuss training for parents and health matters at its next meeting. So, at its next meeting the County Nurse spoke on "The Dangers of Disease Lurking in the Common Drinking Cup." Within a short time, the John's Island PTA began to hold fundraisers to support the local school. One such fundraiser was the idea of paying for "half a piano" if the school would pay for the other half and holding a recital to raise money for its purse. School and PTA ended up sharing the cost of the piano, which the association used for entertainment at its meetings and rented out for community events to raise additional money.[16]

Another early task that the John's Island PTA members took on was enlisting a committee of men who would help locate a Scout master to lead a Boy Scout troop at the school. Not only was this a need perceived by the community, but it was not uncommon for parent-teacher associations around the country to work closely with the Boy and Girl Scouts of America; they frequently enlisted local troops to become a part of their opening and closing rituals. Thus, the parent-teacher meetings became one of the main social events on John's Island as it united citizens around the school calendar and through school and other shared activities.[17] Entertainments were a central feature of the John's Island PTA meetings, which helped build community through members' engaging in shared activities and projects. Often, school-children provided the entertainment by singing or putting on plays. Officers sought to make the duller aspects of meetings lively; for example, the John's Island PTA had members responding to roll call with their favorite flower, vegetable, and once "by slogan."[18]

Local and state unit leaders often attended PTA-sponsored workshops—called PTA Schools—to learn more about the organization and how to run meetings. Mrs. Sherman Roe of Denver, Colorado, a member of the Executive Board of the National PTA and a field secretary, traveled the country in the 1920s and 1930s, teaching local leaders about PTA programs and policies. The classes were open to educators, parents, and anyone else interested in PTA work, and those attending earned certificates confirming their having participated in a National Institute. In the late 1920s Roe gave a series of workshops in South Carolina that were well attended. Her classes covered topics such as PTA history and leaders, its publications, study circles, parliamentary law, and the "Ethics of Money Raising." Roe even tailored her workshop by including information about the origins of the South Carolina PTA.[19]

Mary K. Newton, a South Carolina PTA leader who rose through the ranks in the 1920s, first serving as a district president, then publicity chair, and finally a state board member, attended Roe's workshops and took copious notes about what she learned. Newton learned the importance of district meetings and district presidents—a position of "greater honor" than state vice president, according to Roe, who furthered the organization's interest in having strong leaders close to the ground. Another important lesson was recorded by Newton, to "adapt not adopt National standards," revealing the flexibility of the federation. In addition to the role of PTA Councils (a group of associations rather than individuals in a particular region) and the organization's standing committees, Newton's abbreviated notes recorded the importance of hospitality: "Hospitality necessary in these meetings. Play together. A laugh is worth a dollar to the box office. Never go through a hard and fast program. Song. Chestnut Tree." Further advice included keeping the organizational meeting "snappy" and the importance of a "peppy song leader." The National

PTA used these workshops to circulate its documents on the standardization of local meetings, sharing organizational flowcharts and other items such as "Leadership," "The Parent-Teacher Meeting," "How to Organize," and the "Model Parent-Teacher Meeting." These strategies to standardize the organization's activities and programs were successful, not only in South Carolina, but around the country. Circulating these and other key documents took the guesswork out of organizing local units and, according to PTA policy, helped leaders develop their skills while leading.[20]

In South Carolina, as elsewhere, men appeared in the leadership ranks, but not to a significant degree. Overall, the PTA remained a women's organization. Since the John's Island PTA's founding in 1924, a small fraction of its membership was male, about two or three of the total of forty regular members. Often at the state level, male education professors would be elected to officers' positions, such as Dr. Leon Banov and Dr. Harry Clark, who served as vice presidents of the South Carolina Congress of Parents and Teachers in 1930. In a study conducted in 1934, Elmer Holbeck of Teachers College, Columbia, found that on average men made up 10 percent of the membership of white local units. In addition to being education professors, many of them were community and civic leaders, businessmen, and school administrators. Given the greater percentage of education professionals in leadership positions in the Colored Congress, and the emphasis on race work, men appeared in a slightly larger percentage.[21]

At the local level, men who were not members or PTA officers were encouraged to participate in special "Daddy's meetings" as guests. These meetings were held infrequently, usually once a year. For example, in the case of the John's Island PTA, local units recognized the importance of including men, so in 1927 the group decided to initiate a "Daddy's Meeting," at which coffee and sandwiches would be served. The first of the series was a success, as fathers "were made welcome and given seats of honor." The women members decided to sing "America" instead of the PTA song, presumably because the men knew the lyrics. After an account of the history and work of the John's Island PTA, the fathers listened to a presentation on "children and their daddies." The meeting was seen as a success, so much so that they held another the following year, at which the school principal appealed to the fathers to "be companions and buddies to their sons." Including fathers periodically in special meetings brought them into the fold of PTA business without handing over to them the work of running the association. They were available in an advisory capacity in limited numbers in the white PTA, which contrasts with their more regular presence as leaders in the Colored Congress.[22]

Men's involvement in PTA leadership reveals the partnership in education between laypersons and professional educators, as it was not all that uncommon to find men serving as officers at the local, state, and national levels.

For instance, Dr. John C. Moffitt of Provo, Utah, was both superintendent of schools and a vice president of the National Congress of Parents and Teachers in 1959. Also, Dr. Kenneth E. Howe, dean of the School of Education at University of North Carolina at Greensboro, was also a vice president of the white PTA in 1965. In the black PTA, Charles W. DuVaul served as the Georgia Colored Congress president from 1952 to 1954. After his term he remained with the NCCPT as an advisor to help train new leaders. These examples reflect a general acceptance—though not a preponderance—of male professionals in the association who served as leaders. Men also were invited speakers at annual conventions at both state and national levels, a trend begun by Birney and Hearst at the founding meeting in 1897.[23]

Nonetheless, women remained the overwhelming majority of PTA leaders and members. Like the national level of the organization, state and local PTA units enlisted an energetic corps of women leaders who threw themselves into PTA work with great dedication and enthusiasm. Many were community leaders who belonged to various civic associations such as the General Federation of Women's Clubs, the Daughters of the American Revolution, and the League of Women Voters. As discussed in chapter 1, there was much overlap in membership in the PTA and GFWC, which continued throughout the twentieth century. PTA work offered white women a means to express their civic selves by volunteering for the betterment of the community and the country—as opposed to a means to further their own self-interests and their children's educational advancement, as is often argued in the scholarship—and also was a way to express democratic ideals through participation in legislation reforms and curriculum development. PTA work was virtually the same for black women, but with the added urgency of race work. The leaders of the Colored Congress, many of them teachers and school administrators, assumed the role of PTA organizing as part of their professional responsibilities.[24]

As the white PTA grew exponentially mid-century by creating local units with apparent ease, the black PTA toiled to establish a network to serve far-flung local schools. Nonetheless, the NCCPT quadrupled its membership, growing from 3,000 in 1926 to nearly 12,000 two years later. By the mid-1930s, despite the report by the white PTA at this time that the black PTA "had not grown numerically," the NCCPT membership reached 45,000, representing roughly 0.05 percent of the black population in the South (see figure 3.4). At the same time, however, the white PTA enlisted over 1 percent of the U.S. population in its membership, a significant accomplishment for a voluntary organization. Over time, the Colored Congress continued to grow as it gave black members a civic space for electing leaders, debating educational matters, and exercising rights denied them by white school boards and

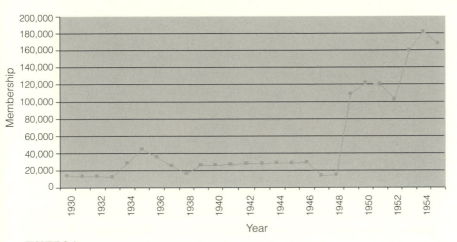

FIGURE 3.4

NCCPT membership, 1930–55. (*Source:* Data from *Coral Anniversary History* and *Our National Family*)

administrators. Thus, membership offered black citizens a "surrogate political role," in which they could hone leadership skills that would serve them in civil society.[25]

The absence of a fully established black PTA network, however, was not an indication that collaborative parent-teacher work at the local level was not being undertaken. Many local associations were organized very much like the ones Narvie Harris coordinated in DeKalb County, Georgia, out of an educator's desire to more effectively teach and improve the lives of her students, their parents, and the community at large. A critical component to her success was spreading home-school groups elsewhere, as Harris gave advice to other teachers on how to start parent-teacher associations. She told one interested organizer, "Well, Honey, you do the same thing I did. . . . There's a handbook that the National put out, and it has everything in there what to do." As more and more local units were established, they became increasingly invested in the work of supporting schools and the NCCPT program which, like the NCPT program, was flexible enough to allow for activities that served particular community interests. In the early 1920s, the NCPT's Special Committee on Colored Parent-Teacher Associations encouraged black citizens to "organize their own Parent-Teacher Associations if possible" according to local traditions and needs. In the early years, communication was uneven across the various levels of organization as black teachers and principals had to face racism, prejudice, and separate and unequal facilities on a daily basis. As one NCCPT worker explained, "Problems of illiteracy and segregation, together with the denial of basic rights to Negroes, made difficult the job of establishing an effective, ongoing national-to-state-to-local unit program."[26]

Even though white PTA leaders attempted to establish a separate organization for black members, the founding of the NCCPT in 1926 presented logistical and structural challenges to the organization. Immediately after the founding meeting of the black PTA, the NCPT created the Committee on Extension Work among Colored People and appointed white PTA worker Adeline Wessels its chair. To prepare for her new role, Wessels collected data on the status of African Americans in the PTA to "give the newly appointed members of this committee an idea of the work that has already been accomplished." Wessels found that even though black members were welcome in PTA units outside the Southeast, few held officer positions or other leadership roles. One of the main questions facing the organization's leaders at this juncture was whether existing black members should be "retired" from the NCPT, as Wessels put it, and encouraged to join the newly formed National Congress of Colored Parents and Teachers. Wessels deferred to the white Board of Managers, which debated at its September 1926 meeting the suggestion that state units "neither solicit nor admit members who are eligible to membership" in the NCCPT. With no way to resolve the issue, the NCPT deferred to individual state units to handle the matter on a case-by-case basis: "Where schools have an attendance of both white and colored members, it is suggested that a friendly spirit be retained between the races, each state branch deciding for itself the advisability of organizing separate colored associations, and colored state branches."[27]

Wessels thereby established a structure by which each state president would appoint five members to serve on a statewide extension committee to aid Colored Congress units. She drew up parameters for organizing state branches of the NCCPT that required ten associations with a minimum membership of 300, and all state and local units were directed to follow the NCPT constitution and bylaws. Keeping in line with PTA practice of collaborating with other organizations, Wessels suggested that the NCCPT join forces with American Child Health Association and Home Demonstration Agents and County Nurses. The Colored Congress experienced growing pains during these early years as it became part of the federation. An early incident resulting from confusion over who qualified as a delegate at its fifth annual meeting prompted Wessels and her committee to draft a grievance policy for the NCCPT. It required Colored Congress units to bring their disagreements to the NCPT, which in turn would be handled by the Committee on Extension Work among Colored People. The Committee also added, however, that the NCCPT should "settle all disagreements within its ranks, the responsibility of our advisors being merely advisory."[28]

As the newly elected president of the NCCPT, Selena Butler was deliberate about organizing her association according to the guidelines of the NCPT. She was well versed in PTA bylaws, since the black parent-teacher organizations had for years worked under the guidance of white units. One of Butler's first tasks was to circulate literature that promoted and disseminated organizational policy and activities in an effort to educate black PTA leaders on the expectations of the NCPT. Colored Congress officers at the local level were instructed to obtain a copy of the leaflet *Reasons and Objects* for information on how to organize and sustain an association. Butler urged her growing list of workers to meet with school principals, church pastors, and other influential individuals in the communities in which they resided. In addition to relying on the white PTA for assistance, she preferred to work with the organizations she knew best in establishing the NCCPT: the Urban League and the National Association for Teachers in Colored Schools. These organizations, rather than the American Child Health Association and Home Demonstration Agents and County Nurses, as suggested by Wessels, would view the NCCPT on equal footing. Both groups had supported the fledgling organization in the early years, helping to establish the state units of the NCCPT. Butler encouraged local units to follow closely the directions for organizing "in order to keep the work standardized," and she encouraged black PTA workers to hold their meetings in the schools so that "parents could become acquainted with teachers and their work." In those states that did not have a recognized (i.e., dues-paying) state congress unit, local units were instructed to work directly with the national leadership of the Colored Congress.[29]

Getting the organizational infrastructure and leaders in place was a challenge for which the NCCPT had to rely on existing networks. The white PTA was available on request, but was not too intrusive. A year after the black PTA was founded, its officers wished to hold an annual convention but knew they did not have enough members, and hence delegates, to secure reduced railroad and meeting hall rates. Therefore, Butler contacted C. J. Calloway, the Executive Secretary of the National Association of Teachers in Colored Schools (NATCS), for help. She asked whether it were possible for the NCCPT to hold its convention two days prior to the NATCS meeting in Nashville in order to benefit from the reduced rates, and her request was granted. However, another problem remained. There was no Nashville branch of the Colored Congress to issue an invitation to hold a convention, a requirement of PTA bylaws. So again Butler made use of another network. She contacted Adeline Wessels, chair of extension work of the white PTA, who in turn contacted the white Tennessee PTA president, Mrs. Herman Ferger. The board of managers of the white Tennessee group unanimously extended the invitation, and black school leaders and clubwomen in Nashville lent their support to the gathering by helping to organize the program and handle the logistics of the meeting. The president of the Nashville Association of Colored Women's Clubs worked with the Nashville PTA leaders to help coordinate the meeting, and some white PTA officers attended what was considered the first convention of the NCCPT.[30]

Foreseeing that her organization would struggle in years to come with building its membership and financial base, Butler encouraged those attending the convention not only to carry out the work of the black PTA according to its ideals, but to do so "in cooperation with other agencies." The first convention subsequently prompted the organizing of black state units, which were added to the original four of Alabama, Georgia, Florida, and Delaware. For example, Tennessee was organized in 1928, a result of the NCCPT's gathering in Nashville the previous year. White and black PTA leaders, along with school leaders and members of the Tennessee Interracial Commission, organized the Tennessee Colored Congress with a membership of fifteen local units and 532 dues-paying members. Butler worked with Missouri's white PTA president, Mrs. W. A. Masters, to organize a segregated unit there the same year, similar to the manner in which the Tennessee unit was created. Missouri, like Tennessee, was organized by Butler and the white state PTA president, Mrs. W. A. Masters. Some states, such as Illinois, California, and Ohio, did not have the minimum number of members and associations to join the NCCPT, so they did not form Colored Congress branches. Those that did, such as New Mexico, Kansas, and Oklahoma, formed state units because of local interest, even though they did not practice *de jure* segregation in those states.[31]

Butler, like many black community activists in the South at this time, viewed her office as working not only for African Americans but also in support of interracial work, something the white association did not explicitly claim as part of its agenda. Michael Fultz argues that black teachers were often called upon to "serve as interracial diplomats and to work at developing support for their schools among influential whites." After the 1920s the white PTA no longer espoused Progressive-era ideals about uniting women across racial lines. That work was carried on separately and became part of the mission of the black PTA. Selena Butler was both spokesperson for her race at such events as the 1930 White House Conference on the "negro mother," and an attendee at the 1931 meeting of the Committee on Interracial Cooperation in Atlanta, Georgia. Butler maintained that the NCCPT was "a fine channel through which effective interracial work could be carried on." Therefore, the black PTA negotiated across the gap between home and school, and between black and white citizens. By 1930, Butler had conceded on the point that separate Colored Congress units could be established in those states without legal segregation (see figure 3.5).[32]

Over time, other voluntary associations and governmental agencies continued to support the work of the Colored Congress. In the early 1930s the

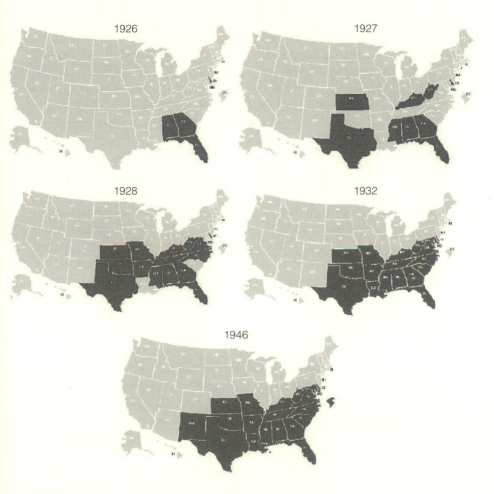

FIGURE 3.5

State units of the NCCPT, 1926–28, 1932, and 1946.[33] (*Sources:* NCCPT, *Coral Anniversary History;* W. McKinley Menchan, "Adult Education Programs of Negro Parent-Teacher Associations," *Journal of Negro Education* 14, no. 3 [1945]: 412; and Georgia Congress of Colored Parents and Teachers, *Our Georgia Family,* [October 1963], 25)

National Kindergarten Association donated literature to and advised the black PTA on establishing kindergartens in segregated schools, and the National Urban League guided the organization on vocational education. During the Depression the white PTA in the South helped out materially. As one black PTA historian explained, "Letters also came to the [black] national office telling of the help and cooperation that the local units were receiving from the white parent-teacher workers—help and cooperation in the form of food and used clothing and aid in contacting welfare agencies. Such reports were encouraging to black national officers, making the load lighter." Each of the Southern states had an advisory committee—as required by the white PTA—that was composed of white and black members. The purpose was to aid NCCPT units and serve as a forum for concerns. However, the committees' work was hierarchical rather than mutually supportive, and typically involved white members giving literature to black clubs and answering questions on protocol and policy as needed. Face-to-face meetings to discuss matters of common concern never materialized.[34]

Both black and white branches were invited to the White House Conferences on Child and Health Protection held each year. In large part, the access to a national forum and leading national policymakers was a major reason the NCCPT was formed as a segregated branch of the white association. Having the ear of American presidents and visibility on a national stage was important to black PTA leaders, who wished to have a platform for the discussion of racial equality. In 1931 Herbert Hoover wrote to Selena Sloan Butler, "The annual convention of the National Congress of Colored Parents and Teachers . . . brings to this city representatives of a very important movement in the improvement of children of the race. . . . I am interested to note that the program of your convention stresses the children's charter as a challenge to better standards of child care and protection."[35]

Five years after it had been organized, the NCCPT had established, with the assistance of white PTA leaders, a network of state and local units across the American South and beyond, with only New Mexico and the District of Columbia creating Colored Congress units later, after 1932 (see figure 3.5). Its membership stood at approximately 15,000, which was not particularly strong but was representative of teachers, community members, and other community leaders. This growth and stability prompted NCPT officers to reassess the nature of the relationship between the two PTA branches. The NCPT's Executive Committee "agreed that the growth and strength of the Colored Congress made desirable a new type of cooperation," and handily abolished the extension committee to coordinate the efforts of the NCCPT. Thus, Adeline Wessels's ties to the Colored Congress were severed. She wrote Butler, "Please do not forget, although I will not be your National Advisor any longer, I am always ready to talk things over with you, if you wish, and to help in any way you may wish me to." Wessels also commended Butler for her work meeting the needs of "your people."[36]

Butler had moved on as well, and although she was no longer NCCPT president, she remained affiliated with the organization to ensure continuity and training in leadership. Butler continued to allow her home to serve as the organization's headquarters through the 1930s. Mary W. Blocker of Florida, Butler's successor as NCCPT president, believed the organization should stand on its own under her leadership, so she attempted to negotiate a new relationship with the NCPT. In 1931 she announced, "The time has come to try our own wings." However, despite the desire of NCCPT leaders to stand on their own, little had changed in terms of their relationship, other than the termination of the extension committee. In its place a Committee on Cooperation with the Colored Congress was formed in which white state presidents and other interested parties assumed the role of guiding and advising the black PTA. Mrs. Charles Center, the chair of the committee, attended the NCCPT's annual meeting in 1936 and found the Colored Congress still struggling: "In hearing their reports we found the most urgent need for a simplified program material and a simplified outline for a health program." Both congresses found the committee beneficial; the white PTA continued to monitor the black PTA's program and development, and the black organization became stronger through the support materials and advice as it continued to work toward a racial understanding.[37]

Building a separate PTA was a challenge through the 1930s, even though it had established practically all Southern state-level offices by 1932. As local PTA units were being organized during the Depression years, it was difficult to enlist them all in state and national membership. Many African American units remained independent of the federation because they would rather donate money to local schools than pay dues to a national association, the benefits of which were not immediately apparent. The distribution of PTA materials by white fieldworkers to local black associations was intended to build the membership base, and was intended only for members of the federation, or dues-paying members. However, since some unaffiliated associations were receiving the materials, the white PTA began the practice of distributing materials only to the NCCPT office, for dissemination to local units. This helped solidify the national level's role as a home base and clearinghouse of materials for segregated state and local units and took some of the control, or direct contact with black local units, away from the national and state leadership of the white PTA.[38]

Despite the challenges of building the NCCPT through the Depression years, by 1940 its membership reached into the tens of thousands, marking a transition to greater independence. Its membership base and network were now strong enough to sustain national and statewide meetings and undertake school improvement work on a wider scale. In 1942 the black PTA had the most state affiliates of its forty-four-year run: twenty associations, which included Washington, DC, and the Virgin Islands. It began to hold its own meetings separate from the American Teachers' Association—formerly the National Association of Teachers in Colored Schools—because it now had enough members to secure reduced travel and conference rates. The two associations did not stop working together, however; in 1954 the headquarters for the Georgia Teachers and Education Association furnished space for the offices of the Georgia Congress of Colored Parents and Teachers.[39] .

The growth of local units began to increase by the 1940s, during the time Narvie Harris was organizing parent-teacher associations in Georgia. For example, a 1940 study of the Alabama Congress of Colored Parents and Teachers revealed that roughly one-third of the state's segregated schools had organized local units and noted that there were more that were unaffiliated with the federation, bringing that number even higher. Of the state's approximately 2,300 rural and 100 urban schools, there were 846 local associations that year. The majority of these associations, of course, were in rural settings, having been organized by the Jeanes teachers' network. The Jeanes teachers of Alabama distributed PTA publications to local units at the opening of the school year, which included "year-round programs recommended by the vice-presidents in charge of organization, extension, welfare, education, home service, and health activities." Black local associations employed the strategies mentioned in the publications to build their membership base, of which serving refreshments, holding attendance contests, and hosting social hours were "the most popular and effective." Nonetheless, it remained a challenge to get rural Alabamans to PTA meetings. Several reasons accounted for this, such as the great distance parents had to travel, as well as work and other family obligations. Many mothers revealed that they could not attend PTA meetings because of domestic service duties.[40]

At this time, black associations adapted another staple of the PTA program, Founders' Day, with one distinct difference. Many local black PTA units celebrated only the founding of the Colored Congress and honored Butler and the other early officers. When white PTA leaders at the national level learned that black local units were celebrating only the founding of the NCCPT, they cited PTA bylaws and instructed them to celebrate also the Congress of Mothers conveners, Birney and Hearst. While the local units of the Colored Congress began to include the white PTA founders in its celebrations, no suggestion was made to local white PTA units around the country to also celebrate the founding of the Colored Congress. The white PTA found itself with a new challenge: to ensure that the black association honored the founders of the National PTA.[41]

In addition to abiding by the program and policies of the white PTA, the black PTA was able to craft its own agenda. Black leaders argued that because of their particular race needs, their PTA program and interests were necessarily "broad and complex" as they kept members abreast of the organization's program, activities, and officers through their publication, *Our National Family*. These needs included an emphasis on fundraising, voting and voter registration, encouraging literacy, and teaching black history in the schools. For example, at the NCCPT's founding convention of May 1926, one of the first items of business was adopting a resolution that denounced the deplorable train depot and railcar conditions facing black patrons. What white PTA workers saw as part of their own association, the freedom to allow white local and state units to adapt rather than adopt PTA policies according to their own particular interests and needs, they had difficulty accepting as part of the black PTA agenda. Such additions to the PTA program, such as voter registration drives, the centrality of fundraising, and other matters, were viewed by white PTA leaders as a "deviation from the standard" and a "false interpretation of objectives."[42]

For black citizens, the gap between home and school was much less pronounced than for white PTA members, as schools were viewed as a part of the community and essential to racial uplift. The 1940 study found that many black PTA units in Alabama extended their work beyond the school. Its author argued, "While the association does much in connection with school problems, its unique opportunity seems to arise from those problems of an educational nature growing out of home and general community life or out of the relationship between these environments on the one hand and that of the school on the other." Black PTA leaders such as Georgia's Narvie Harris knew they could not begin to teach if basic needs were not being met. Harris felt that "you couldn't separate . . . educational from personal basic needs that people have." Therefore, PTA organizers reached into homes and into businesses as well. For example, local black units during the Depression set out to meet with business leaders to investigate "why they refused to employ Negroes in large numbers." The national officers of the Colored Congress, challenged by the flexibility of the organization and the projects that local units took on, decided not to endorse this particular initiative. Caught between the potential of alienating white PTA leaders and supporting their commitment to race work, they instead "urged the local units to compliment those who were responsible for these [job] opportunities."[43]

Mary Blocker, the NCCPT's second president, (1931–35) who, like her predecessor Selena Butler, was educated at Spelman, made the needs of African Americans in the South an explicit part of her association's program. She explained to her constituents that "the race and the individuals must develop through their own initiative." Blocker led the charge to place blacks on school boards and as assistant superintendents of education in segregated school systems to protect the interests of African Americans in the education of their youth, a goal that went largely unrealized. What remained central was fundraising, especially through the Depression years, since without a solid financial base the NCCPT could not continue to build schools and its membership.

Successors Essie D. Mack of Louisville, Kentucky (1935–39), and Mary Foster McDavid (1939–42) continued Blocker's agenda of developing black community and educational leadership. PTA workshops for the Colored Congress were typically hosted by local universities and coincided with in-service workshops that provided training for black teachers. For example, Essie Mack enrolled at Louisville Municipal College while at the helm of the organization in order to "increase her own efficiency as a leader." Through the mid-1930s, the association's leaders paid their own expenses and sought to enlist increasing numbers of volunteers in leadership roles. Also during those years, despite admonitions to focus on educational programs, the majority of the activities of local black and white PTA units were fundraisers to support local schools.[44]

The Organization "Gives and It Receives": Fundraising in the PTA

In 1928 Cornell professor of education Julian Butterworth concluded in his study of white NCPT units, "It is not the responsibility of the parent-teacher association to finance the schools." That PTA workers spent so much of their time doing so was proof to him that they did not understand "the basic principles of public school financing, as now generally accepted by progressive thinkers." Butterworth's position that volunteers' involvement in school fundraising overstepped professional boundaries is reflective of school leaders during a time of PTA organizational growth and stabilization. In the most positive light, parent-teacher groups in the early twentieth century helped build bridges between the schools, which were becoming increasingly professionalized and centralized, and the broader community. Butterworth himself noted that their "material contributions . . . have been commendable." However, by the mid-1920s, the ability of PTA workers to raise funds began to challenge the professional domain of school administrators, who sought to contain and direct this power into projects of their own choosing. As the line of demarcation was becoming clearer between women volunteers and professional educators, white PTA women were accused of being out of touch with the latest educational developments and contributing to schools as though they were still, as one educator put it, "in the days of the little red schoolhouse." PTA workers' fundraising was portrayed as quaint and obsolete by Butterworth, but in truth these contributions, inasmuch as they continued to fund materials and the building of schools, challenged the newly institutionalized means of funding for public education. This tension was reflected in male school leaders' comments that they were concerned with the "meddling attitude" of PTA women and therefore preferred to work with individuals rather than groups. Generally, however, male administrators struggled with the idea of which was easier to manage: groups of women or individual women volunteers.[45]

In the 1920s and 1930s two education scholars, Julian Butterworth and Elmer Holbeck, commented on the white PTA's overreliance on fundraising, and attempted to change this practice by parsing different aspects of PTA work into "acceptable" and "unacceptable" categories. That they commented at all is a testament to their concerns over the influence of the organization on local schools. In particular, they sought to make a distinction between the educational function of local units and their fundraising efforts. Elmer Holbeck of Teachers College, Columbia, echoed Butterworth's claim that white women's PTA work focused too heavily on purchasing school supplies and equipment, hosting fundraisers, and what he called engaging in "other non-educational activities." Butterworth cautioned that the PTA could potentially endanger schools if the associations continued their policies of raising and giving money as they saw fit, and concluded that the energies of local white organizations "were directed into new and in many ways less important fields."[46]

Yet, instead of advising PTA leaders to cease all fundraising efforts, Butterworth suggested they continue these activities with administrators' approval and guidance. He noted that his recommendation to focus on educational work did not "preclude the parent-teacher association from engaging in certain types of activities to finance the school more adequately." Therefore, Butterworth drew up parameters for raising funds under special conditions, which he attempted to limit to providing satisfactory facilities in the poorest school districts that lacked adequate tax money to cover costs. Other than that, he explained, "it is preferable for the parent-teacher organization to create public recognition of the need for better standards than to raise the money through its own efforts." Additional approved activities included raising money for operating expenses. To Butterworth the most egregious offense was the use of PTA contributions to raise a teacher's salary, because it usually contradicted the salary schedule of the school. White PTA workers generally complied with this request and, after 1930, began to hold teacher appreciation lunches and dinners instead of supplementing their paychecks. In other cases, the PTA applauded salary standardization efforts. In 1927 in Cincinnati, the PTA publicly commended the superintendent of schools for creating a standardized salary schedule. By cautioning PTA workers against raising money for local schools, Holbeck articulated the fear on school leaders' minds: that fundraising afforded PTA workers "a greater opportunity to influence policies, legislation, and educational practice."[47]

Even though many school leaders saw fundraising as beneficial, the efforts of both white and black parent-teacher associations were imbued with gender and racial dynamics. White women volunteers' strength in numbers challenged the rising male administrative hierarchy of schools in the 1920s, posing a threat to the male power structure that sought to manage and control women through parent-teacher associations and women's clubs. This threat did not originate in the 1920s; it had existed since the Mothers' Congress was organized in the late 1890s, during the heyday of the women's club movement. For example, in Denver in 1897, the women of the mothers' clubs were "denounced as 'faddists'" for their support of kindergartens and nature study. Denver's male school administrators were so concerned with the potential power of an organized group of women that they successfully forced the nearly 4,000 members of the city's educational union to disband by running a successful smear campaign in the 1890s. However, in the twentieth century, as the PTA grew stronger as an organization, members had the benefits of training and a well-organized network to coordinate more expansive and successful fundraisers. Thus, as Holbeck observed in 1934, the "efforts of local [PTA] units were directed into money-raising activities and other fields which had no connection with the original need which had brought the organization into being." Therefore, educational leaders such as Holbeck and Butterworth sought to make use of the network to inform volunteers about appropriate means to raise cash.[48]

Why did black and white PTA workers spend so much time and effort raising money? Women volunteers, in their desire to put children and child welfare first, perceived many school needs to be addressed and a curriculum that warranted their influence. For instance, fundraisers helped build new schools or renovate them, purchase books and materials for schools, provide uniforms for sports teams, and pay for hot, nutritious lunches. Holbeck found that most of the money raised by PTA workers came from sponsorship of entertainment programs, donations, and various sales. White PTA workers were so dedicated to fundraising that, according to Butterworth, providing cash donations accounted for more than 50 percent of all activities ranked in his 1928 study.[49]

Fundraising was a universal activity among PTA units around the United States, and regional differences called for a variety of needs to be addressed. Butterworth explained that in poorer communities there was a greater reliance on PTA fundraising, "either because a reasonable tax rate does not bring in enough or because the citizens are more reluctant to raise funds for school purposes." For example, not only did the John's Island PTA in South Carolina purchase "half a piano," which it then used as a moneymaker; it successfully led a campaign to install a power plant to light the school. Its Light Committee was formed in 1924, shortly after the association was organized. At the meeting at which the idea was first proposed, members passed a hat to get the fund started. By 1926 the committee had convinced the County Education Board to put up half the money for an electric plant to run the lights for the school, while the PTA agreed to raise the other half by soliciting donations from community members and businesses. In April 1927, only six months later, the John's Island PTA reported that it "had a nice sum to pay toward our electric plant fund. Let us hope that in the near future we will be able to make the final payment." By the start of the next school year they had done so.[50]

Similar ventures were carried out around the country, especially in Southern white associations. PTA units in the three Southern states in Butterworth's study, North Carolina, Texas, and Virginia, ranked the highest in providing money for schools. Conversely, because of Butterworth's attempt to separate acceptable (educational) from unacceptable (fundraising) activities, these states ranked at the bottom of the study in the category "directly concerned with the promotion of educational objectives." White Southern PTA women saw local schools as being in need of their constant support and attention. As a result, their voluntary efforts were political acts, as white women as a group challenged the authority of male school administrators more than the individual taxpayer ever could. In large part, the influence of white PTA women far exceeded the power of taxpayers because the former were well organized and widely networked, and because they walked the line between outsider and insider. Not only were they connected to a major educational organization, but the typical association also held its meetings at the school and enjoyed a fair representation of teachers in its membership. As a result, male administrators around the South and the nation questioned whether such extensive fundraising was the best use of volunteers' time.[51]

Although the amount of time spent on fundraising activities by white parent-teacher associations was significant, it was far surpassed by black teachers and community members in the segregated schools of the South from the turn of the twentieth century through the 1960s. As black teachers made organizing local units a top priority, they, along with volunteers, believed that the PTA's primary purpose was to provide for the financial needs of the school. Continuing to contend with double taxation well into the twentieth century, black citizens gave money, materials, and their time in order to build the schools they wanted for the children in their communities. Around the South, parent-teacher associations paid for the land on which new elementary and high schools were built. After schools were up and running, black citizens continued giving in order that there would be enough money for books and materials, maintenance, and transportation. This "resource development," Carter Julian Savage argues, was a central feature in the lives of black community members at least until the days of desegregation.[52]

Black PTA workers continued to work closely with local schools as their networks expanded across state lines through the Colored Congress. As the organization continued to grow, the national office struggled with having enough money to coordinate the efforts of local and state units. Dues trickled in—members paid as they could—but the shortage of money was not a reflection of the level of commitment of PTA workers in segregated schools. Founding president Selena Butler expressed her concern with the heavy focus on fundraising while her own office suffered because of a lack of adequate financing. She sided with white National PTA officers when she told her constituents that she feared the "real spirit of the work for children would be lost if the organization converted into a purely money-raising machine." She cautioned delegates at the second convention in 1928 "not to make money the object of their parent-teacher work. Money [is] necessary to carry on the work but needed more [is] sympathetic cooperation between parents, teachers, and school authorities." By supporting the guidelines of the majority organization, Butler echoed the sentiments of Butterworth and Holbeck that PTA work should not focus on fundraising, lest it detract from more legitimate educational purposes. However, what sustained the black PTA's commitment to fundraising over time was the belief that giving had mutual benefits for leaders and the membership, and that it was a way to strengthen the federation. NCCPT leaders explained that the organization "gives and it receives." It furnished guidance, materials, and a clearly defined program to its members, who in turn built the association and raised money in order to carry out its program.[53]

Black national and state PTA officers nonetheless remained significantly underfunded and, therefore, had little to work with and even less to give to members in need. Even though the NCPT gave small cash donations to the black organization, its leaders were more inclined to donate publications and other materials to NCCPT local and state units. In its second year, the NCCPT main office remained without a typewriter and other office equipment. The executive board approved the purchase of a typewriter and, as an NCCPT historian explained that "because the organization was young and without funds, the committee felt that the other expenses of the national office should be left to the discretion of the president." This meant that Butler purchased for herself and her office what she needed out of her own pocket. Even though she did not have the same travel funds as the white PTA president, her ability to attend state meetings was not curtailed; she merely paid her own way.[54]

In addition to traveling, Butler kept in touch with the membership through correspondence and the NCCPT magazine, *Our National Family,* which helped the black PTA maintain a collective consciousness. In its pages were shared the activities of local units, the expectations of national and state leaders, and the history of the organization in each February issue, during the time of Founders' Day celebrations. By establishing its own means of print communication in the late 1930s, the NCCPT took another step in standing firmly on its own to the extent that it could. The journal was free for members until later that decade, when leaders decided it would sell subscriptions to raise money. Unlike the white PTA, which enjoyed financial solvency courtesy of an endowment fund established in the early 1900s by its second president, Hannah Kent Schoff, the black PTA struggled to secure enough funds in order to provide leadership to its local units through the mid-twentieth century. Yet, despite such challenges, the NCCPT managed to remain a viable organization, accomplishing much with little money, not unlike the schools it was supporting.[55]

After 1930, as the NCCPT infrastructure gave black civic leaders and educators a means by which to generate greater political and moral support of PTA work, they also had a network to coordinate and train members in fundraising techniques. During these years the black PTA faced the challenge of following the program of the white PTA while attending to the specific material needs of its constituency. A 1929 report by the chair of the Extension among Colored People Committee, Adeline Wessels, revealed the patronizing attitude of the NCPT leadership toward its black counterpart on the matter of fundraising. Wessels expressed concern that black PTA leaders could not be trusted to follow the program of the PTA: "The work done by local colored parent-teacher associations should be along the same lines as those pursued by our own parent-teacher associations and in our capacity as advisors, we should see that nothing detrimental to the welfare of home, school, community, and church be undertaken by their associations." Wessels's use of the word "detrimental" shows her belief that an emphasis on making money took away from the mission and ideals of the PTA. Such seemingly quotidian activities, such as bake sales, Halloween parties, popularity contests, and other moneymaking events, were viewed by white PTA leaders as embracing a "politically subversive character within southern society," as black citizens gained power and control by raising money for education.[56]

In the 1930s white PTA leaders continued to disparage the Colored Congress over the very issue school administrators were criticizing *them* for: too much time spent on fundraising. Throughout the Depression years, the black PTA struggled to retain members, since the majority of its membership base was drawn from wage earners. As unemployment increased, income for the black PTA decreased. Therefore, the membership of the NCCPT dropped and "its work suffered serious setbacks," at least at the national level. Even though many state units stopped holding annual conventions from 1931 to 1936, local parent-teacher associations continued to meet whether dues were paid or not. A study conducted in 1938 of the black PTA units in Alabama found that not only were local units still meeting and conducting PTA business, but there was an overwhelming commitment to fundraising. In fact, it was the most popular activity, followed by scheduling speakers to appear at meetings. Of the 184 local units surveyed by white University of Chicago graduate student Bishop Montgomery, "money raising efforts" was the topic most often reported in meeting minutes. However, Montgomery failed to take into account "sundry contests," which she reported as a separate category; their inclusion would have made her calculations even higher for fundraising. Contests were often, if not always, fundraisers for black local PTA units. Other items of business did not appear with as much frequency, such as musical programs (30 references), open forums (16 references), and study courses (14 references), which were the educational activities promoted by Butterworth and Holbeck.[57]

Even though the main purpose of fundraising in the early twentieth century was to create schools, either by building them or purchasing existing structures, black PTA units continued to hold fundraisers long after schools were built. For NCCPT units in Alabama during the school year 1938–39, after dues were paid to the state and national units, funds were used to supplement teachers' salaries, maintain school buildings and grounds, and purchase school equipment and supplies. In addition to providing nutritious lunches and paying for books and other school materials, black parent-teacher associations collected, repaired, and distributed clothing to schoolchildren and provided eyeglasses and medical examinations for children. Like the white PTA, the black PTA noted the low salaries paid to teachers and sought to "upgrade teaching salaries and to recruit persons for teaching careers." However, because of the relative absence of friction between black principals and the PTA members of a community, contributions to supplement teachers' salaries were often welcomed. PTA members also collaborated with school principals on other spending decisions. Thus the NCCPT contributed as it could to the salary equalization drives, though it may have undercut the endeavor by contributing voluntarily and unevenly, while not working to make the salary increases permanent and part of school districts' salary schedules.[58]

Also, once lower schools were built, school-community groups focused on securing high schools (see figure 3.6). In Mississippi, local PTA units built the first black high school in the state in the 1940s in DeKalb County and later built one in Scott County. Following this, it financed lunch programs and bought uniforms for the school band. In Caswell County, North Carolina, the parent-teacher association approached State Supervisor of Negro Education, N. C. Newbold, in 1938 to lobby for a high school. Newbold agreed, even though the high school was not built for another thirteen years. Since white administrators and boards of education often required black citizens to come up with matching funds, it sometimes held up the process of building a school, as in the case of Caswell County.[59]

Narvie Harris used a variety of approaches to raise money and to get the resources she needed for the schools in her purview. She networked with

FIGURE 3.6

Groundbreaking for a new high school in Georgia, n.d. Avondale Elementary and High School PTA President Gussie Brown is second from left, holding the shovel. (*Source:* Photo reprinted with permission from Narvie J. Harris and Dee Taylor, *African-American Education in DeKalb County,* Arcadia Publishing, 1999; http://www.arcadiapublishing.com)

parents and other agencies to coordinate donations of much-needed items, often being directed by white supervisors to raise the money herself. She explained that in the 1940s she "had invited Mr. Nelson [Superintendent of DeKalb County Schools] to one of our county-wide [PTA] meetings at Avondale, and among the things the teachers asked, you know: 'Can we get some construction paper; can we get some pencils and tablets,' et cetera—and he said to them that day that [we would] if we raised the money. . . . [T]his was the thing in the South, you raised the money—when I was teaching, we would get peanuts from the children and then have a carnival and sell them to them."[60]

As with white PTA units, sometimes the money raised by black organizations was used to prepare the next generation of teachers and community leaders. The black PTA of Alabama, like other state units, had autonomy in developing and awarding college scholarships. The Alabama Colored Congress of Parents and Teachers gave three full scholarships at its annual meeting to the top high school students in the state to attend teachers' colleges. However, its leaders wanted to give more but could not, given the lack of funds, so it successfully encouraged other civic, social, and fraternal associations to award scholarships as well. Full scholarships were rare, though. In the 1930s the Maryland Congress of Colored Parents and Teachers awarded what it called "senatorial scholarships" to supplement the tuition for high school students who wanted to attend Maryland colleges, and in the 1940s Arkansas began to give $100 scholarships to students entering colleges in that state. At least as late as 1961, the South Carolina Colored Congress awarded two scholarships a year. Another common way for black PTA units to help students get to college from the 1930s to the 1950s was to create student loan funds, in which students were charged low interest rates; Texas had such a fund, as did Maryland. In the late 1930s Maryland initiated an annual scholarship loan fund, which lasted into the 1960s.[61]

In her survey of principals and PTA officers on the seven aims of the Alabama Colored PTA, Montgomery found virtual unanimity around promoting the welfare of children, uniting home and school, and helping citizens better understand the workings of public education. Like white PTA workers and white school leaders, black PTA workers and black administrators differed in their opinions on the centrality of fundraising to support local schools. Black principals were much more supportive than black PTA officers of these activities, whereas white school leaders tended to be less supportive of fundraising than white PTA officers. As the leaders of segregated schools, black principals knew their successes depended on the money that could be raised by the PTA network. In Vanessa Siddle Walker's study, when Principal Dillard decided he wanted a regional high school to be built for the people of Caswell County, he invited the parents and patrons of the Yanceyville PTA to school meetings and then, in 1933, enlisted them in the effort. He needed their advocacy with the state board of education to get the school built. After the PTA was told the funding would be approved if enough students could be found, the parents canvassed the county. The Yanceyville PTA saw the school through to completion, and even as late as 1952 it continued to support the school, supplying Venetian blinds worth over three thousand dollars.[62]

White PTA leaders remained critical of the fundraising activities of black units, in large part because they were concerned that it would lead to gambling or other immoral acts, and they could never have the organization associated with such unseemly activities. As Montgomery observed, "This unusual emphasis on money raising, despite its justification on other grounds, may divert the attention of parents from the main purposes of the parent-teacher organization. One favorable aspect of these financial efforts, however, is revealed in the fact that associations have not resorted to gambling, raffling, and other forms of entertainment detrimental to character building in communities." This assertion echoes Adeline Wessels's concerns of a decade earlier, that black PTA units potentially might initiate money-raising activities that were illegal or immoral, reflecting racist beliefs about black citizens' inability to manage their finances and channel fundraising efforts in proper, acceptable ways.[63]

Such attitudes about black PTA fundraisers continued into the 1950s, when a similar study conducted by Marguerite Taylor, a white PTA officer at the state level in Missouri, argued virtually the same points. Taylor surveyed the 75 local units in elementary and high schools—representing roughly 3,400 members—of the Missouri Colored Congress for her master's thesis. Taylor's objective was to "propose or recommend ways or means of improving the programs of the Colored Parent-Teacher Association." She examined the activities of these local units and compared them to the approved activities of the white PTA, noting in her conclusions that activities deemed secondary by the white PTA were quite primary for black units, especially fundraising. Taylor, like other white PTA leaders, overlooked the necessity of fundraising activities for segregated schools and concluded, "Although entertainments and money making devices often contribute valuable and legitimate services to the school and the community, care [should be] exercised to keep such activities in proper relationship to the real purpose for which the organization is structured—the welfare of children."[64]

Sometimes, however, fundraising and the welfare of children intersected in ways other than monetary contributions to local schools, which was something Taylor had overlooked. In 1951 the officers of the Missouri Congress of Colored Parents and Teachers learned that the Missouri State Department of Education was about to organize a Citizens' Commission for the Study of Education to examine the scope, content, and quality of educational programs in the state. Infuriated that none of their members was "allowed active representation on the Commission," they decided to conduct their own study of the "inequalities of facilities and services" for black children, which they would submit to the State Commissioner of Education. Similar studies were taken up around the South to protest unequal conditions with increasing frequency in the late 1940s and early 1950s and were often initiated by whites who wanted to maintain segregation. Overcrowding and inadequate facilities were typical findings that resulted, and they were published in *Our National Family* so that all NCCPT members could be aware of the results. By 1952 the Missouri Colored Congress began to spread the word to other state congresses in the federation, arguing that "the elimination of bad community influences and conditions as well as the removal of unequal educational opportunities in all school districts are the responsibility of the [PTA] Council." This effort shaped its platform in its sunset years, as the Missouri Colored Congress became more outspoken about unequal educational opportunities for children in the state. In 1952 it launched its "Pennies for Opportunity" project, which had the goal of funding the statewide study of "educational opportunities available to Negro children."[65]

Raising enough money at local, state, and national levels of the organization remained a constant concern for black PTA leaders through the middle decades of the twentieth century. One NCCPT historian summarized years of financial struggle, challenging its focus on raising money for its operations:

> The question of finance has long been a problem for the National [Colored] Congress as well as for its state branches and local units. As is often the case with budding organizations, many local units were prone to borrow too much time from their programs for children for fund-raising projects. Little of the money they raised, however, was converted into parent-teacher dues and often the expense of carrying out the work of the Congress exceeded the dues forwarded to the national treasury by the state congresses. Some local units, too, were poor and needed to look to the National Congress for aid, financial and otherwise, which it was not in a position to give. If the Congress had been better financed it could have given more attention to the needy areas.

Nonetheless, the black PTA carried out its work as many needy communities benefited from its leaders' and members' efforts in supporting education for African American children in underfunded schools. White PTA workers continued fundraising as a main activity at least through the 1950s, when the organization decided that its role in schools and communities had to change once and for all, and it shed the emphasis on raising cash. While fundraising certainly was central to the work of black and white local-level units from the mid-1920s through the 1940s and beyond, other educational concerns were shared by the various levels of leadership. In particular, a major area of concern for black and white parent-teacher associations was the school curriculum.[66]

"Offerings That Are More Functional": The PTA and the School Curriculum

Despite Margaretta Willis Reeve's public pronouncement that the PTA was not a crusade to reform the schools, the organization had been doing just that, and continued to do so through the mid-twentieth century. The most significant contribution the PTA and other women's clubs made to the school curriculum during the Progressive era was initiating curriculum innovations—such as kindergartens, vacation schools, school lunches, and vocational education programs—that helped to transform schools into social service institutions. Through the mid-twentieth century, curriculum reform continued to be as central to local-level PTA work as fundraising, even though members were cautioned to defer to the expertise of professional educators. Even Bishop Montgomery, who criticized the emphasis on fundraising of Alabama's black

PTA units, noticed "quite clearly that the activities of the organization are not devoted exclusively to the matter of raising money for school buildings and equipment." She was referring to the many citizenship and character-building clubs the Alabama Colored Congress coordinated around the state. These clubs were not unique; they were a project commonly undertaken by black and white PTA units around the country.[67]

By the late 1920s the National PTA took inspiration and direction from a major document drawn up by one of the curriculum committees of the NEA in the 1910s, the Cardinal Principles report. The Cardinal Principles were conceptualized by the NEA's Committee to Reorganize Secondary Education in 1918, and they intended to rework the school curriculum around seven ideals: sound health, vocational effectiveness, wise use of leisure, ethical character, worthy home membership, mastery of the tools and techniques of learning, and useful citizenship. These principles emerged in the early twentieth century as part of a movement to prepare citizens for different yet complementary tasks—thus the emphasis on relevance and differentiation in the school curriculum. While historians of education give credit to the Cardinal Principles for shaping the comprehensive high school in the early twentieth century, they have overlooked their wider role in elementary and secondary education and, in particular, their popularization by civic groups such as the PTA. Having lost the battle to reform the school curriculum around parenting and childrearing in the 1910s, and agreeing with professional educators that the school curriculum should prepare students for life beyond school, the National PTA placed the Cardinal Principles at the center of its program, in large part as a result of the focus on worthy home membership, but also because of its valuing of health and character and citizenship education. In other words, what others saw in the revised school curriculum—vocational preparation for future roles—NCPT and NCCPT members welcomed as an opportunity to prepare students to be family members and citizens, with a particular emphasis on their future roles as parents.[68]

The Cardinal Principles anchored PTA programs and activities as the organization was able to further publicize them to the American citizen. In a series of meetings to determine what each of the principles meant for PTA workers and the organization, committee members discussed the meaning of "worthy home membership." This aim was welcomed by PTA members who believed it could help members improve their family lives and work for "laws raising the requirements for marriage," better housing, better building codes, better neighborhood parks and playgrounds, and also better municipal planning. Worthy home membership, PTA leaders hoped, was also the justification for high school courses on homemaking and parenting. However, the organization's leaders promoted the notion that such courses were to be more expansive than cooking and sewing classes and should, instead, be "a broad study of the home and the family living in the home and their relation within the home and in the community." They hoped that the courses would become "a highly desirable part of the program of study of every girl and boy."[69]

In 1928 the white PTA formally developed its own "Sevenfold Program of Home and School," which essentially was a restatement of the Cardinal Principles of Education. The Sevenfold Program was promoted in PTA magazines and at workshops in the late 1920s, to let members know that the "Seven Cardinal Principles of education [will be the] permanent platform of Parent Teacher work." This revised platform guided the association's activities at all levels, was reproduced in PTA publications, and provided topics at meetings and for speakers for decades to come. Each of the seven points was considered essential to a "Program of Work for a Good Citizen." The justification for the Sevenfold Program was made clear by an officer of the PTA at its September 1928 Board of Managers Meeting: "In spite of the fact that these objectives have been before the country for some time, great numbers of parents and teachers still think of education in terms so narrow that many children are denied a fair start in life." However, an emphasis on vocational education was not to be entirely embraced by the middle-class women who served as NCPT leaders at the state and local levels. Even though women such as Eunice Harper Leonard of South Carolina promoted the Sevenfold Program, they did so mainly for other people's children. While Leonard was fond of statements such as "It is better to be an expert blacksmith than a failure in law," her four children were college-educated professionals.[70]

The black PTA also, of course, put the Cardinal Principles front and center in its program, which eventually caused it to further question the organization's racial policies and practices. In regard to the Cardinal Principle "wise use of leisure time," the NCCPT sought to give African American youth appropriate and wholesome recreational activities. Its leaders felt that "Negroes had a greater need for recreation facilities than did other groups. Because of their generally low financial status . . . [t]hey had few parks, community centers, and supervised playgrounds in their communities." The association wanted municipalities to fund such wholesome endeavors as recreational dancing because, in part, "Municipal recreation was democratic and inclusive." Another issue, health, was of critical importance to black PTA members, so it became one of the most central curricular issues. The NCCPT defined health as more than physical wellness: "it was emotional stability, a wholesome outlook on life, the ability to adapt one's self to society and the environment, the capacity to create and enjoy happiness." The Colored Congress of Alabama had a wide range of health initiatives in the late 1930s, which included the Summer and Pre-School Round-Ups, checkups by county nurses for preschool children, vaccination of all school students, the provision for hot lunches at school, and special health programs such as cleanup campaigns and pictures and features for the schools. Montgomery, the graduate student who analyzed the Alabama black PTA's program, remarked, "Recognizing that health is one of the cardinal principles of education, the Alabama Branch of the National Congress of Colored Parents and Teachers contributes to the health program of the public schools."[71]

In practice, however, black PTA leaders wanted schools to include liberal arts, or what they called the "more traditional" courses, and even suggested that they replace the "offerings that are more functional." Therefore, local units emphasized two seemingly disparate matters in the school curriculum: vocational education and the liberal arts, including black history. NCCPT leaders, the majority of whom were teachers, did not distinguish between the two and saw both as critical to success in a democracy. Adopting the slogan "Train People for Jobs," the black PTA pushed for an extensive program of vocational education "to prepare youth to take their places in the labor world; for the full development of the pupil and to continue the ideals of democracy." Local units also promoted the teaching of black history. For example, in the late 1920s the West Virginia Congress of Colored Parents and Teachers donated books on black history to school libraries. The association also passed a resolution urging that "Negro history become a required subject in the school curriculum." This initiative was there from the start, when the first president Selena Butler reiterated what other black educational and civic leaders were calling for: "Hang upon the walls of your homes pictures of the men and women of your own race[;] . . . fill your libraries with books that are the product of the Negro brain." The importance of teaching black history was clear to PTA members, as it was related to a positive sense of self and group identity that would impel young African American students to be successful and to fight inequality. Such was the meaning of one black PTA leader's statement in 1952 when she asked, "Can we, in spite of some sort of strategy which has omitted the Negro from the American History textbook, motivate our boys and girls to go on?"[72] In this sense, the attention paid to history can be considered the rare liberal arts curriculum issue the PTA took on. In general, white and black PTA units did not interject their opinions on the formal curriculum, though they did engage in a small way in the turf wars around textbook adoption.[73]

The centrality and importance of family, citizenship education, health, and wise use of leisure were the elements that most appealed to black and white PTA workers and ended up shaping policies and programs beyond the World War II years.[74] Therefore, the PTA was in large part responsible for the success of the Cardinal Principles in the schools, since it included them in its literature and publications and promoted them to its ever-growing membership.

Attention to citizenship by the association never waned, though the ways PTA leaders construed citizenship and its goals changed over time. In general, however, what began in the 1920s as a commitment to democratic ideals by cultivating character and virtue was replaced with an emphasis in the 1940s on cultural understanding and, for the black PTA, civil rights.

From the mid-1920s to the end of World War II, the two branches of the National PTA grew steadily and enlisted many volunteers around the country. By the end of the war, the two PTA branches had fully developed infrastructures with separate local, state, and national levels of leadership that followed the same program. While the white PTA sought to ensure the black PTA's compliance with its program, it nonetheless recognized the flexibility of the federated structure in letting local and state units cultivate their own interests around the core ideals of the National PTA. However, despite PTA and school leaders' insistence that the purpose of the organization was not to fund the public schools, black and white PTA workers continued to hold fundraisers through the 1960s as a central activity. During the twentieth century, the PTA based its program on the Cardinal Principles of Education, as health and civic education pervaded the work of the association. Emphasizing the role of citizens in a democracy led the black PTA to be increasingly outspoken about inequalities in education and society and led to their questioning the NCPT's policies on racial segregation.

CHAPTER 4

Making America
"Strong from Within"

School Lunches, Civics, and Intergroup Relations

IN A 1940 article in *National Parent-Teacher,* the magazine produced by the white PTA, the author reminded readers, "As parents and as teachers we cannot neglect the opportunity to make America strong from within. In brief, this building of America through its children and youth is the *unique* function of the parent-teacher movement in American democracy." With 2.4 million white members and 26,000 black members that year, the PTA was a growing force with a well-established federated infrastructure. White PTA leaders positioned the organization as a patriotic institution on the vanguard of upholding American ideals such as prosperity and clean, wholesome living. In the South, the days of building schools were generally over, since black local units had successfully created a viable system of schools in the early twentieth century. During the middle decades of the twentieth century, white and black PTA members, steered by the Committee on the Reorganization of Secondary Education's (CRSE) Cardinal Principles, focused on increasing membership and attending to educational matters such as study circles and parent education programs. Local units continued fundraising activities as national and state leaders led campaigns for legislation to benefit children and families, such as school lunches. As this chapter reveals, while both PTA branches supported the principles of democracy, each interpreted and applied them differently. The separate paths, however, led to the same conclusion by the end of World War II: a segregated PTA was true to neither the nation's nor the organization's founding principles.[1]

Both branches of the PTA experienced their greatest growth trajectories from the mid-1920s through the years after World War II, although the black

PTA continued to lag behind in the proportion of members of the African American population. The work carried out by each Congress in the early decades of the twentieth century had set the foundation for a strong intra- and interstate network of units and regenerating corps of leaders. In the 1930s and 1940s, as R. Scott Baker explains, the "tempo of African American educational activism quickened," to which I would add that the infrastructure of the black PTA allowed for this activism in an organization that whites perceived as nonthreatening. The biggest increase for the NCCPT occurred during the 1951–52 school year, with a membership drive that far exceeded its goal of a 10 percent increase, bringing instead a 21 percent jump. The momentum around civil rights activity contributed to black citizens joining in increasing numbers after World War II. During the mid-twentieth century, the white PTA grew from 3.5 million to over 8.8 million in 1954, while the membership of its segregated counterpart doubled, from approximately one hundred to two hundred thousand.[2]

As Crawford and Levitt argue, during these years, the PTA "reaped the rewards of a societal emphasis on traditional families . . . and concerted membership drives."[3] Awards given to state and local units with the largest membership increases allowed for parent-teacher associations around the country to enjoy growing rosters. These competitions—in which members were recruited through door-to-door canvassing, media advertisements, and publicity announcements—as well as the PTA network and publications, illustrated to members around the country what other units were doing. One white state officer from South Carolina, making a case for a membership drive in the Palmetto state, revealed that some PTA units were aided by state boards of education. West Virginia doubled their membership in two years, she explained, because "Their State Department of Education has ruled that no rural school may be ACCREDITED without PTA that is a Congress unit, and DOES it bring in the bacon?" By 1950, however, leaders within the organization questioned the intensity of membership drives and wondered whether it came at the expense of having PTA workers dedicated to other organizational pursuits. They argued, "Large memberships should not be our goal, but more efficient understanding members who desire to have a share in the work of this child welfare organization and are eager to do their part." On the home front, between the two World Wars, many were anxious about juvenile delinquency, crime, and poverty, which helped the PTA position itself as an agency to help ameliorate society's ills through parent education, support of local schools, and legislation.[4]

The black PTA continued its focus on fundraising in an effort to generate enough of a cash flow to cover costs and support local schools while having enough money to run the state and national offices, which remained a cause for concern among the organization's leaders. The NCCPT struggled with bankruptcy over the years and sought various means to remedy the situation as financial solvency varied across segregated state units. For instance, Georgia enjoyed fiscal stability and maintained a support staff and state office, while others struggled with bringing independent units into the fold. Alabama reported that their "total State membership is unknown because many local units are operating under the name of PTA but are not taking part with the State organization." Because of poverty in many rural areas, some local organizations did not join the federation and remained independent, but the NCCPT leadership discovered this trend in more densely populated areas as well. This hesitation is a subtext in the history of the PTA, as some black local units resisted joining what was generally perceived as a white organization. Nonetheless, the main reason remained financial: why send dues to state and national governing bodies when tangible results were not immediately apparent? As a result, during the middle decades of the twentieth century, the national office of the Colored Congress was very much concerned with building a stronger network of parent-teacher groups.[5]

In addition to local-level fundraisers, other efforts raised money for state units. In 1950, pressed for ways to generate income, the NCCPT started charging an annual subscription rate of fifty cents for its quarterly, *Our National Family*, and increased it to one dollar two years later.[6] Founders' Day celebrations were also moneymakers for the organization, and the NCCPT saw them as especially important to financial solvency, given that dues were low and membership proportionately small. One officer reminded members of the rationale for Founders' Day celebrations: "Remember, we are trying to run a National Office and dues alone cannot do this and carry out our program thus planned. . . . [M]oney is needed, much money."[7] Nevertheless, NCCPT leaders prided themselves on the fact that less attention was being given to fundraising and more to educational projects by the early 1950s. The leaders of the Colored Congresses in North Carolina and West Virginia heralded the fact that "There has been a tendency to reduce the amount of time devoted to money-raising activities and concentrate the efforts on home-school cooperation, community betterment, and youth participation." West Virginia state president A. L. Younger argued, "To place emphasis on fund raising campaigns throughout the year thereby neglecting to set aside time at each meeting to study problems affecting the development of youth is indeed a serious charge to those who are responsible for leadership." In spite of this, some state units organized major fundraisers. The Texas Congress of Colored Parents and Teachers raised a thousand dollars to give to the American Red Cross Fund in 1952.[8]

Beyond fundraising efforts, the PTA agenda from the mid-1920s to just after World War II focused on two interrelated ideas of the Sevenfold Program of Home and School: health initiatives and civic education. Each of these interests eventually led black and white PTA leaders to consider the matter of race and inequality in the organization, schools, and U.S. society in general. Even though successive white and black PTA presidents introduced new platforms after each election, the organization's agenda remained remarkably consistent over time and across region. In particular, PTA leaders continued to draw on the core ideals of the CRSE's Cardinal Principles of 1918 at least until the early 1950s, and into the 1960s for the NCCPT.[9] For instance, when white PTA leader Mabel Wilhams Hughes took office in 1946, her administration implemented a Four-Point Program that included strengthening the school curriculum, improving the health of the nation's children, promoting world understanding, and stressing parent education. Black PTA leaders also revised their programs around the same principles. In 1951 Virginia's Twelve-Point Program included vocational education, health, and social and mental adjustment. In many respects the social service initiatives implemented in schools during the Progressive era did not disappear as the twentieth century wore on. Instead, the National PTA took the lead among civic associations in strengthening its connection to local schools with such issues as lunches, civic education programs, home economics, and other such matters that forged greater connections among school, society, and home. Therefore, the PTA became a supporter, promoter, and mobilizer of educational reform initiatives by virtue of its location in civil society, in the interstices of schools and the public.[10]

A major concern of Americans during the Depression was the significant number of unemployed youth, which prompted educators to rethink how the school curriculum could address the dual challenges of eradicating juvenile delinquency and preparing young people for gainful employment. Beginning with Roosevelt's New Deal initiatives, the federal government began to play a greater role in public education in the 1930s. These efforts culminated in the National Defense in Education Act of 1958, which increased federal involvement in the school curriculum in terms of preparing citizens for a modern, technological society. During the war years, the curriculum changed from critiquing capitalism and the social order to emphasizing patriotism and national cohesion, and the PTA followed suit by supporting and promoting the new curricular emphases and helping with war projects. Voices of concern could be heard in PTA meetings around the country. Kentucky's white PTA president summed up these changes in society, schools, and the PTA:

> Chet Huntley of N.B.C. Television team really woke us up with some astonishing statements in his speech on the last night [of the PTA convention]. Some agreed and many disagreed on his accusations of the P.T.A. being responsible for so much being spent on recreation and fine cafeterias; and so little being

spent for the actual teaching of our children. It seems that nearly all children of foreign countries can speak our language but we are unable to speak theirs. With everything changing and the world shrinking so fast it seems that we have plenty food for thought concerning the education of our children.[11]

No matter what the PTA agenda emphasized, and no matter how many points it included in its programs year after year, citizenship and democracy remained as core ideals. This emphasis, along with the postwar interest in international relations and the growing Civil Rights movement, challenged the organization ultimately to face its complicity in perpetuating discrimination, prejudice, and segregation by maintaining a separate and unequal organization. During the mid-twentieth century, the National PTA was forced to look again at itself in terms of what ideals it espoused, and while the white PTA emphasized tolerance and the eradication of prejudice, its focus was on international, not domestic, relations. The black PTA, conversely, focused on the United States and called forth the founders' ideals, challenging the entire organization to return to one of its original principles, racial inclusion. Beatrice Morgan, the NCCPT's president from 1949 to 1953, was fond of restating Alice Birney's call that the PTA was open to all, "irrespective of creed, color, or condition." Yet Morgan maintained a position of self-sufficiency as she challenged black PTA members to act on these words, telling them, "We must stop looking to the white people and to God to do for us what we can do for ourselves."[12]

The NCCPT embraced the organization's mid-century emphasis on rights, tolerance, and equality, as evidenced in the materials it circulated to members and the Intergroup Relations committees it coordinated. In large part, the publications of the two PTA branches helped shape and sustain the discussion about race, difference, and tolerance. The role of black periodicals helped inform members' civic and organizational vision, as discussions of tolerance and difference were framed in terms of democracy. It is important, however, to remember that these resulted in multiple discourses instead of binary, opposing discourses, as PTA leaders and members interpreted the organization's goals according to their own beliefs. Some white PTA members were allies to the cause of racial equality; some were not. Also, while virtually all black PTA members supported racial equality and desegregation, some wondered what desegregation of schools would do to the organization they had taken years of hard work to establish. Nonetheless, it is important to view the organization and the schools they supported as sites of political activism by members, in particular black members who were allied with a large-scale, majority-white voluntary organization. In this regard, PTA activities at the local, state, and national levels continued to be political endeavors over time as members worked for or against desegregation of schools and the organization. And the roots of this impulse were found in the interwar years.[13]

Additional subtle changes are evident in the development of both organizations during the mid-twentieth century. The white PTA developed an experienced leadership group that influenced national legislation that had an impact on local schools. White PTA leaders were nationally known, especially in Washington, DC, lobbying circles. Yet both branches enjoyed the visibility of national events, such as the 1950 White House Conference on Child Welfare, which white and black PTA presidents attended. The National Congress of Colored Parents and Teachers came to rely less and less on the NCPT and began to stand on its own as it, too, developed a regenerating group of leaders and recruited teenagers to be members of Junior PTA units in order to sustain leadership and the organization beginning in the early 1950s. Topics such as "Education for Responsible Leadership" were part of the program—for black and white members—that sought to perpetuate the organization through proper management according to PTA policies and practices. A workshop held by the NCCPT in 1949 was described as enlightening leaders who "in turn shall develop similar workshops in their own states and thus increase the numbers of local workers who are qualified to lead." Black PTA officers viewed the establishment of the organization's headquarters in Dover, Delaware, in 1948 as the start of "a new era" for the organization, since it was its first permanent location. For black PTA workers, leadership became an essential element to carry out the work of racial uplift and racial equality as the twentieth century wore on.[14]

One transformation within black local units was that the language of cooperation seeped into its interactions in schools and at meetings. For example, a 1951 report of the Maryland Congress of Colored Parents and Teachers annual meeting noted a "lack of cooperation between the church, the home and the school." The black PTA, by coming into its own, began to reflect the tensions between professional educators and volunteers that had long been a characteristic of white PTA units. Yet cooperation also referred to how the two organizations related to each other, and the two branches of the PTA developed different interpretations of the term. For example, the white Arkansas Congress of Parents and Teachers (ACPT) claimed in 1948 that it had been cooperating with the Arkansas Colored Congress for years because it had donated surplus publications and program materials to the black PTA and offered assistance with workshops, conventions, and district meetings. In contrast, cooperation for black PTA members meant more than charitable giving; it meant working together to solve racial problems. By 1945 NCCPT president Anna Strong requested that the two associations meet regularly to discuss common concerns. Generally, white PTA leaders agreed to meet with black PTA units on occasion, but walked a fine line between welcoming African American members as part of their political base, which could potentially alienate white racist members, and keeping them at arm's length. In so doing, white PTA leaders and members were free to not work for racial equality if they did not wish to. Therefore, in many communities around the country NCPT units carried on without regard for the interests of black members.[15]

"Perhaps I Am Too Interested in This Project": The Politics of Health

During the middle decades of the twentieth century, the National PTA designed its programs and projects around the foundational Seven-Fold Program of the late 1920s and promoted healthful living as a means to a stronger democracy. Improving the health of American children and adults emerged as a primary aim for black and white congresses alike. Both branches of the PTA worked closely with the American Cancer Society, the March of Dimes, and other associations dedicated to eradicating disease during the mid-twentieth century and included health issues in parent education workshops and programs. Yet, while health was a centerpiece of both programs, it was of acute importance for the black PTA because of poverty and lack of access to information and health care among black communities in the South. As white PTA women worked to teach and disseminate information on healthful living, nutrition, and disease prevention, black PTA women viewed improving the health and health education of African American community members as critical to equality of opportunity and the vibrancy of an African American citizenry.

In her first message as president of the NCCPT in 1949, Beatrice Moore Morgan outlined the dual focus of her tenure: better health and increased membership, which could be construed as organizational health. Morgan explained that the "specific objective [of the NCCPT] must be to help in every way possible to produce a generation of healthy minds within healthy bodies." Under her leadership, the NCCPT publicized National Negro Health Week, a nationwide effort it credited to Booker T. Washington. By 1950 it was a year-round program run by the Public Health Service of the Federal Security Agency. With the potential for the desegregation of schools and public places looming as litigation moved through the courts, black PTA members tried to be proactive in protecting their interests, and references to health programs became increasingly linked to the idea of equality. In the early 1950s the NCCPT sought to remove any references to "Negro program" in federal health initiatives for fear of being excluded. If they were in a separate category, they could be overlooked or, worse yet, dropped. Therefore, the NCCPT encouraged members to "work towards a complete oneness in all state health programs." S. M. Burrell, chair of the NCCPT's Health Committee in 1951, explained that "Interpreting . . . the work of your state department to local communities and fostering as many projects as possible [will] bring about a good working relation between the two races from the standpoint of better health for all." In 1952, before she stepped down, Morgan continued to instruct NCCPT local units to plan the new school year around Summer Round-up, immunization programs, and school lunches.[16]

The PTA's commitment to health typically meant getting involved in federal legislation; at mid-century the PTA was aggressively political in terms of its ability to mobilize members around legislative causes. The PTA relied on strategies that had been developed by women's associations in the late nineteenth century that, by the second decade of the twentieth century, became part of the skill repertoire of the organizations as they combined forces to agitate for legislation on behalf of women and children. The NCPT had cut its activist teeth in the 1910s with the fight for the passage of the Sheppard-Towner Infancy and Maternity Protection Act. PTA leaders' experience with this major piece of federal legislation helped develop their lobbying abilities and strengthened the communication network of the organization. The Sheppard-Towner Act, which was passed in 1921, sought to reduce infant mortality rates by providing federally subsidized prenatal clinics and health care education to mothers. The National Congress of Mothers and Parent-Teacher Associations was one of several women's groups, along with the General Federation of Women's Clubs and Association of Collegiate Alumnae, to lobby extensively for the passage of the act, which was repealed in 1929.[17]

Even though maternalism had become outdated as an ideological framework after 1920 with the fight for women's suffrage having been won, the PTA continued to work for national legislation in the interest of child welfare, having honed its political lobbying skills and extended its federated network across the country with millions of members united through a well-coordinated infrastructure. Elizabeth Tilton, the chair of the NCPT's Legislative Department in 1922, set the tone for PTA legislative efforts for decades to come:

> Legislation is the high-tide of all Civic work. Good things are tried out in local communities and when their worth is proved, the call comes to give them to everybody and the only way to do this is to pass a federal law. There is no better investment of energy than that put into the passage of a beneficent law, it is so-far-reaching in its effect.

From this point, the National PTA made the commitment to focus on education bills in the U.S. Congress.[18]

By the end of the 1920s it became apparent that a female voting bloc was not going to materialize as expected, and concomitant changes occurred in terms of the ability of organized women to influence legislation and social policy. However, the PTA continued to focus on legislation through the twentieth century, since it had built its program around child welfare and had the organizational strength to effect change in the U.S. Congress. Moreover, focusing on legislation, according to PTA members, was one aspect of the "practice of citizenship" or, as one PTA officer put it, "in a democracy legislation should be designed to accomplish the greatest good for the greatest number."[19] PTA members were notified about critical issues and were frequently called upon to publicize them to the rest of the membership and the public and to write to elected officials. The major issues on which the legislative committees of both PTA branches focused at mid-century included federal aid to education, the School Lunch Act, the Child Labor Act, and national defense matters, such as the creation and promotion of the United Nations in an effort to support international peace.[20]

All the while, the NCCPT did not have the numerical or political force on its own to rally its members around legislation, which was one of the reasons black educational leaders remained as a segregated branch of the PTA for so long. As part of the PTA, black educators reaped the benefits of an alliance with a powerful organization that had the ability to make significant change and to reach citizens across the South as well as politicians and policymakers. However, the NCCPT did not just publicize the white PTA's legislative agenda verbatim but amended each proposal, increasing its appeal to disenfranchised citizens and working to further racial equality. This was the reason the NCCPT supported such initiatives as the equalization of schools and salaries for teachers in the 1940s. By 1951, the organization was recognized for its ability to mobilize citizens by becoming the first black organization invited to join the Women's Joint Congressional Committee, a nonpartisan agency designed to bring women's organizations together around legislative matters of common concern. African American PTA leaders endeavored to show their political lobbying in the best light, not as agitation but, in typical PTA parlance, as supporting the tenets of child welfare and democracy. As William I. Lee, chair of the NCCPT's Legislation Committee in 1952 put it, "[Being involved in federal legislation] is not political interference, but a helpful force which should always exert its influence at the right time and in the right place to balance our national scales and do justice as far as it is humanly possible."[21]

The proposal to support federal aid to education, an issue taken up by professional associations and civic groups, was a major agenda item for the PTA's legislative committees and can serve as an example of how the black PTA infused the initiative with the language of racial equality. Following the NEA's lead, both branches of the PTA backed the federal aid issue, but the NCPT did not explicitly mention race when explaining its support for the measure to its membership. At its annual meeting in 1949, however, the NCCPT added the proviso that such legislation "will guarantee to all children, regardless of race, creed, or color the same financial assistance without discrimination on the part of the states which are recipients of such Federal Aid."[22] Through the 1950s the NCCPT used the fight for federal aid to education as one way to work for equal school facilities and opportunities for black children, hoping and expecting that if enacted, it would "apply equally to all school children without regard to race or color." In so doing, they joined forces with the NAACP, the American Teachers' Association, and the National Association of Colored Women. Yet black PTA leaders knew that their support, hopefully, would make segregation so expensive that it would "die of its own weight," as was the intended goal of the NAACP's equalization suits in the 1930s. Members had learned to be outspoken about these matters, since earlier experiences, such as with the Sheppard-Towner Act, had raised their suspicion as to whether the argument for states' rights was bolstered by such legislation with matching appropriations for reform measures.[23]

Another major campaign for the PTA was the support of federal legislation for school lunches. The project culminated in the U.S. Congress's passing of the School Lunch Act, which was touted as a "nation-wide effort to improve health and nutrition of America's school children." Spearheaded by committee chair and South Carolinian Eunice Harper Leonard, the passage of the School Lunch Act reveals the effectiveness of the PTA network in legislative matters mid-century. Leonard, like most white PTA workers, rose through the ranks by taking on leadership roles at increasingly higher levels of the association. And, like other PTA leaders, by assuming these positions she developed skills and attributes through her affiliation with the PTA and the other organizations with which she was active, such as the American Association of University Women, the American Cancer Society, the Carolina Business and Professional Women's Club, the Daughters of the American Colonists, and the South Carolina Federation of Women's Clubs. After graduating from Winthrop College and taking graduate courses at the University of South Carolina, she married Paul H. Leonard, who was elected to the state's House of Representatives and later served as South Carolina's hotel inspector. Leonard began as a local unit president in the early 1930s and by the end of the decade (1937–41) was South Carolina's state PTA president. She later became NCPT vice president of Region III (1941–44), in the Southeast, and ended her run as a PTA leader as national chair of the School Lunch Committee (1947–50). Of her many accomplishments, Leonard was most proud of the role she played in the National PTA in promoting school lunches nationwide and getting the School Lunch Act passed in 1946. In the midst of her leadership of the school lunch initiative, Leonard confessed to NCPT president Minetta Hastings that she was, perhaps, "too interested in this project." However, the single-minded devotion to PTA objectives and enthusiasm of members such as Leonard were responsible for the success of its legislative initiatives.[24]

In the Progressive era, organized women started serving meals in public schools as an extension of their municipal housekeeping efforts. Lunch programs were first run and maintained by women's clubs, who later relied on local school boards and municipal funding to ensure their continued implementation. William J. Reese argues that school lunches, part of the school health movement of the turn of the twentieth century, were not always imbued with democratic ideals about giving the poor and marginalized an equal chance at thriving and learning. He posits that some elites viewed health initiatives as a form of capital investment, "a response to the allegedly inferior biological makeup of the native poor and certain ethnic groups." This notion was carried beyond the Progressive era as the PTA and other civic organizations continued to work to institute the school lunch, justifying it as a means to a stronger nation. With citizenship ever at the core of PTA ideals, the organization's leaders viewed promoting good health and nutrition as an important aspect of its program, arguing that it was "a chief factor in creating responsible citizens of high integrity."[25]

The institution of lunches in schools as comprehensive and equitable did not happen during the Progressive era, despite clubwomen's best efforts. It took the Depression and extreme poverty and destitution to prompt Franklin Delano Roosevelt's New Deal programs focusing on recovery, relief, and reform to bolster the school lunch initiative. In the 1930s, with a stronger and wider organizational network, and supported by its investment in the Cardinal Principles of Education, the National PTA backed the federal government and stepped up its push for health and nutrition in the schools. As Eunice Leonard went from leading a local unit to serving as president of the South Carolina Congress of Parents and Teachers, one of her first actions was to request that the white national office coordinate a study of school lunches in order to make recommendations to the federal government. The results presented a convincing argument: "hungry, underfed children could not do their best at school." Consequently, Leonard was appointed chair of the School Lunch Committee and began working with the U.S. Office of Education to help find a way to make school lunches available to all children. Thus, the PTA ended up positioning itself at the forefront of a national effort to get lunches in the public schools, and even though it was one of many voluntary organizations involved in the endeavor, it was one of the largest and most widely networked. The federal government recognized the organization's ability to mobilize volunteers around the country and invited it as the only civic organization to serve on the National Cooperating Committee on School Lunches in the early 1940s.[26]

The U.S. government had plenty to gain by passing the School Lunch Act. In the midst of the Depression it was looking to solve the problems of hunger and poverty while increasing the consumption of its abundant agricultural commodities by expanding markets nationally and abroad. Propaganda of the era argued that much went to "waste on the farm while millions were hungry for these products in the cities."[27] Beginning in 1936, the U.S. Department of Agriculture began to distribute surplus farm products to local and state relief administrations which, through the Works Progress Administration (WPA), the Federal Surplus Commodities Corporation, and the National Youth Administration, turned the foodstuffs over to local educational and welfare agencies and civic organizations—such as the PTA and American Legion—for distribution in communities. The benefits were immediately apparent in remote regions in the South. African American PTA members in the School at Society Corner on James Island, South Carolina, brought vegetables to school for lunches, while the WPA funded the purchase of cooking utensils and paid for a cook. The program—nationally coordinated and much more connected to and supported by the U.S. government than the disconnected local efforts of the Progressive era—became the framework for the school lunch program in decades to come.[28]

The federal government became more invested in providing school meals as the United States entered World War II and the national draft was instituted, having found that nearly half of those drafted could not pass the physical exam, which was blamed on a lack of nutrition during their childhood years. With the presumed threat of national security in jeopardy, the federal government expanded the existing lunch program in 1942 to include any child who would "*benefit nutritionally* without reference to financial status." The program lasted only a year, ending on June 30, 1943. The WPA, an important liaison between the government and civic organizations, was dismantled in April of that year, as a result of the war and transportation issues. Moreover, agricultural surpluses had waned, leaving little for distribution to local communities. To protect against potential problems that would result either financially or nutritionally from the immediate removal of lunch programs from the schools, an indemnity program was established in March 1943 that reimbursed school districts for purchasing the agricultural commodities used for lunches. The U.S. government supplemented the school meals on occasion as it distributed surplus foodstuffs that could not make it to troops overseas because of shipping and transportation lapses.[29]

It became clear to educational administrators and PTA leaders that in order for school lunches to become instituted nationally, they needed to be funded by the U.S. government and could not depend on the availability of farm surpluses. Therefore, Leonard and her committee took the lead in reviving the bill and wanted it placed under the aegis of the U.S. Department of Agriculture. Instead, the government wanted local communities to handle it as they had in the past. When the school lunch committee met in September 1944, its members declared their intention to keep "before the public the importance of continuing to make and keep the school lunch a permanent part of the education program and to emphasize the fact that it is a permanent institution needing permanent support." Leonard's committee used the networks of voluntary civic associations to get an amendment passed with the Annual Appropriation Bill, which earmarked $50 million for school meals. Meanwhile, state boards of education and the PTA successfully convinced the federal government to extend the Program for School Lunch Aid on a year-by-year basis, while states such as Illinois passed legislation to appropriate funds that supplemented federal monies. This gave the PTA, state education authorities, and the U.S. Department of Agriculture time to come to a workable solution to the school-lunch funding issue.[30]

School leaders, in the meantime, found that the School Lunch Program was reaching more and more children. Whereas the program had served 342,000 children in 3,800 schools in 1937, it grew to feed 6.5 million children in 44,000 schools in 1945. Over the next several years, Leonard worked with representatives from the Office of Education and the U.S. Department of Agriculture in drafting a bill for nutritious lunches to be made available to all children and asking for matching appropriations from the federal government. As they had done in the past, PTA leaders contacted "every member of Congress" in order to get the bill passed. The bill went through many revisions and ultimately included the requirements that school lunches make use of agricultural surpluses and be made available only to children with limited means, although local communities could supplement the lunches. The School Lunch Act was signed by President Truman on June 6, 1946, and Leonard was elected National Chair of School Lunches in order to see the program through to 1950, when it would be implemented nationally.[31]

In her report for 1947–48, Leonard commented that thirty-four states and Hawaii each had a state supervisor of school lunch programs, many of whom were trained nutritionists. That year, her committee estimated that "parent-teacher members were wholly responsible for or were assisting with school lunches" in 10 percent of the schools serving lunches nationally. Other groups that pitched in included church and civic groups and patriotic organizations. In reflections of Progressive-era efforts, the PTA and other civic organizations even set up school gardens to provide produce for lunches and, following the trend begun in homemaking clubs, the PTA directed canning and food preservation efforts in no fewer than fifteen states. School meals thus became a staple in the PTA's health program mid-century as black and white PTA workers led health and nutrition efforts in local communities. The NCCPT created its own network of local and state "Health Chairmen," who helped members sponsor health clinics and lunch programs.[32]

In the late 1940s, PTA volunteers did not just help make lunches; they promoted the idea that education about nutrition should be a part of the school curriculum.[33] For example, the white PTA School Lunch Committee in Leland, Maryland, gave advice on the lunch menu and procedures. In Leland and other schools in Maryland, teachers studied ways to include nutrition in the curriculum and helped teach parents how to plan meals. In Louisiana, one superintendent required his schools to teach health and nutrition, using the school lunch as a laboratory. The interest in nutrition seeped into training courses for parents in the PTA and at state colleges and universities, where county and district supervisors took graduate-level courses in nutrition and home economics. The Georgia Colored Congress showed the film "The School That Learned to Eat" at its annual convention in 1949 and encouraged local units to study the School Lunch Program at its meetings. School lunches were so important to both PTA branches that the topic was included on a rare joint committee meeting of NCPT and NCCPT representatives held in August 1950 at Tuskegee, during which both sides worked out the details on holding more frequent meetings between them and creating a list of topics common to the two organizations.[34]

The school lunch was just one of a number of health issues that the PTA took on. Both PTA branches were still conducting Summer Round-Ups at mid-century and were continuing to work toward federal support of well-baby and maternal clinics, programs that had begun in the Progressive era with the Sheppard-Towner Act. Moreover, the NCCPT supported better dental health and dental education, an improved foster care system, and more nursery schools. Through the 1940s and beyond, the NCPT focused its efforts on legislation to safeguard the health and well-being of children and families. It continued to direct its members to be informed on current bills the organization supported and to "urge members to discuss proposed legislation with candidates, seeking their support ahead of time." PTA members were instructed to contact legislators to get their position and support. Even after bills were passed, PTA members were told to "Follow up on the administration or enforcement of laws enacted, looking toward need for improvement by amendment." External agencies recognized the PTA's extensive role in promoting health matters. For example, Ben F. Wyman, the State Health Officer of the South Carolina Board of Health, remarked that the South Carolina Congress of Parents and Teachers was one of the most "effective organizations in the state for the promotion and development of education—especially for one of education's most important phases, health education." Wyman echoed the sentiments of PTA workers "that education is dependent on good health."[35]

Reports submitted to School Lunch Chair Eunice Leonard from schools in North Carolina sum up best the PTA's belief about the connections among health, citizenship, and education, revealing how the organization remained true to the Cardinal Principles report. For educators and PTA members in that state, the school lunch program "has taught democracy and how to work together harmoniously. It has laid the foundation stone for personal, social etiquette, enabling children to eat with ease and relaxation, converse with others comfortably and intelligently. This program pays dividends now and for the future—dividends in better scholastic averages, fewer absences from school because of illness, and in countless ways building stronger more mentally alert citizens." For PTA and school leaders, children who ate well-balanced meals grew to become thoughtful, concerned citizens. Such goals were at the top of the PTA agenda for the middle decades of the twentieth century.[36]

Meeting New Needs:
Civics, Citizenship, and the Tenets of Democracy

The CRSE's Cardinal Principles of Education, in addition to emphasizing health, placed civics and citizenship education at the centerpiece of the school curriculum. The United States was a different place between the wars; with immigration quotas in place, the onset of the Depression, and a proliferation of ethnic cultural groups and associations, civic education was transformed from emphasizing assimilation to incorporating the experiences and perspectives of minority groups who had been outsiders to American political, social, and educational life. Moreover, the threat of totalitarianism in Europe prompted educational leaders to develop programs that highlighted the advantages of democracy. This new vision of civic education emphasized the notion of cultural pluralism, and the new programs were engineered to teach how democracies dealt with ethnic, racial, and religious difference.[37] Yet cultural pluralism existed in different forms. Inasmuch as it was intended to promote open-mindedness about various cultures and ethnicities, Jonathan Zimmerman reminds us that it also was used in some instances to support ideological conformity. Therefore, no one version of cultural pluralism won out, as theory was interpreted and applied by different groups in a variety of settings to suit any number of political standpoints.[38]

In the middle decades of the twentieth century, PTA workers—positioning themselves as popularizers of the latest educational theory and practices—

endorsed cultural pluralism in local communities and schools. Citizenship
had always been a central goal in the organization's program, but the PTA's
stance on civic education was a complex one—melding a variety of political
perspectives—that changed only slightly over time. In the years leading up to
World War I, the Congress of Mothers promoted peace and the "outlawry of
war," based on maternalist notions that the mothers of the nation could never
support military aggression. In this regard they were in step with educators
and political leaders who saw educational reform efforts as part of international restructuring efforts. Even though the organization continued to support peace over the course of the twentieth century, it balanced these ideals
with an emphasis on patriotic duty. In the late 1920s, the NCPT's citizenship
committee developed a definition of what they meant by citizenship and "citizenship training"; they observed what other agencies were doing and how they
construed citizenship before deciding to craft a new platform that sought to
"encourage voters to vote."[39]

The emphasis on voting as a civic duty did not end up being the centerpiece of the revised civic program but nonetheless was important for black and
white PTA members in local units. White PTA women in the 1920s persuaded
newly enfranchised members to vote, and in later decades asked members
to guide their fellow citizens in voting on issues of particular interest to the
organization. Voting rights were especially important to black PTA leaders, as
they joined other civil rights and civic organizations in the effort to enfranchise
black adults. In the 1940s and 1950s, the NCCPT assisted with voter registration drives and helped bring voting machines to schools as part of their civic
education programs. Narvie Harris, the PTA worker in Georgia introduced in
the previous chapter, claimed that she registered high school students to vote,
which in turn resulted in her registering their parents. Therefore, voting as
a central dimension of citizenship held much more salience for the NCCPT,
as references to citizenship and civic duty in black PTA publications almost
always included a statement on racial equality.[40]

In 1928 the NCPT committee on citizenship put forth its four-point platform, which included encouraging members to register to vote; teaching laws
and the necessity of obeying them; aiding in Americanization efforts; and cultivating "Junior Citizenship" among children, which meant teaching children
to obey laws. The emphasis on a law-abiding citizenry was a change in direction from its promotion of peace and community activism just two decades
earlier. Revealing the political leanings of the NCPT, the committee suggested
that local units carry out certain activities, which consisted of inviting "well-
informed, competent, and conservative speakers for citizenship programs,"
celebrating citizenship by holding festivals for new citizens, and giving awards
for students' citizenship essays. As always, NCPT leaders encouraged coop-

eration with other civic groups in these endeavors. The pillars of citizenship continued to guide the association's program at least thirty years after they were outlined in the late 1920s. The PTA's committee on citizenship drew up virtually identical activities in its 1943–46 plan, with the added component of wartime activities. For instance, it suggested that local units build "wartime citizenship through the High-School Victory Corps" and "begin postwar planning now" in teaching the tenets of democracy.[41]

During the Depression, the white PTA emphasized patriotism as it took more seriously its own role as preserver of American values. In some ways, this contrasted with the school curriculum, which advanced a critique of capitalism. The PTA joined other civic organizations in promoting patriotism but did not challenge school authorities as had the United Daughters of the Confederacy, the American Legion, and others who suggested a revised history canon. The PTA leadership created, through words and images, an organization that embraced patriotic ideals. Around the country it was not uncommon for local school meetings to be part business, part patriotic exhibition. A November 1934 meeting of the white Jamestown, New York, Parent-Teacher Association included tables decorated with American flags and red, white, and blue candles, and speeches on the work of the school boy patrol and the importance of keeping dues current. Throughout the 1930s, at the monthly meetings of the Jamestown PTA, members took part in different patriotic and civic-oriented activities: they sang the "Battle Hymn of the Republic," and they discussed "The Home's Responsibility in Developing the Fundamental Standards of Good Citizenship." The emphasis on patriotism and teaching citizenship continued through the 1940s as the Jamestown PTA listened to schoolchildren sing the "Star-Spangled Banner" and debated whether to order new china for their monthly meetings, given the importance of rationing and doing away with nonnecessities during World War II.[42]

Yet in the 1930s the citizenship committee had begun to incorporate the language of "world good will" into its discussions. The PTA continued to focus on educating law-abiding citizens, but reintroduced an emphasis on peace that it had retreated from temporarily in the early 1920s, because that stance was associated with communism and subversion. Moreover, the PTA was helping to promote to the American population the thinking of liberal educators and social scientists who positioned the school as the ideal place to teach harmonious democratic relationships and world citizenship. PTA committee members explained, "Peace should know no boundaries. There should be international understanding, and universal good will among peoples. . . . Every parent-teacher should study the peace movement, so that there will be no question as to whether children shall be trained in the ideals of peace or the habits of war." For white PTA leaders, world goodwill and patriotism went hand-in-hand, as the good citizen educated herself about and respected other cultures. However, acting on these principles was challenging, because PTA leaders would be forced to reconcile the organization's commitment to racial inclusion with its policy on segregation. During the 1930s and 1940s, even though the white PTA began to emphasize tolerance and understanding, it circumvented the matter of racism within its ranks by placing these ideas in an international context. State-level meetings of white units reiterated the focus on international understanding over domestic race relations. In contrast, the black PTA accepted the new emphasis and acted on it, using the platform of cultural pluralism to promote racial equality and understanding in schools, to the white PTA, and in the public at large. The NCCPT also had embraced the growing intercultural education movement and incorporated its ideas and activities into its program.[43]

As the United States entered World War II, the PTA took on world tolerance and understanding as part of its platform, as organization leaders expressed renewed interest in improving the school curriculum to "meet new needs." It was a reflection of concerns about the welfare of children around the globe, as well as an interest in protecting American patriotic ideals. Even the NCPT's Committee on Reading and Library Service declared, "Only when there is an educated public, fully informed and able to make wise choices, is the nation safe from the forces of ignorance, fear, intolerance, and greed. Such a public is dependent for its existence and maintenance upon good reading habits and an adequate supply of reading material."[44]

When the United Nations (UN) charter was drafted and ratified in the early 1940s, the PTA seized the opportunity to promote the idea of the care and protection of children worldwide. The organization's leaders were especially interested in the founding of the United Nations Educational, Scientific and Cultural Organization (UNESCO). The NCPT's Committee on International Relations, led by Lucille L. Jesse, stepped up plans to raise the standards of political education among PTA members and youth in schools. Jesse declared, "We must educate ourselves and our neighbors so that we have a nucleus of informed and understanding citizens, whose vigilance will produce intelligent public opinion to give support to our leaders at the peace table." In particular, the committee called for understanding others' viewpoints, exercising tolerance toward different beliefs, and studying other cultures and nations. The committee suggested that in order to become more informed on these issues members at the local level peruse articles on international understanding in the organization's magazine, *National Parent-Teacher*.[45]

This was a pivotal point at which white national-level officers began to examine the hypocrisy of maintaining a segregated organization. During the middle decades of the twentieth century, *National Parent-Teacher* published fewer than a dozen articles on tolerance and cultural understanding that challenged white members to consider their own complicity in racism and discrimination.[46] The articles reflected NCPT leaders' awareness of the global sociopolitical context, in particular of Britain and France declaring war on Germany, in relation to citizenship issues for youth. NCPT leaders announced they were revising the organization's original philosophy and programs to meet "present social needs," reminding members, "A spirit of genuine tolerance permeates every phase of the work" of the organization. However, discussions of tolerance were in reference to religious tolerance, as a result of the outreach efforts of the National Council of Christians and Jews.[47] Features in *National Parent-Teacher* reflected this renewed direction. A 1939 article by Annette Smith asked, "Should a democracy permit any kind of propaganda? Should it permit pleas for dictatorship, for violence, for 'race' prejudice?" These questions were intended to link world events to what was going on in the United States. Smith's true objective is revealed at the end of the piece, in which she advised parents and teachers of ways to prepare young people for "responsible citizenship in a democracy": by examining assumptions and prejudices, reflecting on American ideals, and teaching about the "contributions of various racial and national groups to American life."[48]

Another article, Ruth Benedict's "Let's Get Rid of Prejudice," was more explicit in terms of addressing racism. Benedict asked parents—mothers, really—to begin by looking at themselves and their habits and comments to see whether they were perpetuating bigotry by making comments such as "'What can you expect of Negroes?'" or complaining about "Mr. Angotti in the corner grocery store," because "all Italians . . . cheat." The author linked such comments, and those denigrating statements directed at ethnic minorities, to Nazism and the belief in racial superiority. By using a strategy that associated prejudice and discrimination with genocide and mass murder—a tactic Smith used in the earlier article—Benedict left no gray area for the reader: bigotry of any kind was wrong. Her piece stood out among the other articles in *National Parent-Teacher* because it took on racism in the United States directly. The other articles connected race obliquely to the problems of discrimination against other nationalities without discussing racism within the borders of the United States. Despite these calls for an end to intolerance in the pages of the NCPT periodical—and perhaps because there were so few of them—little changed in the day-to-day activities of local-level white units.[49]

At the national level of the organization, white PTA leaders' thinking about difference, race, and tolerance was furthered by their involvement in a series of conferences convened by the State Department toward the end of the war on the formation of the United Nations. NCPT President Minnetta Hastings was invited to attend meetings held from August to October, 1944, which came to be called the Dumbarton Oaks conferences. The result of the conferences was a proposal for a new international peace organization, the United Nations. Hastings was most enthusiastic about PTA involvement at this level and her having been invited to the 1945 conference held in San Francisco, at which the UN charter was signed by fifty nations. The high-security gathering included representatives from the leading national women's organizations, such as Margaret Hickey of the National Federation of Business and Professional Women's Clubs, and La Fell Dickson, the GFWC president, as well as men's veterans' organizations and service clubs, such as the Kiwanis, Rotary, and Lions clubs, in an effort to get their input regarding the United Nations. In particular, the PTA was one of several education organizations asked for their feedback on the feasibility and purpose of an international office of education. It was the government's way of getting in touch with the American public, by tapping into civil society and the reach of civic associations. With the inclusion of the PTA, a vast communication and action network was at hand. In her report to the NCPT, Hastings bragged about the ability of the PTA to reach across the United States at lightning speed. While in San Francisco she had sent telegrams to the state PTA presidents of New Jersey, Michigan, Texas, and Minnesota, states that had congressional representatives among the U.S. delegates at the San Francisco conference. She explained, "Within twenty-four hours each state [PTA] congress had sent a fine telegram to its [U.S.] congressman delegate. The president of the American Council on Education, the N.E.A. consultant, and the others just couldn't believe it. They said, 'It has been no time at all since we talked about the possibility of doing this—and here it's done! Whenever the P.T.A. people say they will do something, they come through all over the country.'"[50]

Attending the UN organizing conferences helped shape the NCPT leader's thoughts and led her to rework the platform of the organization; Hastings was exposed to new ideas that challenged the head of the Judeo-Christian-oriented PTA. She remarked on the religious differences presented at the San Francisco conference: "The meeting opened with a minute of silent meditation. With Moslems and Buddhists and people of many other creeds represented there, it was not quite politic to say a word of prayer." Also, while at the conference, she along with the other attendees watched international films on such countries as the Netherlands, France, and the USSR that depicted the atrocities of war as well as the customs and lifestyles of other people. At the end of the conference Hastings noted the importance of coming to understand "peoples of other lands," an insight she took back to her role as leader of the PTA. Most importantly, the experiences she had in San Francisco led her to question the PTA's approach to difference in its membership and programs.[51]

Hastings returned to her work invigorated about getting the word out about the importance of the United Nations. One PTA member wrote, "Thousands of letters were written to congressmen urging adherence to the principles of the UNO" as a result of having attended the conference. Moreover, the PTA took it upon itself at this time to educate its membership and the public. The "vast resources of the National Congress of Parents and Teachers were mobilized into a gigantic educational project to explain the structure and scope of the UNO, not only to its own membership but to the citizens of every community where there is a P.T.A." The NCCPT followed suit and promoted UN Day, asking members to remember "that education for freedom will make a nation free indeed." The PTA stepped up efforts to teach about foreign lands and people, claiming that pageants have proven to be "unusually successful as a means of fostering appreciation of other cultures." These pageants, a staple of early intercultural education programs, were becoming increasingly common in schools around the country. Likewise, food and clothing drives were promoted as a way to involve children in reaching out to the less fortunate and teaching them to be thankful for American abundance.[52]

As a result of the war and the creation of the UN, the national leadership of the white PTA began to question its commitment to all children. In a rare acknowledgment of the NCPT's inconsistency regarding racial equality, Hastings made a statement that was celebrated by the black PTA; at the annual meeting of the NCPT in 1943, she announced, "If 'all children are our children,' it follows that there can surely be no inequality among the children living in a country that proudly calls itself the arsenal of democracy. The first step toward citizenship in an interdependent world must be the elimination of all prejudice and bias toward minority groups within our own border."[53]

White units at the local level, however, did not have to heed Hastings' call, because there was no direct pressure on them to do so. While their objectives needed to match the platform of the national level, the flexible federated infrastructure of the PTA allowed them the freedom to interpret those objectives according to their own interests and local contexts. Therefore, at the local level, white PTA units carried on with business as usual, except in those regions that already were doing interracial work through the PTA, such as Delaware. In the South, white units included world citizenship in their state programs and at annual meetings; they had to, just as other regions did, but avoided any direct mention of racial understanding in the United States. For example, while the 1947 annual meeting of the South Carolina Congress of Parents and Teachers (SCCPT) featured health and citizenship prominently in the program, it downplayed cultivating friendly feelings toward other nations and encouraging "peoples of different origins in a community to participate in community affairs." Despite the white South Carolina PTA's recounting of the earlier theme "all children are our children," its focus remained on children of other lands. This pattern continued through the 1950s, as the SCCPT reiterated the NCPT's central ideas but refused to acknowledge Jim Crow segregation and other forms of racial discrimination.[54]

The focus on world citizenship was embraced by the NCCPT, which began to infuse the idea into its programs and publications, with a special emphasis on eradicating racism stateside. Intercultural education became the vehicle that would help the black PTA address such issues. Black PTA leaders were much more willing to take action than their white counterparts, as they took an interest in the intercultural education movement that was growing in popularity and entering the school curriculum in the United States. From 1936 to 1941 the local units of the black PTA were encouraged to study the economic, social, and educational needs of their communities in order to make recommendations for change. One of the outcomes of this effort was that local units began to institute intercultural education programs in their communities. Beginning in the 1940s the association successfully encouraged state and local units to form committees on intercultural relations with the white PTA representatives in Southern states. Little is known about how racial and ethnic minorities felt about the goals of intercultural education or how they adapted its programs. Stephanie J. Shaw examines the involvement of black professional women in intercultural and intergroup relations efforts and argues that black women were exploited by white managers who enlisted them in cultural sensitivity groups because of their orientation toward social justice and racial uplift and their willingness to work on behalf of these issues for little or no wages. She claims that those white managers who embraced intercultural education did so out of fear of the emerging radical left. However, the black PTA's use of intercultural education shows another application, as African American members sought to use the Intergroup Relations committees to their advantage by employing such groups in gaining equal resources in schools, and especially after desegregation became inevitable. By 1945 intercultural education was a staple of the adult education programs sponsored by the NCCPT.[55]

Initiated by Rachel Davis DuBois, a classroom teacher from New Jersey, intercultural education was intended to cultivate sympathetic attitudes in schoolchildren toward people of other races and ethnicities. In the 1920s and 1930s, DuBois designed and led assemblies and lessons that highlighted the contributions of minority groups, in particular African Americans. She drew on her Quakerism and status as an active member of the NAACP to seek to improve relations between the races. In 1934 DuBois organized the Service Bureau for Intercultural Education (SBIE) as a center for teachers. Later criticized for glorifying ethnicity and fostering divisiveness among Americans, the SBIE was wrested from her control and redirected under new leadership toward a focus on "respect for a national culture with limits to expression of cultural differences." DuBois continued her work, however, by creating the Workshop for Cultural Democracy in 1941. For the rest of her long life, DuBois worked with community groups and schools, implementing her "group conversation method," which involved different groups of people getting to know one another socially in order to overcome stereotypes and prejudices. The group conversation method was adapted by civic groups, educational institutions, and churches in an effort to build racial and ethnic understanding.[56]

In 1946 the PTA convened its first meeting of the Group Relations Committee that was composed of members from the NCPT and NCCPT. However, the committee met only once, revealing the difficulties in bringing the two parties together. Leaders of both PTA branches met at Tuskegee in the summer of 1950 and decided to revive the committee. A photo of the gathering, with the committee posing under the statue of Booker T. Washington, made the cover of the NCCPT's magazine, but the gathering went without mention in the pages of the *National Parent-Teacher*. The Group Relations Committee met again at Tuskegee the following year and decided to attempt to build on the plan of work outlined five years earlier. By this time, the national officers of both branches decided they would work together for the common good, claiming it would be "one of the biggest contributions" the PTA could make "to the national welfare and to the future good of all our children." In so doing, the committee resolved to make Group Relations a standing committee of the two PTA branches and instructed its state units to do the same. The committee was determined to work on equity issues, such as regularly scheduled conferences on race relations, equity in education—especially in terms of personnel and school facilities—and adequate housing. The NCCPT found additional benefits of having the Group Relations Committee as a newly formed part of its infrastructure; in 1951 it used the new mechanism to request that the NCPT not usurp its authority by sending materials directly to its local units.[57]

Having adapted a model—the group conversation method—that enabled the leaders of the segregated branches to communicate, the PTA formalized the Group Relations committees to coordinate and promote intercultural education programs among its membership. The committees thereby carved out a "discursive arena" within the National PTA that was not there before. That is, while civic organizations enjoyed the benefits of face-to-face meetings, such interactions were not possible in a segregated association. A structure had to be imported to bring leaders of the two branches together. Needing a committee chair, the group selected the dynamic Deborah Partridge, a black scholar, to fill the job. At the time, Partridge was a visiting professor at New York University and an assistant professor at Queens College, and was doing postdoctoral work at the University of Pennsylvania. Within a year of her appointment

as chair, Partridge began to push for the "integration of all people into the
[PTA] program," calling for joint meetings between the two congresses beyond
what had already been established. However, her call to action and the Group
Relations Committee met with limited success. Within months, she was able
to report that nine state units had developed programs on human relations,
but little else transpired, as white Southerners were resistant to being active on
the Group Relations committees.[58]

Nevertheless, the NCCPT made the ideals of intercultural education part
of its program and formed groups to work on racial harmony and educational
equity. African American PTA leaders viewed intercultural understanding
as "basic to the development of both character and citizenship." Throughout
these years, black and white local units were directed to utilize the talents
and abilities of the different cultural groups in their communities, but the
white PTA continued its focus on world cultures—promoting the purposes
and activities of the UN and asking all members to support food and clothing
drives for poorer nations and to show "unending patience in compromising
differences within and among nations"—while the black PTA sustained its
focus on racism in America. By the 1950s Rachel Davis DuBois had become a
featured speaker at the annual meetings of the National Congress of Colored
Parents and Teachers. She was among a list of well-known scholars to speak
at the twenty-fifth anniversary of the NCCPT, along with Horace Mann Bond
and local dignitaries such as Oscar J. Chapman, president of Delaware State
College, and William J. Storey, the mayor of Dover, Delaware. In northeastern
urban communities that experienced racial conflict, DuBois was called upon
to lead group conversations to solve problems. When the conflict involved
schools, DuBois favored having local PTA groups partake in the exchange. In
her memoirs DuBois recounts one such day in the early 1950s in New York
City:

> After ten weeks of working together and sharing, a mothers' group gathered
> in the coffee canteen of a West Side public school in Manhattan to celebrate in
> January's zero weather the birth of two babies on the same day—one black and
> one white, brought to the PTA when a month old, by their mothers. The fun
> of sharing old-wives' tales about birth and babies moved into a deep feeling
> of joy when they sang each other's lullabies, while passing the babies around
> the circle.

In this recollection, DuBois romanticizes her hopes for intercultural education and the group conversation method. It was a scenario that was, if at all
accurate, rarely replayed in local PTA units around the nation and particularly
in the South.[59]

Nonetheless, the NCPT could not, by 1950, ignore the importance of race relations in its program and objectives. "Human relations" became one of the points of the NCPT's Four-Point program that year, and the black PTA devised programs and enlisted speakers to serve the goal. That year, Delaware conducted a program titled "Human Relations through the Parent-Teacher Program," and Georgia's president, Ethel Kight, emphasized "human understanding" during her tenure (1946–52). NCCPT leaders considered with irony the white PTA's rhetoric on global understanding and the continuing existence of segregation and prejudice in the United States. Dr. John W. Davis, president of West Virginia State College and keynote speaker at the 1952 annual meeting of the NCCPT, connected world understanding to the plight of African American youth for the delegates: "It is important that not only the salvation of the Negro be considered; this means salvation of all peoples, black, white, yellow, brown. The growth of the youth in Georgia has something to do with the total growth of youth in Indonesia, China."[60]

Unlike *National Parent-Teacher,* the NCCPT journal *Our National Family* featured discussions on prejudice, tolerance, and racial equality in virtually every issue, and local units remained focused on race work through curricular initiatives and community projects.[61] Thus NCCPT leaders interpreted the PTA platform as supporting race work and capitalized on the emphasis on democracy to further equal educational opportunity. For example, in a piece titled "Problems of Prejudice," Mrs. Charles L. Williams, an NCCPT officer, used war imagery in a manner similar to her white counterparts, but did not avoid critiquing the United States. "In our nation, the minorities are still behind the barbed wire fence of prejudice," she wrote in 1952.[62] Like the authors of the articles in *National Parent-Teacher,* Williams called for members to turn inward and examine their own lives and prejudices. Guest speakers at the black PTA's annual meetings echoed the refrain, challenging democracy as "weakest in the field of racial equality." The journal promoted special events in the community around racial pride, furthering the activities of Carter G. Woodson's Association for the Study of Negro Life and History, such as Race Relations Day, Brotherhood Day, and Negro History Week. Beatrice Morgan, the outspoken president of the black PTA from 1949 to 1953, helped come up with the theme for the organization's twenty-fifth anniversary that made clear the organization's position: "Every Child an Equal Chance." Morgan gave her reasons for choosing this theme: because "three million Negro children in America are handicapped by the incident of color." NCCPT leaders did not just state their beliefs; they encouraged local units to speak out against inequality in constructive ways: "Develop the courage to speak up when things are unfair" and "Be cooperative," they instructed members. As always, the burden was on the oppressed, as black PTA members worked to build interracial bridges. Maryland's Colored Congress reported in 1951 that it had "increase[d] its efforts to promote more inter-racial activities in the State and local associations." Black PTA leaders believed that the one of the best antidotes to racial discrimination was education for citizenship, what Morgan defined as "responsible citizenship[,] . . . the kind of education that will enable persons to make a confident, satisfactory, happy adjustment anywhere on this globe."[63]

Such efforts always had to be balanced, however, with the conservative political stance of the white PTA. As a result, black PTA officers found themselves in the difficult position of using the organization and its platform to challenge the status quo while seeking not to offend white PTA officers and members. The balancing act became all the more demanding as civil rights litigation heated up in the South and the prospect of the desegregation of schools appeared. The school equalization movement, begun in the 1930s, was favored by both blacks who wanted to make segregation expensive to force the issue and whites who wished to maintain a separate system of education. School desegregation became a contentious point for PTA leaders at the state and local levels, which national officers had a difficult time managing. In 1950 the NAACP fought for the desegregation of schools in South Carolina with the *Briggs v. Elliott* case, but lost. Instead, Governor James Byrnes was instrumental in maintaining segregation with a $75 million school equalization program, which the South Carolina's Colored Congress of Parents and Teachers vowed to "carry out to the letter." Black local units were instructed to "make inventories of their respective educational facilities on county and local levels and . . . [to present] their findings . . . to the education officials." The Colored Congress responded, "We further urge the institution of court action, if that becomes necessary, to secure our objectives."[64] The white state PTA endorsed the measure as well, since it would help maintain separate schools. The white members of the South Carolina Congress of Parents and Teachers were implored to "act now" in making sure every member was registered to vote and did vote on "legislation that will provide equal educational opportunities for our children in South Carolina." Overall, the effort failed to equalize school facilities for African Americans because only 57 percent of the money collected through the special sales tax went to the separate schools. It was not enough to equalize the value of school properties in South Carolina, which stood at $19.7 million for black schools and $83.9 million for white ones. The South Carolina Colored Congress of Parents and Teachers (SCCCPT) would take on Governor Byrnes and the state legislature at least once more in the 1950s, condemning the "vindictive action" proposed by his administration to remove the law providing for public schools from the state constitution. A handful of religious groups, the NAACP, the Palmetto Education Association, and the state's Colored Congress fought the attempt to deny blacks public education if desegregation became the law of the land. South Carolina's white PTA remained silent on the matter. Eventually, South Carolina's Colored Congress backed away from the school equalization efforts to follow the lead of the NAACP in fighting for the desegregation of schools.[65]

As civil rights organizations were gearing up for the battle in the courts to desegregate schools, members of the Colored Congress watched, listened, and volunteered when they could. The pages of *Our National Family* kept the membership informed by featuring articles by prominent civil rights leaders. A 1953 article by NAACP field secretary June Shagaloff argued that the movement to equalize school facilities was "Superficial, because construction materials are not always of the best quality, school curricula, student-teacher ratio and teaching materials are often ignored." It is ironic that Shagaloff's piece appeared in the same issue—on the same page, no less—in which NCCPT president Beatrice Morgan reported, "The shining new and up-to-date school plants, the rehabilitation of old ones, and the modern school supplies which I have observed as I have traveled over the states, dictate that a new personality may be born in the Negro boy and girl." Nonetheless, one cannot assume that Morgan's comments are to be taken as accommodationism; instead, such statements were often intended to deceive—or at the very least, there was more to Morgan's position than what appears at face value. NCCPT leaders knew that if schools and facilities were to be truly equalized, that would be a setback in race relations and equality. Morgan and other NCCPT leaders nonetheless reflect a tension that was a constant in the organization's history. Whereas the NCPT advocated a "race-blind" approach to child welfare work, black PTA leaders understood that one could not raise young people and educate them without paying attention to race and racial inequality. In the pages of *Our National Family*, therefore, Morgan's comments and other essays collectively represented a site of resistance within a white-majority organization and offered a public forum for challenging segregation and racial equality.[66]

However, even though the black PTA gave more time and attention to intergroup and intercultural relations than did the white PTA, it was not the foremost issue on local units' agendas. Overall, by the 1950s little had changed in the National PTA program and activities, except that the NCCPT and its state and local units began to become more outspoken about racial equality. Black and white local-level meetings in the early 1950s looked similar to those of decades prior, with fundraising and social events dominating the monthly meetings. The all-white Sixth District PTA of South Carolina reported in 1953 on its activities and accomplishments of that school year. One unit, the A. C. Moore PTA, explained that the theme chosen for that year was "The Child in a Democratic Community." It held a series of Fathers' Nights, and students put on plays; officers gave reports on membership drives, school inspections, and fundraising activities. "Three paper drives and two coat hanger drives have been held. From these drives we have given $250 to the Library to purchase books." The Arden PTA, in the same district, reported that a representative group of members attended a parent education workshop at Winthrop College that July. The theme was "Partners in Child Development" that year, and they had heard local judge J. T. Sloan speak on the "Function of Juvenile Courts and Synopsis of Juvenile Bill." The Arden PTA also conducted a fair amount of fundraising: "A set of books were bought for the library and each room given $10 to be used for room improvement." These reports were repeated around the country, each one detailing the ongoing efforts of women volunteers and their contributions to local schools.[67]

"Plan for a Changed PTA": Transitions at Mid-Century

In the middle decades of the twentieth century, the modern PTA was forged with a membership in the millions, a far-reaching network, and the ability to sway national legislation. The organization was viewed by others, in particular the U.S. government, as a force to be reckoned with and an organization that could rally the average American around supporting such causes as the United Nations, school lunches, and the ubiquitous fundraisers. The NCCPT began to rely less on the NCPT for direction and guidance as it came into its own by the 1940s. With a relatively small but growing membership, the black PTA was developing its own program, based on the NCPT's platform but informed by race and the fight for equality. The white PTA, too, began to include tolerance and understanding in its guiding principles, but tended to speak in terms of world tolerance and the understanding of peoples of different nations. Nonetheless, the NCPT began again to consider racial inclusion and what it meant for the organization.

By the early 1950s, the black PTA, in the manner of civil rights organizations, had become more vocal about the need for racial equality in all facets of American life. After World War II, conflict in Korea caused concern among the American public because the United Nations forces—with a considerable representation of American troops—had been deployed and were facing the formidable Chinese communist army. Americans' hopes for worldwide peace were dashed as truce negotiations dragged on for years. NCCPT leaders followed closely the cases being tried in the Supreme Court and kept members apprised of each new development. In 1952 Beatrice Morgan vacated the NCCPT president's office in the association's new digs in Dover, Delaware, as Mayme Williams of Florida took over the leadership position at a crucial time. Referring to the issue that was on everyone's mind, school desegregation, Williams established a committee "to study the problems and to formulate helpful policies, for the Congress planned to be ready with a definite but flexible program whatever the decision of the United States Supreme Court might be." Williams urged greater cooperation between the two PTA branches on a more level playing field. With her tenure began the tradition of the two PTA presidents speaking at each other's annual meetings. During this time, the black PTA sought to show the white PTA it no longer needed it as an advisor, but as a peer. African American leaders, such as U.S. Circuit Court of Appeals Judge William Hastie, informed black PTA members at one annual meeting that they could ably serve the role of developing "reason and understanding in their own communities." He thereby helped PTA members see themselves as an important part of the process of school desegregation by educating the public. Portending challenges for the association in years to come, Hastie could not have been more right when he advised black PTA members to "plan for a changed PTA."[68]

Overall, by the early 1950s the PTA's valuing of difference, race, and inclusion had returned after not having been addressed in any public way for nearly fifty years, since the organization's founding in 1897. At this time, however, the PTA was more directly challenged by society and its own members when it came to the *Brown v. Board of Education* decision and the enforcement of desegregation in the ensuing decades. With the passing of *Brown* the PTA faced the challenge of supporting desegregation not only in the schools but also within its own organization. After the Supreme Court's decision was rendered, both PTA branches issued their own statement of support, encouraging local and state units to work toward the integration of schools and PTA units.

During the mid-twentieth century the black and white leaders of the PTA had created an administrative structure that would help facilitate integration: the Intergroup Relations committees. However, the committees were limited in their reach and effectiveness in uniting the two PTA branches and offering guidance on the desegregation of schools. Some committees addressed regional interests, such as religious diversity, while others did not meet at all. In some instances, the committees were effective, as in some border states, where the Intergroup Relations committees successfully negotiated desegregation of local units. While the white PTA's national-level officers were opposed to segregation and tried to encourage the membership to work toward unification of the PTA, they faced violent opposition from the white PTA units in the Deep South. By allowing each state to determine the pace of the desegregation of its units, the white PTA leadership set the stage for a protracted process of integration that lasted nearly twenty years.

CHAPTER 5

Diminishing as It Advanced

The Unification of the PTA

T HE LAST president of the National Congress of Colored Parents and
Teachers, Clara B. Gay (1967–71), signed the organization's unification
plan in June 1970 without the unanimous backing of black PTA leaders across
the South. Even though she supported desegregation, she struggled with the
understanding that it meant the end of the Colored Congress. Despite her
willingness to unite with the white PTA, Gay maintained, "Only black parents
can speak for black children." A Georgian who was educated at Knoxville College in Tennessee and who received her master's degree at Atlanta University,
Gay was active in the Georgia Teachers and Education Association and the
YWCA. Known as a steadfast leader, she negotiated the merger between the
two parent-teacher associations in 1970 with white PTA president Pearl Price.
Press releases from the NCPT headquarters in Chicago championed the move
as being true to the founders' original intentions of racial equality, but the
merger was no partnership. It dissolved the black PTA and gave only a handful
of its leaders token representation on the state and national levels of the organization. Black PTA leaders' belief that the sacrifice was worth the long-term
advantages was summed up in a statement, published in *Our National Family*,
that the organization was "advancing as it diminishes."[1]

What NCPT president Pearl Price called the organization's "finest hour"
was, in fact, its most challenging one, and an event, after the decades of separate work, that was the culmination of its racial practices and pronouncements. As Price's speech at the unification convention echoed the well-known
Negro spiritual and Civil Rights era refrain—"At long last we have overcome

the barriers and surmounted the obstacles that kept us apart. We have overcome, and we have come together to become one"—desegregation, in fact,
spelled disaster for both branches of the PTA. Not only did black units lose
the influence they had over separate schools, but membership dropped precipitously overall. The black and white PTA branches experienced their largest
membership bases in the early 1960s, with a combined total of just over 12
million members. However, by 1970 membership had declined to 9.5 million and continued on its downward slide to a low of 5.2 million members in
1982. With desegregation and other forces, such as the women's movement
and changes in the workplace, PTA membership was cut by more than half in
just two decades.[2]

This chapter examines the effects of the *Brown v. Board of Education* decision on the PTA and how its members reacted to the watershed ruling. Following the lead of David M. Callejo-Pérez, who argues that the "Civil rights
historiography has tended to emphasize the extraordinary and the exciting
over the mundane," I explore the commonplace interactions between and
among black and white PTA leaders as some Southern units supported *Brown*
while others challenged it. Taking the form of debates and discussions—all
within the organizational infrastructure, such as at meetings and through
proper communication channels between the two branches—black and white
members deliberated whether to remain with the federation. At this time, the
PTA was forced to face one of its key founding principles: that in the interest
of child welfare, it would not discriminate based on race. Racism and discrimination played out in the discursive arena offered at PTA meetings at the local
level, in state-level intergroup relations meetings, and through the journals of
both PTAs, as the NCPT and NCCPT directed Southern units to desegregate
in May 1954. However, the discursive arena, or public space allowed for by
the PTA as a civic association, was never fully realized, because of the organization's completely segregated federation. After decades of separate work, it
was too difficult to bring black and white members together in a common
setting to have them ponder the advantages of an integrated association.[3]

The process of desegregating the PTA, which meant including the Colored
Congress in full membership, took nearly twenty years, because the white
national-level leadership remained true to its well-worn policy of deferring to
state and local units to manage their own affairs. Therefore, the timeline for
desegregation was to be determined by each state unit's leaders. What transpired was the state-by-state annexation of black PTA units beginning with the
border states. By the late 1960s, a few hold-out state units remained in the
Deep South, as white PTA units refused to allow for the full participation of
black members. Even when unification went smoothly, black members left the
association because they did not feel welcome at local meetings. In some areas,

white PTA membership dropped because of members' refusal to serve in the same civic organization with African Americans. The PTA, therefore, did not become officially integrated until the unification of the national-level offices in 1970.

The *Brown* Decision and the PTA

The experience of fighting overseas in World War II led African Americans to become increasingly radicalized and intolerant of inequalities on the home-front. The battle to desegregate schools had begun but was slow and haphazard, with each local community dealing with its particular needs and interests. Each case was fought separately until Thurgood Marshall and the NAACP decided they would challenge the constitutionality of segregation once and for all. In *Brown* four states were represented: Kansas, Virginia, Delaware, and South Carolina. The landmark ruling maintained that "Separate educational facilities are inherently unequal," which thereby quashed the earlier precedent of *Plessy v. Ferguson*. The decision, however, did not give a timeline for desegregation, nor did it outline how the feat was to be accomplished. As a result, the Supreme Court issued the ruling known as *Brown II* in 1955, which is characterized by the phrase "all deliberate speed." *Brown II* put the onus on states and their courts to oversee and enforce desegregation; however, as one historian put it, "Under these circumstances 'deliberate' inevitably outweighed 'speed.'"[4]

The *Brown* decision was just as much a watershed ruling for the PTA as it was for schools, because it forced the association to face its own segregationist practices. The organization responded rapidly to the Supreme Court's decision as white leaders outside the South supported the mandate and viewed the desegregation of schools as a worthwhile and significant achievement to be attained. White PTA leaders were already heading in that direction anyway, given their increasing calls for tolerance and understanding in the organization and U.S. society as discussed in the previous chapter. At the White House Conference on Children and Youth in December 1950, the NCPT publicly stated its position that "racial segregation in education be abolished." Less than one week after *Brown* was announced, the Board of Managers of the white PTA convened in Atlantic City for its annual session and drafted a response for members. It read, in part, "Educational integration of different races is proceeding rapidly in some communities; it will require a longer transition period in others. The National Congress urges parent-teacher leaders, in cooperation with schools and other governmental authorities in each community, to study and pursue effective means in working toward integrated education for all children." Thus, the NCPT's position was unequivocal. While other segregated educational associations, such as the NEA, took longer to react publicly to *Brown*, the PTA was among the first to make a formal statement supporting its directive, although it took years to put those words into action.[5]

Since the white and black PTA branches were coexisting by this time as virtually separate entities united by a common agenda, the NCCPT issued its own "Resolution on Integration" instead of just reiterating the NCPT's proclamation. Adopted at the NCCPT's annual meeting in Oklahoma on June 22, 1954, the decree commended the actions of the Supreme Court and directed state units to "develop an action program to achieve the goals of complete integration within its state." Black PTA leaders maintained that the organization's Intergroup Relations Committee would continue to meet with that of the NCPT in an effort to integrate the organizations, and they encouraged each state-level committee to do the same.[6]

The years immediately following *Brown* were characterized by cautious optimism in the black PTA and among African American leaders and educators. In the aftermath of the *Brown* decision, NCCPT president Mayme Williams announced, "In spite of wars, atomic bombs and frustrations, these are wonderful days for one to be alive." Her state units reported on the themes of their annual meetings, such as Virginia's focus on "What Kind of Education for Integration?," and the journal *Our National Family* began regular features on the Supreme Court's decision and the impact of *Brown*. The journal included suggestions on how black parents could help their children interact in integrated settings by encouraging them to take trips and tours to acclimate the young people to the wider community. The years of NCCPT leaders' calling for democratic practices to be followed in the PTA and in schools and communities was finally coming to fruition; the reality was catching up with the rhetoric, or so NCCPT leaders hoped. At least one member raised the unthinkable question at a PTA workshop in West Virginia: "What is the Future Role of the National Congress of Colored Parents and Teachers now that the Supreme Court has ruled segregation in public schools unconstitutional?," but the question did not prompt any major concerns among the NCCPT's leaders at the time.[7]

However, as many soon realized, change was not going to come easily or quickly in the schools or in the PTA. By the time the *Brown* decision was rendered, *de jure* segregation was practiced in the District of Columbia and seventeen states, which had segregated PTA units: Alabama, Arkansas, Delaware, Florida, Georgia, Kentucky, Louisiana, Maryland, Mississippi, Missouri, North Carolina, Oklahoma, South Carolina, Tennessee, Texas, Virginia, and West Virginia. Kansas and New Mexico also practiced segregation, so these states had officially organized Colored Congresses as well, bringing the total of black

PTA units to twenty overall. As Thurgood Marshall called for completely integrated school systems in the United States by 1956, Southern states resisted, claiming that local interests needed to be respected and suggesting that "the problem required something more than a judicial decision for its solution." Rabid segregationists in what Tuskegee sociologist Lewis W. Jones called "the hard-core states" of Mississippi, Alabama, Georgia, South Carolina, and Louisiana undertook intense extralegal action to defend separate schools. In these same states the parent-teacher associations were the last to desegregate, as the NCPT's response to *Brown* stunned white units in the Deep South who refused to act on what they perceived as a mandate to integrate. A Supreme Court ruling was one thing, but to be told what to do by the leaders of a voluntary association was an entirely different matter; within the framework of the federation, members had considerable power to resist the authority of national-level leaders. Because letting local interests drive the PTA agenda was a commonly accepted practice, white units in the South dragged their feet, refusing to join with black units.[8]

In the border states, school desegregation was proceeding by late 1955 in such places as Washington, DC, Baltimore, and Kansas City. In fact, most states did at least make some attempts at beginning to desegregate, with the exception of the hard-core states—Alabama, Georgia, Louisiana, Mississippi, and South Carolina—as well as Florida, which put up the strongest opposition to desegregation.[9] Within a decade, school desegregation was proceeding so slowly that the Civil Rights Act of 1964 was passed, in part, to speed its pace by linking federal funding to integration. However, even the law and financial incentives could not sway pro-segregationists, who found ways around the Civil Rights Act and *Brown* by trying various tactics with mixed success, such as pupil placement plans, freedom of choice plans, neighborhood zoning plans, and parental preference statutes. Private schools grew during this time as well, leaving Southern schools with still only 2 percent of the South's black students in schools with whites.[10] Yet, after 1965, with the Civil Rights Act and the Elementary and Secondary Education Act (ESEA), which included similar provisions, change became noticeable as most Americans came to accept the idea of integration, which meant having a handful of black students in schools with white children.[11]

Arguably, the greatest impact the *Brown* decision had on the PTA was on its membership. While both black and white congresses grew steadily during the period 1920 to 1960, the Civil Rights movement and desegregation affected the membership of local and state associations in the South. What transpired, though, is counterintuitive. With desegregation, one might expect the membership in the white PTA to increase as it began to include black members in its tabulations. Following this, one would expect membership in the black PTA overall to decline, given that it was being absorbed into white PTA units. Quite a different phenomenon occurred; beginning in the early 1950s, black units increased—some significantly—while by the early 1960s, white Southern units registered declines in membership. This trend continued for each branch of the PTA through 1970, the point of integration—or unification as PTA leaders called it—of the organization.

Although the NCPT units in Louisiana, Kansas, and New Mexico experienced declining memberships beginning in 1961, the largest exodus of white members began in the mid-1960s, with the majority of states beginning to show significant losses in 1966 (AL, AK, FL, GA, MO, NC, SC, TX, VA, and DC). Crawford and Levitt reveal that the losses in the South were proportionately larger than in other areas of the country. They calculate that in 1970–71, while the National PTA membership declined by 5 percent, 28 percent of this loss came from seven Southern states, and "close to 18 percent came from Mississippi, Florida, and North Carolina alone." By the mid-1960s, because of the Civil Rights Act and the ESEA, the pace of desegregation in the schools picked up. However, instead of the integrated National PTA growing by a quarter of a million members—the total membership of the National Congress of Colored Parents and Teachers in the mid-1960s—membership in the PTA overall dropped. With the push for desegregation, whites in the Deep South left the PTA by the thousands, showing that they did not want to be in an integrated organization. While other scholars have suggested additional reasons for the declining membership, such as the women's movement, the consolidation of school districts, the rise of competing organizations, and dues increases the PTA enforced during those years, I maintain that the desegregation of schools stands out as having had the greatest negative impact on PTA membership. It struck a blow from which the organization has never recovered.[12]

A most striking development was the growth of black PTA units in the Deep South from *Brown* to the late 1960s, which reveals leaders' wishes to maintain a measure of control over the education of black children during a period of great uncertainty. Even though the NCCPT supported the integration of schools, the organization's state and local units did not desegregate swiftly; ten years after *Brown* the NCCPT had lost only six of its twenty state units to desegregation. Black state units instituted successful membership drives in the post-*Brown* years, in large part to strengthen black representation in what was hoped would be a more integrated and equal society. It was a time of building the organization, as numerous PTA workshops and "schools of instruction" were offered and three states—Mississippi, Florida, and Louisiana—established permanent offices. The rise in membership can be read as resistance, with many African American citizens anticipating the challenges they would face; these losses mirrored those of black principals and the teaching force. While teachers in larger urban districts were less likely to lose their jobs once schools desegregated in their area, those in smaller districts experienced great attrition as their schools were absorbed by white schools that were bigger and had better facilities. Therefore, black teachers and principals were displaced beginning shortly after *Brown,* and a similar phenomenon happened with PTA members. However, the situation was different because one cannot fire a volunteer. Instead, black members felt that they were unwelcome at integrated PTA meetings and that meetings run by white PTA local leaders did not address their needs.[13]

Despite the knowledge of the losses that black communities and schools would experience, the majority of black PTA members nonetheless supported school desegregation as the greater good. Around the South, black PTA leaders vocalized support in their own meetings, periodicals, and other public venues. The Tennessee Congress of Colored Parents and Teachers, which was 15,000 strong at the time of the *Brown* decision, sent a statement to the Tennessee General Assembly expressing their view that "the feeling of blacks [is] that the best interest of all people of Tennessee will be served if the Supreme Court Decision outlawing public school segregation is implemented without an attempt at circumvention." African American educators and PTA members knew, however, that much more than employment was at stake; no longer would schools be filled with black teachers to instill racial pride. Many believed a dearth of black teachers would inhibit black children from "expressing themselves naturally," as white teachers would not understand them. Hence, many knew that desegregation signaled the end of the cultural leadership of black teachers.[14]

The NCCPT membership drives of the 1950s and 1960s were remarkably successful. For example, from 1955 to 1956, Florida increased its membership 96.6 percent; South Carolina 44.6 percent; Louisiana 20 percent; Alabama 15 percent; and Arkansas 12.7 percent. The Texas Colored Congress of Parents and Teachers had a respectable increase around that time, its membership having gone from 4,800 to 8,700. Its membership chair set an ambitious goal of 60,000 that year, which was never attained but signaled a desire to strengthen its presence in schools and communities. Overall, the membership of NCCPT units grew steadily during the 1950s and 1960s as the organization's leaders in 1955 decided on the "ultimate goal" of one million members, aiming for a quarter of a million members by 1957. It did not reach a quarter of a million until 1961, which turned out to be the highest recorded total in the NCCPT's history. In many of the state units, such as Virginia, Tennessee, and Georgia, membership continued to increase until the late 1960s, when the NCPT announced plans to unify with the NCCPT. This surge in membership offset the losses to desegregation of the black PTA state units as the border states

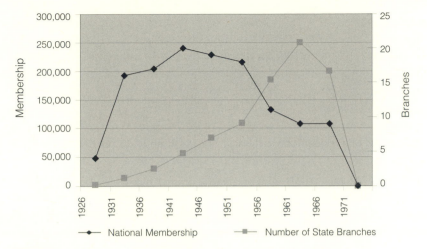

FIGURE 5.1

State branches of the NCCPT, 1926–76 (*Source:* NCCPT, *Coral Anniversary History,* 57–81)

began to integrate immediately after *Brown.* In other words, a comparison of national membership figures with the number of state units reveals that black PTA membership was at its peak in 1961 with only half of the original twenty state units remaining (see figure 5.1).[15]

Throughout these years, intergroup relations agencies stepped up resources and staffing to meet the challenge of desegregation and improving race relations. Although the PTA's national-level Intergroup Relations Committee had been meeting annually since it was formed in 1946, both black and white officers wanted greater participation at the state level. The state-level committees, which were to be composed of representatives from the black and white congresses, were a means to bridge the ethnic and racial differences among members. As organizational guidelines explained, the purposes of the committees were to provide members a chance to "get to know members of both races" and to "plot signs of progress and discuss difficulties faced by each group, and explore ways of overcoming them. . . . [and to] set aside suspicion and misunderstanding as to the motives of each group." They also were to come up with a plan of action and invite speakers of "both races" to lead discussions and join study groups.[16]

In practice, the Intergroup Relations committees enjoyed mixed success. Predictably, the committees in the border-state units were the most productive, while the white members of the Intergroup Relations committees in the Deep South were the most resistant to change, with members even refusing to attend meetings. Black PTA histories note that Maryland and Kentucky had Intergroup Relations committees that focused on "interracial harmony," while the Kansas black branch reported that their officers established "Excellent intergroup relations as study groups and workshops were emphasized." In the best-case scenario, Kentucky's committee became a part of the white state PTA infrastructure. Kentucky had a relatively open-minded approach to the process, as Intergroup Relations committees around the state were coordinated by a group of educators at the University of Kentucky, who began holding annual summer workshops in 1950. In other states, such as Alabama, Intergroup Relations committees were not as effective as national-level PTA leaders had hoped. Moreover, Alabama's white PTA officers had to be prodded to hold regular meetings, and when they did, they were secretive about them: they kept the committee meetings and minutes off the official record. In contrast, Alabama's black PTA leaders viewed the Intergroup Relations Committee as important, documented its activities and proceedings, and often held meetings without white members.[17]

Therefore, PTA units in the South had a scattered and uneven investment of Intergroup Relations Committee members. By 1965 black and white national leaders devised a means by which committee members could call on a national liaison as needed, echoing the extension efforts of the 1920s. Also, using the federated structure, they encouraged the formation of county- and city-level Intergroup Relations committees to carry out the work, and asked that reports be submitted on a regular basis. As calls for desegregation were stepped up after the Civil Rights Act, both PTA presidents requested written updates on Intergroup Relations committees' activities and plans. The NCCPT reported to its membership in 1967 that the ultimate goal of the intergroup relations committees of the remaining nine state units was to "play an integral role in facilitating a merger that will be effective and functional." Yet the Intergroup Relations committees of the PTA were much more effective in the border states than in the Deep South in coordinating a smooth transition to a unified organization.[18]

"You Must Earn Your Place": PTA Desegregation in the Border States

As the border-state units successfully employed their Intergroup Relations committees in negotiating unification and took on the role of educating the public about the virtues of integrated school systems, desegregation of the PTA in those states became a relatively unremarkable event. From 1954 to 1955, the NCCPT lost six state units, in New Mexico, Missouri, Oklahoma, Washington, DC, Maryland, and Kansas, with the desegregation of the PTA in those states. The Delaware PTA remained atypical: even though its black and white state units did not officially merge until 1966, they worked closely together since the relationship between the two congresses had always been congenial.[19] New Mexico, which had created a black PTA unit in 1944, was the first to desegregate, because of the low numbers of black members.[20] In 1954 the Washington, DC, Intergroup Relations Committee took only a year to work out the details and merge its two organizations, tackling the white parents' central concern: "Would educational standards be lowered because of integration?" John R. Gilliland, the white president of the newly unified Congress of Parents and Teachers, sought to "bring all parent-teacher association members in to one group because their purpose and standards were the same," and announced that the idea of two separate groups was "ridiculous." The Washington, DC, Colored Congress noted that the merger increased the membership of the integrated organization by fourteen thousand.[21]

In some areas, even though the transition to unification came with ease, black PTA leaders began to experience an erosion of power. In Missouri, the Colored Congress reported on its unification with the state's white PTA in 1955: "integration proceeded smoothly, without difficulty or friction." Following this, the Kansas Congress of Colored Parents and Teachers held its final convention in the spring of 1955, at which it willingly voted "to dissolve and become part of the Kansas Congress of Parents and Teachers." However, as black units were accepted into the Kansas City, Missouri, PTA Council, they became increasingly concerned about maintaining representation in leadership positions. Mrs. Walter Curnett, the white president of the Kansas City PTA Council, informed black PTA members, "When you come into a majority group . . . you must earn your place. We would not be sincere if we gave you an office just because you are a Negro and held an office in a Negro P.T.A. group. If you proved qualified for office, rest assured that you will be chosen to serve." This became the main question on NCCPT members' minds: would black members be given adequate leadership representation in an integrated PTA? Within those integrated state units, some black members were appointed to chair committees, while many more waited and hoped to be elected at some point in the future.[22]

In general, it is difficult to establish just exactly what PTA members experienced during the period of unification beyond the basic facts because of considerable gaps in the historical record. In some locations—typically the border states—white PTA members initiated the unification of the PTA in their state, while in others, usually in the Deep South, whites resisted. Overall, black PTA members were supportive of integration but wanted to maintain a voice in the unified organization. The white PTA had the freedom not to have to address race, while the black PTA wove discussions of race and equality into virtually every facet of its work. For instance, while the NCPT in 1956 adopted as its slogan "The Family and the Community: Each Shapes the Other; the PTA

Serves Both," the slogan for the NCCPT that year was far more parsimonious and focused on the central task at hand: "Building Together."[23]

Discussions of race and desegregation almost never appear in the minutes, proceedings, and other organizational papers of white PTA units, especially in the South, and when such matters are addressed, they are given only cursory mention. To compound matters, few black PTA records were saved for posterity. The Kentucky Congress of Parents and Teachers (KCPT) typifies this fact: although an active and robust Kentucky Colored Congress existed, I could locate hardly any documentation of its work and leaders. It was created in 1921, just two years after the white Kentucky PTA was organized, and joined the National Congress of Colored Parents and Teachers in 1927. In 1954 it enjoyed its peak membership of 4,000 and approximately 80 local units, after which membership declined. In contrast, Kentucky's white PTA was founded around 1919 with 16,000 members and had over 150,000 members in nearly 700 units in 1954. Membership for the white organization continued to increase to a high of 227,000 in 1969, after which it began a slow but steady decline.[24]

Membership data tell only one side of the story; one may trace the contours of the relationship between the two organizations in Kentucky from the reports of the Group Relations Committee, though it is a mere sketch. On April 25, 1955, the all-white KCPT convened a state-level Group Relations Committee to respond to the NCPT leaders' request that all state units act on the Supreme Court's ruling. Its Board declared:

> No issue will face us in this generation which will be a greater challenge to living in accordance with our moral and spiritual values than that of how we react to desegregation in our schools. . . . We will work, therefore, to implement the integration program in whatever way the court decrees, realizing this is not just a matter of school administrators, but for the parents of the children and for other citizens.

Thus it was the intention of the KCPT to comply with the NCPT's request to work toward integration.[25]

The Kentucky State Board of Education met in June 1955 and passed a resolution that school desegregation should proceed as rapidly as possible, given that overall conditions in Kentucky were favorable regarding the desegregation of schools and social spaces. In September of that year, the KCPT's Group Relations Committee had convened once again and recommended that local PTA units "cooperate fully in carrying out whatever plans for integration" superintendents and boards of education were making for districts around the state. By the end of the following year, school desegregation in Kentucky was beginning to have an impact, with approximately 25 percent of the state's 180 school districts implementing some form of desegregation. Resistance could be found in some places, such as Louisville, where a white Citizens' Council was formed to challenge integration, though as one contemporary observer noted, no "critical incidents" were reported.[26]

In the spring of 1956, the white members of the Group Relations Committee decided to arrange a meeting with representatives from the Kentucky Congress of Colored Parents and Teachers (KCCPT) to discuss desegregation and how to implement it both in their own ranks and in the schools. Members of Kentucky's two PTA branches discussed the challenges of desegregation and considered the importance of parents' responsibility in shaping attitudes about race, ethnicity, and difference. Inasmuch as the KCPT supported school desegregation and wanted to work with the members of the black PTA in their state, they did not wish to cede control of the organization to African American officers. They planned a meeting to "discuss plans for solving the possible integration problems inherent in the future of the two Congresses," as they maintained that "the selection of Discussion Leader be left to the discretion of the president of the Kentucky Congress of Parents and Teachers."[27]

The KCPT met with black representatives in September 1956, only to find out that the Kentucky Colored Congress voted to continue as a separate state unit because, its leaders argued, a separate organization "could still be of great service" to African Americans in that state. The decision reflected a trend throughout the South among local and state black PTA units: the wish to remain segregated in order to maintain control within black communities and over the education of African American children. Similar lines of reasoning could be found in the state units of Delaware and West Virginia. One participant at a workshop in West Virginia contended, "The problems that face Negro youth in the period during which public education is being desegregated makes an organization like the National Congress of Colored Parents and Teachers necessary, but its objectives must be expanded to meet these problems." Ironically, one of the suggestions was that the NCCPT help cultivate "wholesome attitudes toward the integration of public education." By this time, black state units were fully developed in their own right with capable leaders, a growing membership, and successful programs and activities in the schools. The decision of Kentucky's Colored Congress to remain separate left the white PTA between a rock and a hard place; the National PTA's official pronouncement was clear that that all Southern PTA units should work toward desegregation. At the KCPT Board of Managers' next meeting, concerned about accusations that they were not following the guidelines set forth by the national leadership, state officers went on record as "being in accord with the statement of policy of the National Congress of Parents and Teachers on the United States Supreme Court decision regarding desegregation." White state leaders interpreted the statement as official PTA policy and wanted the state's black PTA to comply. Kentucky's Colored Congress continued meeting

separately over the next fifteen years as contemporaries noted that the state had
made "astonishing progress in the desegregation and integration of students."
KCPT's Group Relations Committee met and reported on its activities, but it
was largely ineffective. It put forth one pronouncement after another in favor
of desegregation, but was powerless to bring about action since the KCCPT
wished to remain separate, even as the majority of Kentucky's schools were
integrated between 1958 and 1960. White state-level PTA members remained
concerned; at the January 1958 meeting of the Group Relations Committee,
leaders stated, "It is the feeling . . . of the committee that desegregation and
integration of the White and Negro ethnic groups (or races) is Kentucky's
number one problem as far as group relations is concerned."[28]

The KCPT continued to pay expenses for the black members of the Group
Relations Committee, an incentive endorsed by the national office since the
Colored Congress still struggled with financial solvency. The committee continued to meet through the 1960s to address what they called "problems of
mutual interest" but did not elaborate on in meeting minutes. Then, in 1961,
the two Group Relations committees met to again discuss the matter of integration. The meeting was difficult, as both sides presented their positions and
discussed the difference between integration and absorption, two terms ban-
died about by Southern state units during this time. KCPT leaders posited
that integration was the "law of the land" and based their argument on the
citizenship tenet of the PTA program, claiming members should be "law-abiding citizens" and work for desegregation. KCCPT officers did not disagree,
but shared their concerns that the Colored Congress continue as "a training
ground for leaders of the race to intelligently battle the problem of the day."
Furthermore, black PTA leaders explained that they felt "strongly that they
could minister to the spiritual, social, and cultural and educational needs of
the parents and students at least until integration became an accepted thing."
The only matter on which the two organizations could agree was to continue
meeting on a regular basis.[29]

Kentucky's Colored Congress continued to remain independent and maintain a national presence in the larger NCCPT through the mid-1960s. State
leader Minnie Hitch, who had served on the Group Relations Committee, was
elected president of the NCCPT from 1964 to 1967. Hitch's presidential platform was "Aspiring for One World," revealing to black PTA workers in Kentucky and around the South that the two PTA branches intended to become
one before long. At the fortieth convention of the NCCPT, Hitch articulated
black PTA leaders' hopes that they continue to maintain a voice and a presence in the unified organization: "Yes, we know the time is close at hand when
P.T.A. will be one organization with many sub-groups in many regions. As
we welcome one world so we welcome one P.T.A., but I want to live until I'm
counted, until my qualities are seen, felt and are notable among the accom-

plishments of other organizations that are included." White PTA workers in Kentucky were thrilled and sent congratulations to their fellow PTA worker on her national leadership role. Realizing that time was short, Kentucky's Colored Congress tried to strike a compromise that would keep its membership base, and, hopefully, with it the control it had in the black community, by employing a novel strategy. Since it did not want to be absorbed by the white PTA and lose members as a result, it left the federation, became an independent association, and changed its name to the Kentucky Parent League. Then it applied for membership in the KCPT. It was an attempt to keep its leadership, members, and activities intact as it joined with the white association. KCPT leaders welcomed the Kentucky Parent League in 1966, signaling the beginning of a unified PTA in that state. Ultimately, however, the tactic did not work, since few African Americans rose to leadership positions over the next decade in Kentucky's newly integrated PTA.[30]

In the fall of 1967, the school year began with only nine remaining state units of the National Congress of Colored Parents and Teachers, having dropped from twenty in 1954 as a result of desegregation. The NCCPT had lost five over the summer of 1967: Delaware, Kentucky, Maryland, Tennessee, and West Virginia. Black and white national PTA leaders were growing increasingly frustrated with the remaining segregated state units as they began to realize that it was ineffective to defer to Southern state leaders to determine the pace of and plan for unification. As a result, they stepped up the pressure to merge black and white units while working within the constraints of the organization and its bylaws. They began to require state-level Intergroup Relations committees to submit progress reports to the white national office. By this time, the national leadership of both PTA branches were becoming more outspoken about the inevitability of the unification of the two organizations. The NCPT did not have to become as involved with the situation in Kentucky as it did in other states, particularly in the Deep South, where resistance to desegregation was much stronger and the reactions of white segregationists much more volatile. Moreover, members and leaders in black units in those states had mixed feelings about their willingness to unite with the white PTA, just as they had become ambivalent by the late 1960s about school desegregation.[31]

"This Request I Cannot Submit to": The *Brown* Decision and PTA Units in the Deep South

The desegregation of PTA units in the Deep South took much longer—until 1970 for the last four units—to integrate than in the border states, as the response of white-segregationist PTA members varied from silent evasion to outright defiance. In Georgia and Alabama, two states that refused to integrate until the 1970 national merger, white and black PTA leaders held different stances and attempted different strategies with the push for unification. In Georgia, specifically in Atlanta, the white PTA did not take part in the public debate over the desegregation of schools, while the black PTA remained a vocal presence (see figure 5.2). In neighborhoods in which white PTA women were supportive of integration, they hoped it would be limited. In contrast, Kathryn Nasstrom argues, black parents viewed schools as "institutions where family and community met, each reinforcing the other, [while white] segregationists saw integrated schools as a threat to families." In Alabama, the white PTA fought at the local level against desegregation of the PTA and schools, based on the Southern tradition of states' rights. Black PTA leaders, despite knowing that much control and leadership would be lost in their association, worked to end segregation of schools and the PTA in that state. Their means were not direct or explicit, for that would prove too dangerous, but they acted through existing channels of communication within the organization to take on Alabama's white PTA and its racist practices. In Atlanta, a more liberal approach to race relations offered a different context for the unification of the two PTA branches, although interactions between black and white PTA leaders in Georgia were not always genial.[32]

The case of Alabama after the *Brown* decision illustrates the reaction of white segregationist PTA members in the Deep South. Like other Southern states, Alabama has a history of inequitable distribution of funding for black schools because of laws put into place during the Progressive era. The provisions of the Apportionment Act of 1891 gave local officials the discretion to distribute school funding as they wished, leaving black schools grossly underfunded into the twentieth century. In the early twentieth century, a system of schools was established, and enrollments increased through the first half of the century. From 1900 to 1930, enrollments of white students in public schools grew from 55.9 to 76.9 percent, and of black students from 43.4 to 61.0 percent. In 1920, the average length of the school year in rural areas was 87 days for blacks, and in 1938 it grew to 142 days. In urban areas over the same period it went from 155 to 175 days. As the schools grew, so did Alabama's parent-teacher association. Black and white PTA units were active over the course of the century in this vastly rural state.[33]

The all-white Alabama Congress of Parents and Teachers (ACPT) was organized in Alabama in 1911, uniting the local mothers' and women's clubs around the state. A network of black clubs developed in a fashion parallel to the ACPT during the same time. The African American Alabama State Mothers' League was founded in 1914 and changed its name to the Alabama State PTA in 1924. In 1926 representatives of the black State PTA attended the

FIGURE 5.2

Atlanta PTA district workshop at Wheat Street Baptist Church, 1959. Narvie Harris, president, is in the center seat in the front row. (*Source:* Photo reprinted with permission from Narvie J. Harris and Dee Taylor, *African-American Education in DeKalb County,* Arcadia Publishing, 1999; http:// www.arcadiapublishing.com)

organizational meeting of the National Congress of Colored Parents and Teachers and became one of the original four states to join. Thereafter it was known as the Alabama Congress of Colored Parents and Teachers (ACCPT). The white PTA in Alabama was active in the usual activities, from holding canning demonstrations during World War I, to selling war bonds during World War II, giving scholarships to students who wanted to become teachers, and networking with other associations to more effectively carry out its program. Also, the Alabama white Congress implemented civic education initiatives from the Depression years until the 1970s. The Colored Congress of Alabama undertook similar pursuits, such as planting trees to honor the organization's founders, awarding college scholarships, and coordinating health initiatives around the state.[34]

The example of how the PTA in Alabama reacted to the *Brown* decision reveals state-level machinations of white segregationists, white PTA leaders who sought to appease various constituencies, and black PTA members who worked for desegregation even as they knew the cost would be great to their own organization. Alabama was typical of the holdout states in regard to the reaction of its black and white members. White PTA members in these states sought to stave off desegregation in order to preserve what they called the Southern way of life and to maintain control over schools and curricula. Black PTA workers in the same states debated what would be lost with unification and ultimately came to the conclusion by the mid-1960s that to do so was the greater good. All the while, black PTA leaders increased their membership base in order to facilitate a strong transition to an integrated PTA. However, Alabama is unique among PTA units in the holdout states in at least one respect; a splinter group of white leaders sought to undermine the federation by convincing local units to drop out of the organization and cease to pay dues. It worked for a short time, as the ACPT lost 10 percent of its members from 1956 to 1957. It was the only state in the Deep South to experience such a decline in membership directly after *Brown*. The case of Alabama may just have set the stage, though, for later membership declines, as the merger of the two associations became imminent and as schools in those states began to desegregate as a result of the ESEA and Civil Rights Act.[35]

The NCPT's appeal, issued on May 22, 1954, for its state and local units to "study and pursue effective means in working toward integrated education for all children" set off shock waves through Alabama. While the Alabama Congress of Colored Parents and Teachers celebrated and discussed how to develop a "Wholesome Attitude toward Integration" at its fortieth annual meeting, white PTA workers reacted to what they perceived as a threat to a well-established tradition. Other segregationist organizations joined the debate; Olin Horton, the President of the American States' Rights Association, which was based in Birmingham, circulated a letter to all PTA members in the state imploring them to take a stand against the NCPT. Misinformation spread around the state despite the organization's well-oiled communication system. One PTA member wrote a local paper insisting the organization "has no policy on integration," revealing members' desire to know whether the statement was a suggestion or directive. The ambiguity prompted Mary N. Sellers, president of the Bellinger Hill [Alabama] PTA to write to Ethel G. Brown, the NCPT president (1955–58), to ask for clarification on the matter. Sellers wrote, "As you have probably read our State is in the midst of a turmoil concerning integration in our schools. We in our local PTA would like to know the National Policy and feeling of the National Parent-Teacher Organization on the question of non-segregated schools." Brown's response was parsimonious, reflecting national officers' unease with the situation and their lack of direction on how to address segregation and racism in their ranks; she merely responded by sending a copy of the official statement without elaboration.[36]

Segregationists feared that the NCPT was dictating policy to their state and imposing integration on their organization and the schools, while white state-level leaders were conflicted between adhering to organizational policy and following the tradition of segregation and Jim Crow in the South. Therefore, they said little publicly out of fear of alienating an already agitated membership. However, knowing they had to respond to members' concerns, they issued a statement that challenged the national PTA's stance on *Brown*. The ACPT Board of Managers met on April 22, 1956, and, referring to the "unrest and grave concern" around the state, passed a resolution that asked the NCPT to strike out the section on encouraging integration and replace it with the following: "The National Congress urges parent-teacher leaders, in cooperation with schools and other governmental authorities in each community, to study and pursue effective means of *constructively solving the problems* resulting from the Supreme Court's decision." White PTA workers thereby sought removal of the phrase "work toward integration of all children." Their position was based on a states' rights argument that placed much independence and decision-making power with state and local units. Moreover, PTA workers had additional ammunition in a PTA policy that directed units to neither "seek to direct the administrative activities of the schools nor control their policies." ACPT officers sent their recommended changes to the Chicago headquarters of the national association and requested a written acknowledgment of acceptance. The NCPT leadership merely responded that their resolution was on file and took no action.[37]

Leaders and members of the ACPT wondered about the NCPT's true position on integration. A rumor circulated that local and state dues sent to the national office were being used to fund the legal activities of the NAACP.

Since the NAACP needed every penny it could get for its legal activities, the matter of helping to fund it was a volatile one for Southerners who opposed desegregation. NCPT leaders attempted to address the matter, but did so awkwardly. In September 1956, in response to the allegations, the national office dispatched a telegram that read, "Report that the funds of National Congress are used for support of any organization except PTA absolutely false. Records show that we do not contribute to the other groups in any financial *manner*. All National Congress members can determine these facts by examining financial statements." While the National PTA did not admit to contributing monetarily, its leadership was generally supportive of the efforts of the NAACP in desegregation.[38]

Black PTA members, on the other hand, backed the efforts of the NAACP, but prodded leaders of the civil rights organization on whether they had considered other means to desegregate schools, such as boycotts and sit-ins. They also varied in the ways they made their affiliation with the NAACP public, depending on race relations in local contexts. Some PTA leaders, such as Narvie Harris of Georgia, were cautious about publicizing their membership in the civil rights organization. Harris recalls, "In little towns . . . it was not popular to be a member of the NAACP. . . . So it was not popular for us to go and invite somebody from the NAACP and jeopardize so many people's jobs, their livelihood—also the progress we were making, trying to have a coalition between the races. So the NAACP came at a time of need and more or less was kind of independent."[39] At the ground level in urban areas such as Atlanta, black PTA workers gained more psychically from affiliation with the NCCPT; as Kathryn Nasstrom argues, the black PTA "promoted female leadership development on a far larger scale than did the NAACP."[40] In South Carolina in 1956, a series of anti-NAACP statutes were passed making it unlawful for employees of the state and its municipalities to be members of the NAACP. As a result, teachers were required to submit written oaths regarding their membership in the association. At the same time as the NAACP lost members in South Carolina, going from 6,000 in 1954 to 1,400 in 1958, the state's Colored Congress of Parents and Teachers grew from 6,100 to nearly 14,000.[41] In the pages of the NCCPT's journal, *Our National Family*, however, black PTA leaders proudly listed the NAACP among their affiliations. After 1950 the NAACP reported regularly in the NCCPT's journal *Our National Family* and presented at the organization's annual meetings. In 1958 the Virginia Congress of Colored Parents and Teachers adopted resolutions related to strengthening relations between the races and "commended the NAACP for its work on civil rights [and] reaffirmed the group's faith in the NAACP."[42]

Capitalizing on the rancor among local units on the matter of integration, a white PTA worker, Betty Baldwin McLaurine, initiated a movement to withdraw local white units from state and national PTA membership. Her effort enjoyed a modicum of success from 1956 to 1957. At a meeting of the Montgomery County Council PTA on July 24, 1956, McLaurine, the group's president, resigned because the national leadership had not yet responded to the Alabama Congress's request to revise the PTA's *Brown* response and, as she put it bluntly, "I cannot be any part of an organization that has an integration statement or policy as its ultimate goal." The *Montgomery Advertiser* reported on the "tumultuous meeting" at which McLaurine resigned, and she began her campaign to form a new parent-teacher organization independent of the National PTA, the Parent-Teacher Alliance. The Alliance was intended to link together local units across the district committed to segregation. Although state-level officers Fanny Mitchell Nelson and Martha Rutledge were concerned with McLaurine's stand, they took no action at the time.[43]

That year, the press had a field day with the debates surrounding the desegregation of Alabama's PTA units. Local papers reported on the details of McLaurine's resignation, which prompted Alabama's other local units to question their loyalty to the NCPT. While McLaurine had declared her independence, the Montgomery County Council—one of the largest in the state—acted similarly, but as a member of the federation. Its publicity committee sent certified letters to local units asking them join in taking a stand against the NCPT's position on integration. Local units had to decide where to place their allegiance: with the long tradition of segregation or with an association whose ideals they supported. Members such as E. L. White, president of the Baldwin County PTA Council, turned to PTA bylaws for an answer. White wrote to the ACPT secretary, Fanny Nelson, informing her, "This request [to withdraw and support segregation in the schools] I cannot submit to for I feel it is not in order for any County Council to take action on this matter without the approval of the State Board." Nelson and her cohorts were relieved as they responded, "We regret deeply that this matter has come up but if each council president will hold as you are holding we can continue our work for the good of our children and youth."[44]

Yet the unrest continued, forcing ACPT president Martha Rutledge to issue a statement to all PTA-council presidents on August 1, 1956. Her letter was intended to clarify the matter and reiterate the National PTA's position on desegregation, yet it ended up being a nebulous statement about integration in which she recapped organizational policy. Such responses were characteristic of the state and national PTA leadership and ended up prolonging the confusion and restlessness among local units. Rutledge reminded ACPT members that the Board of Managers of the Alabama Congress adopted a statement of position on segregation on April 22 of that year. She reiterated the organization's commitment to work for the welfare of all children in home, school, church, and community and reprinted the national's policy that it would not seek to direct the administrative activities of the schools. Then, in an attempt to head off the letters from the Montgomery County Council, Rutledge concluded, "You will be getting a lot of mail during the year from various sources. Of course, you will want to read it all carefully but remembering [*sic*] to keep a clear head in your thinking about different issues that will come up."[45]

The following day, local papers announced that PTA units were going to receive letters from a group influenced by McLaurine's resignation that had formed in Montgomery County. They quoted McLaurine's letter, which asked that local units withhold their dues from the National PTA. It read, "Only by withholding your membership dues from both the State and National P-TA can you call the State P-TA's attention to your refusal to support this policy of integrated education for all children." McLaurine repeated the rumor accusing the National PTA of channeling dues to a fund that supported integration. She emphasized her point by claiming that the Alabama PTA sent a substantial amount, just over ten thousand dollars, to the National PTA in 1955. McLaurine's letter accomplished what its author had hoped. The Council and State leaders of the white PTA were flooded with correspondence. Some local workers wrote the state office requesting a copy of the white PTA's stand on integration "as soon as possible." State-level representatives agreed to contact local workers and attend meetings around the state to quell the rumors and assess just how widespread was the movement to leave the federation. One ACPT informant reported in late August that a meeting in Montgomery County had been well attended and that the "spirit was good" despite the "weight of their many recent burdens." She observed at another meeting that no one spoke up during open floor time, but in small groups "there were many disturbed people in each group who freely asked questions." One development the informant noted was that local units were no longer interested in paying dues to the state and national congresses.[46]

McLaurine's resignation and the letter that was circulated to local units in her district not only resulted in members' questioning their allegiance to the National PTA but also slowed the creation of new units as the commotion spread beyond the district to other parts of the state. Superintendent R. J. Lawrence of Bullock County in Union Springs, Alabama, responded to Mrs. James Hepburn, the vice president of District Four of the Alabama white PTA, who was interested in starting a local unit in Union Springs. He did not think too many people were interested anymore, because of "the disturbance" in the Montgomery County Council PTA. "All I know about what happened in Montgomery is what I have read in the paper. . . . [T]he people of Bullock County are very much disturbed over the segregation question, and my opinion is that if it gets too hot you will not have any PTA's in Bullock County which will affiliate with the state and national group."[47]

Realizing that her earlier attempts to downplay the situation did not have much of an effect, white state president Rutledge sent another letter to ACPT members. She began by reminding members of the flexibility of the federation, in particular that some statements from the national office "need not be followed to the letter," hinting that the NCPT's pronouncement after *Brown* was to be taken as a suggestion, not policy, and that each state PTA could and should follow its own path. Following this, she reprinted in full the NCPT's stance, after which she pointed out that the ACPT had drafted an amendment that was on file at the PTA headquarters. Finally, Rutledge addressed the rumor that dues were being channeled to support the NAACP's legal efforts. In response to McLaurine's assertion that over ten thousand dollars went to the national leadership in 1955, the actual figure, according to Rutledge, was only $884.00. With this clarification, Rutledge confirmed ACPT members' worst fear, that their dues were being used to support school desegregation efforts.[48]

In late summer 1956, the PTA units of Montgomery County began their domino-like descent as they withdrew membership from the state and national congresses. It began in August, as local workers debated the advantages of belonging to the federation and whether those advantages were worth the price of having to integrate, or at least having to admit to the likelihood of integration. Some, like the Cloverdale PTA, voted to remain affiliated, claiming, "If we withdrew, we would no longer have a voice in the policy making decisions of that group." At this time, McLaurine was not sitting idly by. She did what her PTA forebears had done over fifty years earlier: she traveled around the county to organize parent-teacher units. However, she tried to convince local groups to leave the National Congress and join the Independent Parent-Teacher Alliance. She implored them to cease sending their hard-earned money to an organization that supported integrated schools. Her efforts were met with a measure of success as some local units decided to secede, though many of them refused to join the Parent-Teacher Alliance. Instead, they voted to be independent for one year, as they watched what would transpire in the schools and the PTA.[49]

Concerned with the loss of local units, ACPT president Rutledge took a stronger public stand on the matter. Using the skills honed as a PTA leader by going to the press to use publicity to the organization's advantage, she denied that state and local PTA units were bound by the national's integration statement and claimed, "The National Congress of Parents and Teachers has never in any way even suggested means of integration of schools in Alabama. . . . [S]tate branches and local PTA units have complete autonomy in working out solutions to local problems." A couple of days later she ramped up her position: "We will not concur or be bound by any policies or statements of the board of managers or of any officers of the National Congress of Parents and Teachers favoring anything other than separate schools." Rutledge's decla-rations, however, did not have their intended effect and may, in fact, have done the opposite of what she hoped in creating more excitement and confusion around the matter.[50]

By early September, the controversy expanded across the southeastern part of the state as more parent-teacher groups discussed whether to remain affiliated with the federation. Concerned with the spread of the uncertainty to four additional counties—Crenshaw, Pike, Macon, and Dallas—Rutledge announced in the press that she would be the first to resign if the NCPT insisted on desegregation in Alabama. She called for a "united front" of PTA members in the state to maintain segregation and became increasingly blunt with the press as she asserted that the ACPT was "fighting to maintain segrega-tion in Alabama" and that the association had "no Negro members." Rutledge claimed the reason she was hesitant to take a public stand was that she felt that her beliefs were on record and she did not want to say or do anything that would be counterproductive to education in the state of Alabama. Finally, in an effort to win back the defecting local units, she made her boldest statement to the press, and it was the position that the PTA's national-level leaders feared the most: "As president of the Alabama Congress, I am a firm believer in the Southern way of life. The entire organization of the Alabama congress is made up of people who believe in the Southern way of life. There is no organization anywhere that practices segregation more than the Alabama P-TA or an organ-ization that will work toward maintaining segregation in our schools with any more force." Her audacious declaration had little effect, largely because the momentum that had been generated was too difficult to reverse. Two days later, McLaurine held a widely publicized meeting in which she detailed her reasons for the Independent Parent-Teacher Alliance and blamed the state PTA leadership for being passive and "willing to serve under this policy of integrated education for all children." Tired of waiting for the state Congress to take action, she formed her alliance "independent of national control" and claimed that it would remain "undefiled by ambitious national leaders anxious to promote integrated education for our children."[51]

Alabama's diminishing membership caused the National PTA to capitulate to Southern integrationists in fear of losing its membership base. Local units were confused by the conflicting stances and continued to debate the matter of whether to withdraw from the National PTA. Some decided to remain, but many local units withdrew in county councils around the state, bringing with them a decline in the thousands of members in Alabama. Other organizations joined the secession movement as many of the withdrawals were fueled by the white Citizens' Councils, which sought economic means to squelch the fight for desegregation. The situation became so dire that the NCPT leadership was forced to take action lest it lose more members in Alabama or, worse yet, the phenomenon in that state was repeated elsewhere. In a stunning move in September 1956, it agreed to a wording change of its *Brown* response to appease Southern white members. Representatives of the ACPT attended the meeting at its Chicago headquarters in which both parties agreed on a compromise. The revised statement was not exactly that proposed by the Alabama Congress—to "study and pursue effective means of constructively solving the problems resulting from the Supreme Court's decision"—but did remove the suggestion that state and local PTA units support and facilitate integration. By a vote of twenty-two for and fifteen against, representatives from Alabama and the national leadership agreed that the new position would urge PTA members to work toward "a just solution to the complex problem of segregation in public schools."[52]

It took a couple of months before the tide turned and local units again joined the federation. Even though some local and county units continued to withdraw membership from the NCPT that fall, at least seven counties met at a district meeting in Birmingham to reaffirm their faith in the State Congress. Most did not agree with Betty McLaurine, who called the revised statement "ambiguous" and continued to stump for members to join her Independent Alliance. McLaurine was not garnering any sympathy either, as word leaked out that several county PTA workers had received threatening phone calls accusing them of being pro-integrationists. Between the National PTA's revised position and the assumption that McLaurine's group was responsible for intimidating PTA workers, local units reassessed their commitment to the federation. Some, like the Delraida School PTA, decided to withhold funds from the Congress for one year, after which time it would reconsider the benefits of national membership. The Delraida PTA also announced that it would "at no time throughout this year be affiliated with the Independent Alliance of Parents and Teachers." As 1957 wore on, many units rejoined the ACPT. The Chilton School PTA, for example, decided to do so because, they explained, "About one-fourth of the student body at Chilton School will require aid in obtaining needed clothing and free lunches, which . . . are provided by the national group."[53]

For the second time in its history, the first being during the Depression years, the membership of the white Alabama PTA had declined; it lost 22,000 members, or approximately 10 percent, from 1956 to 1957. As a result of the National PTA's revised *Brown* statement and the benefits of belonging to a federated association, the figure began to grow again in 1958; by 1960 the membership total in the state was back to where it had been in 1956 and continued to increase in the years that followed.[54] Ironically, during the same period, the slogan of Alabama's Colored Congress (ACCPT) was "Building

Together for Our Children," which referred to the segregated association's wish for integrated schools and parent-teacher associations in the state. During this same time, the ACCPT continued to grow, adding 3,000 members from 1956 to 1957. The exodus of white members from 1956 to 1957 had a significant impact on the PTA in Alabama and nationally, since it made the organization's leaders realize that the challenge of desegregating its Southern units was greater than they had thought. What happened in Alabama, however, did not affect the overall membership of the white NCPT at this time, which continued to grow. The state's negative effect on the federation was short-lived, as members decided the benefits of belonging to the federation outweighed the ordeal of desegregation. Furthermore, some white PTA units in the Deep South in the late 1950s were encouraged by ongoing efforts to push back desegregation, which appeared at the time to be successful, while other white units were silent and unwilling to take a stand publicly for or against the integration of public schools. At the same time, the black PTA carried on, increasing its membership base and developing a regenerating cadre of leaders.[55]

"An Honorable Demise": The Desegregation of the PTA

In the 1960s, school desegregation had mixed success in the Deep South, and had all but stalled by the end of the decade. In Alabama, the state government tried to shut down the operations of the NAACP, while in Atlanta, school desegregation proceeded relatively smoothly. During this time, the PTA continued to face the proposition of integrating its Southern units. The organization rebounded from the secession movement in Alabama to enjoy its largest membership ever in the early 1960s: in 1963 the NCPT had 12.1 million members, while the NCCPT had grown to a quarter of a million members in 1961. However, after this point membership in both associations began to decline nationwide. The year 1966 was a watershed year, as it marked declines in the white state units of Arkansas, Florida, Georgia, Missouri, North Carolina, Texas, and Virginia. The association did not regain its strength in numbers from this point on, as school districts were forced to desegregate because of the Civil Rights Act's funding mandate and the ESEA. For example, Georgia's white PTA membership began a steady, slow decline, losing between 5,000 and 8,000 members a year beginning in 1964. The Birmingham County Council in Alabama remarked on its losses: it had 25,000 members in 1963, 7,000 fewer members than the previous year. In 1966 the Alabama PTA dropped from a high point of 232,000, to lose nearly a third of its members by 1971, the year it finally united with the ACCPT.[56]

Although the black PTA units of Alabama and Georgia did not have the numerical strength of their white counterparts, each had a long record of accomplishments. Georgia, like Alabama, was one of the original four to join the National Congress of Colored Parents and Teachers in 1926, though it, too, had been organized earlier. Georgia's state unit was organized in 1921 by Selena Sloan Butler, the founding president of the Colored Congress. Like other states in the NCCPT, Alabama's and Georgia's Colored Congresses were led by teachers and other education professionals. Both state associations were active in schools and communities and were typical of other white and black local and state units. For example, at the Forty-Third Annual Meeting of the Alabama Colored Congress in 1957, the theme was "Building Together for Children." The Boy Scouts opened the meeting with the presentation of colors, which was followed by the typical PTA activities of the Pledge of Allegiance followed by religious devotions and group singing. The discussions included the usual PTA topics such as parent education, home and family living, and recreation and leisure pursuits but also included the matters that the black association focused on, such as job opportunities and voter registration.[57]

Each of the state Colored Congresses enjoyed growth spurts, even though they did not match the white PTA in proportion of the population. For example, the Alabama Congress of Colored Parents and Teachers grew from 24,503 members in 1954 to 33,381 in 1961, under the leadership of Thelma M. Morris. Georgia's growth spurt was coordinated earlier, from 1936 to 1942, during which time it increased fourfold, under the administration of Ethel Kight. Kight was a master at nurturing PTA membership; when she was NCCPT president from 1957 to 1961, the organization enjoyed its last big push to enlist members, increasing by 70,000 during those years.[58]

The 1960s were years of uncertainty for the remaining Colored Congress units, as they struggled with the desegregation of the schools and whether to unify with the white PTA. The state units came down on the side of integration, as they referred to it, and 1966 saw the unification of black and white units in Kentucky, Delaware, Maryland, and West Virginia, and Tennessee the following year, leaving the NCCPT with just a little less than half its twenty state units. As the state leadership of each announced a unified PTA, it helped facilitate the integration of local state units, a process that sometimes took several years. In Tennessee, after the state's black and white PTA officers announced that the two were merging, its Colored Congress began to reassign local unit after local unit during the following year as it planned its last annual meeting. Black state president Draper announced that with half of the school districts in Tennessee officially desegregated, her state could not afford two separate congresses, claiming that with two "our strength is weakened and diminished." However, membership data reveal that with a unified association, strength was significantly reduced; in the same report, Draper announced the loss of 36,000 black members from 1965 to 1966 due to integration, but the white PTA in that state grew by only 750 members that year. Although the Tennessee Congress of Colored Parents and Teachers grew by smaller increments from 1966 to 1969, it began to lose members beginning in 1968, a trend that continued with the unified PTA in Tennessee until 1985.[59]

The NCCPT magazine *Our National Family* encouraged members to work toward the integration of schools and even suggested "concrete preparatory steps," which included getting the cooperation of local political, educational, and business leaders; holding in-service workshops for professional educators; and "upon announcement of the date of integration, employ[ing] an attitude of 'firm determination' towards all opponents and attempt[ing] to reassure them . . . that the dire results which they fear are highly unlikely to come to pass." NCCPT members were instructed to be prepared for isolated instances of violence and to treat them as such—individual incidents that were not reflective of society at large.[60]

The National PTA's having changed its stance on *Brown* essentially gave local and state units in the South free rein to determine the extent to which they wanted to work with each other. As a result, the Colored Congresses of Alabama and Georgia remained separate to the point of unification in the 1970s. Differences can be noted in how each state desegregated its PTA branches that are reflective of local and state political and social contexts. In Georgia, the leadership base of the Colored Congress was based in Atlanta, where the city's main civic organizations, such as the YWCA and Urban League, emphasized interracial cooperation. Therefore, the Georgia Colored Congress of Parents and Teachers was confident in its independence and had worked cooperatively for years with the state's white association. This cooperation was from a distance until the mid-1960s, when the Intergroup Relations Committee began to meet on a regular basis.[61]

By the mid-1960s the remaining black PTA units began to promote the notion that to remain independent and separate of the white PTA was antithetical to progress in a democracy. The leadership of the remaining nine state units, therefore, wanted to integrate, though like the majority of members, they feared it would not be true integration, but rather extinction, dissolution, or absorption of black PTA units. African American PTA leaders expressed frustration over the loss of state associations and claimed that their state units were being "swallowed up" by the white national PTA. With the goal of maintaining a presence in the majority association and representation in leadership roles, the remaining state units continued to work tentatively toward integration. The most common approaches included having the Intergroup Relations committees handle the merger or trying what Kentucky attempted but failed

FIGURE 5.3

The National Congress of Colored Parents and Teachers' magazine, *Our National Family*, presented its theme for the year on the cover of this issue from June 1968: "Unity—Our Challenge." (*Source:* Reprinted with permission and courtesy of National PTA)

at, which was to reconfigure the black PTA branch in the hope of joining the newly unified organization as an equal partner.[62]

When Clara Gay, the last president of the black PTA, took office in 1967, she announced the new and final theme and challenge of the NCCPT: unity (see figure 5.3). Gay, unlike some of her colleagues, promoted the benefits of the merger even though she was well aware that black teachers would lose their jobs. During the 1960s, with the legislation that discouraged segregation by enforcing monetary incentives, the National PTA worked to get its state-level leaders to negotiate and guide the transition to desegregation through the Intergroup Relations committees that had been established in the late 1940s. What came fairly easily in Georgia presented a challenge in Alabama. In Georgia, the committee first met formally in 1966 and the GCCPT used the gathering to share its history. Revealing the divide that had existed between the two organizations, President Narvie Harris remarked, "Most of the members present from the [white PTA were] surprised and delighted to know about our heritage and work for Children." Over the next couple of years, the two groups held several joint conferences that were successful, but the tenor of race relations changed in 1968, as the two National PTA branches pressed for concrete details on when the two would actually merge. The pressure resulted in "strained relations" between Georgia's two congresses, as neither was ready to relinquish control of its association to the other.[63]

At the same time, the National PTA struggled with the lack of action in Alabama, Georgia, and Florida. Its leaders held up North Carolina as a model; even though the state's two PTA branches did not merge until 1968 and school desegregation was a major challenge, each PTA agreed to honor liberal membership policies during a transition period, as did the other state PTA units that were quick to integrate. In the 1960s a black unit could join either Congress as long as it followed PTA policy. The North Carolina leadership explained: "If a new Negro unit is formed and wishes to fulfill all obligations to be in membership with us, we first inform them of the existence of the [North Carolina] Congress of Colored Parents and Teachers and give the president of that Congress an opportunity to be in touch with the new unit. If after this the unit still wishes to be in membership with us, we receive them."[64] On the other end of the spectrum, the white PTA in Alabama continued to refuse to admit black units through the 1960s based on the rationale that as long as there was a separate state unit, the organization was segregated.[65] The Joint Committee on Human Relations at the national level acknowledged around 1966 that it was receiving much information in support of two separate associations, yet it expressed its wishes that soon "there will be no need and no independent opportunity for a colored congress."[66]

In Alabama, white leaders were secretive about the Intergroup Relations Committee's existence and composition. Members joined by invitation of the president, and meeting minutes were kept off the official agenda of ACPT board meetings.[67] In contrast, black members were much more open regarding the membership and meetings of the intergroup relations committee. By the mid-1960s, they began to challenge segregationist practices and press for a merger. In 1966 the ACCPT announced its plans to "have frequent conferences with our sister organization for the purpose of abridging the gap between the two organizations so that we can work together for one common purpose, the child." In 1968, a black PTA member, Mrs. Thomas, who had just been appointed chair of the Constitutional Committee at a new unit at Westlawn Junior High, wrote to white executive secretary Fanny Nelson to inquire about the relationship between the two PTA branches in Alabama, suggesting that her organization might want to cross color lines and affiliate with the Alabama Congress of Parents and Teachers. Nelson's response to Thomas was terse and read, in its entirety, "In reply to your letter of inquiry, the National Congress of Parents and Teachers and the National Congress of Colored Parents and Teachers are separate organizations. Each organization has its own officers, channels of supplies, and communications." The closest thing to integration the national leadership achieved in Alabama at this time was that the two state presidents extended greetings at the other's convention. For example, in 1966, white state president Mrs. John R. Lathram gave the keynote at the annual statewide meeting of the Alabama Colored Congress.[68]

By 1966 the national-level leadership of both PTA branches became increasingly concerned that the state units in the Deep South were not moving as quickly as they could toward integration, so they decided to pressure them to unify once and for all. One of the first public announcements of the plan was made by NCPT president Jennelle Moorhead at the fortieth annual meeting of the Colored Congress that year. She began by saying, "I greet you as fellow members of the PTA, for in spirit—if not in fact—there is only one PTA," after which she announced that a "single, unified PTA enrolling all parents and teachers without regard to race, creed, color, or national origin" was the goal of both organizations. In response, the NCCPT leadership began running a series of essays in *Our National Family* supporting the merger and outlining expectations for what ideally should happen. Still, the national-level leadership had little power beyond making pronouncements, so the decision to unify remained with each state's group of officers and its Intergroup Relations committees. The NCCPT supported the measure, explaining to members that the Intergroup Relations committees of the [remaining] nine states and the nation should play an integral role in facilitating a merger that will be "effective and functional."[69]

In January 1967, Moorhead wrote the nine state offices—black and white—to inquire about the accomplishments of their Intergroup Relations committees. Alabama's white PTA president, Mrs. John R. Lathram, responded defensively to Moorhead, revealing the resistance of her unit to integration. She explained that they did in fact have an Intergroup Relations Committee that met at least once and that she had spoken at the state convention of the Alabama Colored Congress. Following the tactic of gradualism, she concluded, "We have a fine working relationship. I don't believe either group feels that it is time to press for any drastic change." However, the leaders of Alabama's Colored Congress did not feel the same way. ACCPT president Ethel Bell used Moorhead's query to leverage her position; she asked Lathram for a meeting so they could report to Moorhead "that we have taken some steps toward the two organizations working together." Without any other option, Lathram agreed and a meeting was arranged.[70]

In the spring of 1967, Alabama's Intergroup Relations Committee met and discussed the possibilities that lay before them. Even though this was a state-level meeting, several national officers of the NCCPT attended at Bell's request, which made for a somewhat tense gathering, as white state leaders felt trumped in their authority.[71] After discussing less controversial topics such as their common health projects, the group directed its attention to the central purpose of their gathering. As they reviewed the ways they had worked together, black representatives suggested it was time to unify because the PTA was being criticized for moving too slowly in this direction in Alabama. When a white representative suggested the "Only way is [for one association] to dissolve and be absorbed into membership," black representatives resisted because they knew which organization would be dissolved. Since the meeting did not resolve anything, both parties reported back to the National PTA that they came to a "mutual agreement that we recognize there is still a great need for the two organizations." Therefore, the major accomplishment of the Intergroup Relations Committee in Alabama, according to its white leaders, was the agreement to continue to meet on a regular basis, even though "no definite plans" of work were made at the spring meeting. They would not come together again for another two years to discuss the unification of Alabama's two PTA branches.[72]

White and black national-level leaders checked in regularly with the leaders of those state units with segregated PTA units—Alabama, Arkansas, Georgia, Louisiana, Maryland, Mississippi, South Carolina, Tennessee, and Texas—encouraging them to continue convening the Intergroup Relations committees. The terms used by the association and in the press were weighed carefully. Black PTA leaders in these states generally used the terms merger, integration, and unification to describe the coming changes in the Congress, as did NCPT leaders. At the state level, however, desegregation and integration were words not typically favored by white PTA units. Even the word "merger" was problematic because it implied an equal relationship between the two congresses; they expected, or hoped for, the expiration of the black PTA. When the word was used in a news item in Alabama, white PTA leaders were alarmed: the "newspaper article definitely hurt us. . . . [I]t had created some confusion among those who saw that headline with the word 'merge' in it, and . . . we even had Superintendents and other school people telephoning to ask questions about the article." As always, white PTA members returned to the bylaws to figure out how to respond: "we can handle any situation as it arises since our by-laws and policies give us the direction we will need and also will *protect* us all during the transition period."[73]

In the fall of 1967, black PTA leaders released their strongest public statement to date regarding integration of the organization and were able to get the NCPT to agree to certain guidelines. Arguing that the merger "jeopardizes the forty years of dedicated service of the founders, those who worked with them, and the leaders who have continued through the years to keep the doors open for all youth," black PTA leaders called for "an honorable demise" of the segregated system of PTA units. NCCPT leaders outlined a plan of action that would keep the leadership and principles of the segregated organization intact, to serve African Americans through the newly united organization. They requested a full recognition of the history of the NCCPT; an equal representation of black leaders on the NCPT executive board; that all life members of the NCCPT would automatically be life members in the NCPT; and that "the National Congress of Colored Parents and Teachers should exist as long as a state branch has not been satisfactorily integrated." The remaining details, the black PTA decided, should be worked out by a joint committee.[74]

In some cases, white PTA members followed these proposed guidelines. In Maryland, which officially merged in December 1967, the black PTA president was elected to the board of managers of the Maryland Congress of Parents and Teachers, and shortly thereafter Tennessee did the same. Florida's unification ceremony was generally upbeat, as two leaders of the Florida Congress of Colored Parents and Teachers were given honorary life memberships in the state's white PTA. However, in the Deep South, white state-level officers were not so quick to act in Alabama, Arkansas, Georgia, Louisiana, Mississippi, South Carolina, and Texas. At the local level in Alabama, black PTA leaders encouraged African Americans to join the centralized school PTA in consolidated districts, but they did not feel welcome. Hence, the widespread consolidation of rural districts in the South during this period contributed to significant losses of black PTA members. Consolidation, among other tactics used by segregationists to maintain separate schools, was also supported in some instances by white PTA leaders for the same reasons.[75]

By March 1968, NCCPT president Clara Gay announced the theme for that year: "Unity—Our Challenge." As she commented on the race riots and general unrest around the country, Gay returned to a question raised by the PTA two decades prior: do parents teach prejudice? By June, Gay included reflections on the assassination of Martin Luther King, Jr., informing her members that "our youth need us now more than ever before." Later that year, Gay framed King's death as his sacrifice, using it to explain the loss of black educational leaders in the PTA: "If Dr. King can die for a better life, we surely can lose a job." Despite the emphasis on sacrifice, she expressed concern in the pages of *Our National Family* that NCCPT leaders were no longer present in leadership positions in unified PTA state units and at national civic and political meetings on children and violence. She declared, "It is time now for each of us to become concerned about our disappearing image in working in all areas of interest for child welfare." The loss of black leaders was of little concern to white PTA workers in the Deep South. Alabaman Dorothy Wright, a vice president of the NCPT, wrote to ACPT leader Fanny Mitchell Nelson in Montgomery, explaining "that the National Colored Congress was simply going out of business, due to lack of funds, and that there would be a ceremony called 'unification' in June, in Atlanta." White PTA leaders at the state level in Alabama assumed that the black PTA would just go away—or go bankrupt, as Wright put it—and they would carry on as usual. This was not the wish of the national leadership, which attempted to uphold the NCCPT's request to keep a nucleus of black leaders in NCPT and state-level offices.[76]

Since the national leadership was virtually powerless to enforce the integration of PTA units at the state and local levels, some of those units attempted to take matters into their own hands. The Alabama Congress of Colored Parents and Teachers tried different means to force the desegregation issue. Its leaders hoped that if they took the lead in integrating the PTA in that state, they would maintain representation in its new leadership and some measure of control. In so doing, they would also avoid being absorbed by the white PTA. As black local units attempted to join the white state Congress as discussed above, a more explicit move was made by representatives of the black PTA in Mobile County. Reverend R. L. Hope, the president of the Mobile County-Wide [Colored] PTA Council, circulated a letter in October 1969 to all white principals and PTA leaders in his region. In it he detailed a plan for unification, arguing, "Common sense tells us that eventually, all schools will be integrated. I am sure all of us want to be respectfully and justly unified." Hope sought to ensure the financial viability of the black PTA by asking white principals to cover the dues of those black members who had "crossed over," as he called it. He realized that as schools were desegregated, the black organization would lose members, and having membership dues covered would be a way to keep black members in the PTA as well as keeping what remained of the Colored Congress viable. He explained, "The Mobile County-wide [PTA] has any number of schools, that don't have any whites at all, and every time we lose a school, that weakens us to the point where we cannot support our county-wide, state, or national organization."[77]

Like other black civic leaders, Hope knew the effect the impending merger would have: black PTA officers and members would fade away, just as black teachers and principals were losing their jobs with desegregation. Therefore, in his letter he took the notion of dissolution and expanded it to include the white organization, arguing that both should be dissolved and a new organization formed in its place, with a new constitution, leadership, and structure. The letter reached Donna Gibbons, president of the white PTA in Mobile County, who reacted strongly to the idea of creating an entirely new entity.

She composed a letter of response in which she claimed, "I have explained to Rev. Hope on numerous occasions that the Mobile County Council PTA has no authority to merge or unify with any other organization." Quoting PTA bylaws at length on the purpose of county councils, Gibbons took the path of many white PTA leaders by avoiding racial matters and focusing on the PTA pillars of child welfare and public education. Even though the two PTA branches were one organization, separated by race, with the same bylaws and procedures, Gibbons feigned ignorance to make her point: "I am not familiar with the Bylaws and policies of the Mobile County-Wide PTA Council, the Alabama Congress of Colored Parents and Teachers, or the National Congress of Colored Parents and Teachers. . . . [I]t must be that the Bylaws of the Alabama Congress . . . are quite different from ours, as [Hope's] proposals would be in direct conflict with the Bylaws of our State PTA." Gibbons stood firm that no unification was going to take place until she was directed to carry it out by the white Alabama PTA.[78]

Donna Gibbons did not have to wait long. Shortly thereafter, pressure came from the national leadership to desegregate all PTA units once and for all. The "Plan for Unification" was announced by the white national leadership in early 1970. In addition to putting forth a plan for uniting the two associations, it ordered its remaining state units to do the same as soon as possible. The leaders in the remaining segregated units reacted in different ways. While the black and white national leaders planned the unification ceremony, white state-level leaders carried on with business as usual, since it was difficult for the National PTA to enforce its universal desegregation order. The matter of most urgency for black units was how to keep their membership intact and maintain a semblance of control over issues that were most important to them. In an essay in *Our National Family*, former NCCPT president Ethel Kight announced, "our states are diminishing and our numbers are dwindling. . . . Our organization always urged our states to merge as soon as the time seemed feasible. The change is inevitable but what are we doing to meet the transition?" Kight also suggested that in regard to the desegregation of schools, the remaining units of the NCCPT should serve as "lighthouses" by disseminating information to members and citizens as well as "mobilizing all appropriate groups in the community for involvement [in desegregation plans] through a coordinating organization." *Our National Family*'s editors took the lead in providing information by including articles in subsequent years on desegregation plans, intergroup education techniques, and even information such as "Negro Women in the Population and in the Labor Force."[79]

Black and white PTA members in Georgia still did not act; the members of Georgia's Colored Congress spread the word that "in every state where desegregation had taken place the Negro parent was no longer active in PTA."

Therefore, they, like the other remaining black units, feared extinction, as GCCPT President Narvie Harris called it. In 1970, Harris declared to Georgia's members, "We will not be dissolved. . . . We want to move in as one organization with honor and respect." This position contrasts with the integration of the border-state PTA units in the mid-1950s, in which being dissolved was discussed in a matter-of-fact, almost positive, manner. Georgia's black PTA leaders viewed desegregation of schools and their parent-teacher associations as a loss of autonomy, though they held on to the belief that all PTA units were working for child welfare. Harris implored members to remain in the PTA as the membership drives continued in the remaining segregated states through the late 1960s.[80]

Black PTA leaders in Alabama rejoiced, while white leaders continued to avoid any discussions of unification. Lonia Gill, the president of the Alabama Congress of Colored Parents and Teachers in 1970, was thrilled with the National PTA's instructions. She immediately wrote Mary Edith Jones, the president of the ACPT, asking whether she had received the unification plan from the national office and inviting her to attend their annual meeting in April. "I am assuming," she wrote, "that all States that haven't merged or unified did receive this information. If [other PTA branches] have done so successfully, why can't [Alabama's] PTA? Will you kindly think this through and let me hear from you." Jones responded that she could not attend the meeting because of "previous commitments" and thanked her for her "interest and inquiry relative to organization structure." Avoiding any direct discussion of desegregation and race, she informed Gill, "We are working closely with the National Congress in all PTA matters." As the meeting date arrived, Jones sent Gill official greetings for a successful meeting.[81]

Even though the ACPT leaders did not budge, the ACCPT took action. Its leaders proposed resolutions in an attempt to ensure their viability as an organization. Recognizing that the two national PTA branches were going to merge and had instructed the remaining Southern states to do the same, the officers of Alabama's black PTA resolved to continue "to function as an organized body" and to uphold the objectives of the National PTA. Understanding that the changes in the organization and in the schools "mainly affected the black community," the ACCPT resolved that the PTA would "on every level set up orientation programs to help the Black Community to become totally informed and involved."[82]

The white Alabama PTA remained territorial. When its Board of Managers met in late April 1970, they discussed the coming merger of the two national associations and wondered about their future. The Board decided that "In the event the ceremony takes place, the Alabama [white] Congress would continue to adhere strictly to its adopted bylaws and policies during the entire transition period." And it responded yet again with its own "Statement of Position." In contrast to the segregationist stance reflected in the post-*Brown* document, white leaders this time realized that desegregation was a *fait accompli,* so they sought to make a statement about their wishes for public education in Alabama. It read, in part,

> Although we oppose busing of school children to achieve racial balance and believe that Freedom of Choice is a basic right that is, in fact, a tenet of democracy in the field of education, we accept the challenge of whatever change is commanded by the Courts, and we pledge ourselves to the task of adjusting to that change with equanimity.
>
> The future of the majority of our children and of the State of Alabama will depend on our courage now and on our willingness to cooperate with school officials and with each other, regardless of creed or color, to preserve and improve the public schools.

The statement concluded with a suggestion that all parties "remain calm" during the transition to desegregated schools and parent-teacher associations.[83]

"Unity as We Disunite": The Dissolution of the Black PTA

In Dallas in 1970, national leaders drew up a "Plan for Unification" of the two congresses effective July 1, 1970. It explained that unification would be not only of the national-level offices, but of local, county, and state units as well, and it named the seven remaining segregated states: Alabama, Arkansas, Georgia, Louisiana, Mississippi, South Carolina, and Texas. The authorship of the declaration reveals what black PTA leaders had feared, that the white association would remain virtually intact: "[The National PTA] welcomes with its whole heart the unification of the two organizations and pledges its full support and cooperation to make the unification fully effective and successful." The agreement held that the assets and debts of the black PTA would be turned over to the white PTA and that a position on the Board of Managers would be reserved for a black PTA leader, adding that this was done "not in the spirit of tokenism but by way of symbolizing its intention and desire for the unification of the two organizations." Finally, the plan stated that it would "step-up its field extension services" to stave off any decline in services and ordered the seven remaining states to unify accordingly.[84]

In an effort to ease black PTA leaders' fears over dissolution of their association, the merger was scheduled to take place during the annual meeting of the National Congress of Colored Parents and Teachers on June 22, 1970, in Atlanta, Georgia. The preconvention Board of Managers meeting of the Georgia Colored Congress was NCCPT President Clara Gay's biggest hurdle. She struggled with keeping the promise to NCPT President Pearl Price to bring to the table a willing organization. Gay, like other African American educational leaders, was willing to make the sacrifice in order to attain far-reaching goals of racial equality. Therefore, she presided over a brief meeting during which she cut short the discussion in an effort to quell any dissenting voices from speaking out against the planned merger. Gay left the meeting without the unanimous support of the organization behind her. As one delegate recalled, "The first session ended for some in turmoil and disgust.[85]

Two days later, Gay and Price presided over the merger with much ceremony by signing a Declaration of Unification (see figure 5.4), after which all attending joined hands and sang "We Shall Overcome." Resolutions adopted at the convention focused on "human relations" in education and suggested that schools and communities needed to pay mind to diversity and its challenges. One resolution called for education for all children living in a "culturally and racially diverse society that will encourage the development of curricula which create an awareness and appreciation for the problems, aspirations, and achievements of all people." The National PTA's press release announced the news, claiming that the two organizations had "cooperated continuously" since 1926. It explained that the purposes of the Colored Congress "as a separate organization have been fulfilled and that the time has come for all PTA's to join into one unified organization which will continue as the National PTA." Other than a handful of general guidelines, largely those that were drawn up by the NCCPT several years earlier, no specific instructions were given to the remaining state units on how to reconfigure as one organization. Nonetheless, five of the seven remaining units merged immediately after the unification ceremony, leaving just Georgia and Alabama. Confusion was the result among black PTA units in the two remaining states as white units took a business-as-usual approach. Even as Georgia's Colored Congress planned its 1971 annual convention, Narvie Harris was elected to be the chairperson of the School Education Committee for the white Georgia PTA, and another black PTA worker was elected to serve as chair of the Committee on Exceptional Children of the GCPT.[86]

In Alabama, the Colored Congress was left wondering what to do. Frustrated because their hopes for unification continued to remain out of reach despite the national unification, black leaders again sought to take the lead in pressing for the merger. When the president of Alabama's Colored Congress, Lonia Gill, wrote National PTA president Pearl Price, informing her that Alabama's white PTA was being unresponsive to desegregation, Price and

FIGURE 5.4

The unification ceremony of the two PTA branches in Atlanta, Georgia, 1970. Clara Gay is behind the podium, and Pearl Gay is to her right. (*Source:* Photo reprinted with permission and courtesy of National PTA)

her officers bristled at the thought of having to become involved once again in Alabama's affairs. The National PTA leadership had assumed that the Southern state units would act after the unification ceremony in June. Despite Price's nudging ACPT president Jones behind the scenes, Jones resisted and claimed, "Since no specific time schedule has been set we will continue to work with the ACCPT as we have in the past." Thus, Alabama's white PTA wanted to delay the inevitable as long as possible.[87]

Nonplussed, Gill responded that the Intergroup Relations committees should meet soon. She also wrote to her district presidents to apprise them of the situation: "We know some of you are at the cross-roads, not knowing exactly what to do due to the integration of schools which greatly involved and affect pupils and teachers. . . . We are all in the same predicament." Following a strategy employed by the Virginia Colored Congress twelve years earlier, she instructed them to retain their present officers instead of electing new ones, since changing officers at "this crucial time" would disrupt the continuity in leadership. "Please tour your districts, your churches, your clubs, your sororities, your fraternities, any group interested in P.T.A. and let's continue as we have in the past until such notice is given to do different." The Georgia Colored Congress did the same by voting to return their officers for another year at its convention in March 1970. Gill received Jones's response shortly thereafter, and again, white leaders stalled. Its brief reply included a caveat that they should wait so that "all school adjustments have time to be made. After the first of the calendar year all of us should be able to see the direction in which our organization must go."[88]

Gill and other black PTA leaders again looked to the national office for assistance in prodding the white Alabama state leadership to act. They asked about their status in the National PTA and claimed, "This information is badly needed. What is the affiliation of the Alabama Congress of Colored Parents and Teachers with the National Congress of Parents and Teachers since the merger?" Realizing she had done all she could do, national president Pearl Price capitulated to the problems of race relations in the South yet again and responded that the states with segregated PTA units should function separately until those states agreed to a merger. She added, "We realize this can be a period of some uncertainty, but we hope the unification of the two congresses in the remaining few states will take place without too much undue delay."[89]

However, larger forces were at play as desegregation orders were enforced more strongly from 1968 until the early 1970s as a result of the activities of the U.S. Supreme Court and Department of Health, Education, and Welfare.[90] Within this climate, as various measures such as busing were implemented in schools, white state president Mary Edith Jones contacted Gill to arrange for a meeting of the Intergroup Relations Committee in February 1971.[91] At the meeting, the ACPT agreed to a merger in word, but set no date for it, refusing to have it at their annual meeting in March of that year. Black leaders decided to host a unification ceremony in Alabama, and Gill sent word to her membership that the next annual meeting would be the last for the black PTA in Alabama. Inasmuch as the Alabama Colored Congress of Parents and Teachers was pushing for the merger, its leaders realized it would come at a steep cost. Gill wrote her constituents that they must "realistically reinterpret our objectives and work together for all children to have equal opportunities." She announced that there would be no election of new officers.[92]

The unification of the two PTA branches in Alabama was set to take place at the fifty-seventh annual meeting of the Alabama Colored Congress on April 16, 1971. Even though it still took some convincing to get white state leaders to attend, the officers of the Alabama Colored Congress felt they had executed a coup: they would be controlling the unification since it was to take place on their turf. Gill and her officers prepared for the last annual meeting of Alabama's Colored Congress with mixed emotions because desegregation was finally going to come to fruition but, they realized, would result in the end of their organization. Gill referred to the loss they were about to experience in the convention program: "We shall always treasure the memories of an organization that was and will forever be dear to all of us for it is true we are really losing more than most of you have any dreams of, or realize." Gill concluded by imploring her workers to continue to support the PTA through their efforts on behalf of all children.[93]

But as Gill continued to make plans for the unification ceremony, she learned that National President Pearl Price would not be able to make it as originally expected. Also, she faced continued resistance on the part of the white leadership in Alabama. She wrote Jones, asking whether the Intergroup Relations Committee could meet just prior to the meeting, and requested that Jones give an official greeting and announcement about the merger. Jones and her officers refused. They complained to the National PTA office via the district representative, "It is my understanding that she has made plans for unification without consulting her Board or informing us of her contacts with the National PTA." As in the past, the national office tried to remain on the sidelines as state-level representatives tried to involve it to leverage their positions.[94]

Jones and her officers eventually capitulated and agreed to attend the ACCPT's meeting. Pearl Price had nudged Jones prior to the convention, explaining that Gill "is eagerly anticipating your presence and participation in the unification ceremony." She concluded, "I hope it will be a happy occasion, one that will open doors of mutual understanding that will be beneficial to all the children of Alabama." On Friday, April 16, 1971, the unification ceremony of the two PTA branches in Alabama took place, but left the black PTA leadership confused. ACPT officers stayed only as long as they needed to at the convention and signed the "Declaration of Unification." The Alabama Colored Congress carried on its program after they left, with no plan of action as to how the unified PTA would be run. Following the convention, Gill wrote Jones to inquire about next steps. She had been fielding questions from her PTA workers in the state and did not know how to advise them. Of primary importance was the representation of black members on the Board of Managers of the new Alabama Congress of Parents and Teachers. "I am writing to ask if it is possible that a 3rd, 4th or possibly 5th Vice President's office can be added and being the immediate Past President of the Alabama Congress of Colored Parents and Teachers, if I could be considered for this spot and by so doing, unification will have really become a reality." Gill pointed out that other states had set this precedent.[95]

Unlike the appointment of black officers in other states such as North Carolina and Georgia, there is no evidence that Gill and her co-workers in Alabama's Black PTA were invited to serve on the newly unified state Congress. Although Clara Gay assumed a position on the national board, the states in the Deep South were less inclined to follow the suggestion of the NCPT and include black members on the state boards. Gay lamented this lapse in following unification guidelines as she pointed out to her membership that there was very little representation of African Americans at "high-level meetings" of the PTA. There were just two, she pointed out, who were elected to the NCPT's National Board. Even in states "where the dual system of education has never been a problem," there was a dearth of black PTA leaders. For Gay, the challenge was in becoming one organization while maintaining an identity. "When there is no National Congress of Colored Parents and Teachers," she asked, "who will represent the Negro?" Ethel Kight echoed Gay's concerns, asking, "If Negroes are not in attendance at [NCPT] meetings, to voice their opinions from the mergers, what has been gained?" It was a sour and anticlimactic note to end over fifty years of segregation in the PTA. The hopes of a stronger organization to represent the nation's children had been dashed amid confusion, mistrust, and lack of clear direction. Perhaps more surprising, what had once been a strong and flexible federated organization with a swift, streamlined communication network began its quiet dissolution, drowned out by the din of busing concerns, racial angst, and the economic and political woes of the war in Vietnam.[96]

Conclusion

In local and state PTA units, black members did not feel welcome at PTA meetings, parents were left without an easily available way to work with teachers and volunteer at schools, and leaders were passed over for officer positions, even though in some locations, such as Kentucky, there were largely unsuccessful attempts to enlist black members. Given the lack of documentation on what transpired in the black PTA during these years, it is difficult to establish how many black educational leaders remained with the federation at state and local levels. Even though some state PTA units included token representation of African Americans on executive committees, there no longer was a critical mass of black PTA leaders—teachers, parents, and citizens—to guide the education of black children. The dispersal of black teachers and principals with almost two decades of desegregation efforts was mirrored in the black PTA. The white PTA in Alabama, Kentucky, Georgia, and other Southern states carried on as usual with little mention of black members or their interests. Therefore, throughout the South, black communities lost decades of work of training leaders in schools and communities through the disbanding of the Colored Congresses in Alabama, Georgia, and the rest of the South. The pattern was repeated in other black voluntary associations, as the networks of civil society that united communities of African Americans became frayed and torn. Thus, the institutional infrastructure of the NCCPT and other organizations devoted to the education of black children was diminished to the point of ineffectiveness.[97]

Through the process of integrating with the white PTA, NCCPT leaders remained philosophical while they articulated their awareness that life would change forever for families, schools, and communities. As they acknowledged, "Change is part of the growth process of life . . . [and desegregation has forged] new paths, new duties to fulfill and new purposes to carry out," they faced a grim situation. Even Clara Gay, who had supported the merger, announced, "We want integration but we don't want our black children to feel they do not have any of their race to imitate." Gay, one of the two former NCCPT officers elected to the NCPT Board of Managers, was given the charge of gathering unification reports and fiscal information for the former state units of the Colored Congress. It was a task that she described as leaving her mentally and physically exhausted.[98]

In Georgia, the state's Colored Congress closed out its fiscal affairs and completed the process of integration with the white PTA. Narvie Harris issued her last "President's Message" in the organization's journal, *Our Georgia Family*. Like the remaining members of the Colored Congress around the South, Harris was troubled by the way the unification played out and what it meant for black communities. Much of the rhetoric of the white PTA leadership at this time encouraged members to embrace the history of the organization and to march forward to desegregate the remaining local units of the PTA. Harris wrote, "[N]ow faced with extinctness as an organization due to changes in federal laws, we need to explore and see our directions more clearly." She did not remain with the organization long, even though she supported the ideals of the National PTA for years to come. Other NCCPT officers probably ended up like Harris, and continued to work as administrators and teachers, but without the benefits of the networks found in the institutional infrastructure of such organizations as the NCCPT and teachers' organizations. After the DeKalb School System was desegregated in 1969, Harris moved out of her role as a Jeanes teacher and was named district-wide Instructional Coordinator for Elementary Education, where she remained until her retirement in 1983. After her retirement she reflected on the impact of desegregation and remarked, "The adjustment to better conditions was not an easy transition, but a necessary one."[99]

In the final years of the PTA's dual system, black leaders in the Deep South struggled with the realization that uniting with the white organization meant disaster after decades of building a separate organization and developing leadership for the African American community. The last total membership figure for the NCCPT was 200,000 in 1967. Presumably, the total membership would drop to zero with the unification; however, the membership of the newly combined PTA did not increase by that amount in the late 1960s or even in the early 1970s. In fact, the National PTA membership declined by over a half million from 1969 to 1970. Even though it is very likely that after 1970 the association began to count black members, in 1970 PTA membership began a downward slide from 9.6 million to a low of 5.2 million members in 1982.

The many remaining white units carried on as though nothing had ever happened, especially in the South. In April 1973, the South Carolina Congress of Parents and Teachers celebrated its fiftieth anniversary with much pageantry. The lieutenant governor gave the official greeting, and local professor J. C. Holler gave a talk titled "You've Come a Long Way." Membership in the state unit was on the rise again, after taking a dive after unification; it had picked up four thousand new members that year after losing twelve thousand from 1970 to 1971. The program included the usual topics: child welfare, education, and school financing issues. Awards were given for membership, and past presidents and leaders—all white—were honored. It is unclear though virtually certain that no black members or officers attended the event. Black members' attending the event would have added insult to injury, because the event was the anniversary of the founding of the state's white Congress; South Carolina's Colored Congress was not founded until 1931. At the celebration, there were no references to race or the unification, and no greetings extended to the newest members of the National Congress of Parents and Teachers.[100]

Desegregation marked the end of an era for the PTA, as it signaled the end of its central role in American education. With the unification of its two branches and other factors—such as women's entering the workforce in greater numbers and the increasing popularity of nonaffiliated parent-teacher organizations—came its diminished influence over legislation, education, and child welfare. African American parents, teachers, and other community members no longer found a home for their issues and concerns in the integrated National Congress. The ultimate move toward inclusion, desegregation, ended up excluding black members, parents, and citizens. The National PTA, like other civic organizations, has experienced significant declines in membership, as Americans have ceased to appreciate the benefits of belonging to large-scale voluntary associations: face-to-face meetings, opportunities for civic discourse as well as socialization, and the chance to meet others similar to as well as unlike themselves. At the same time, educators and policymakers should wonder what has been gained and what is lost with the diminished role of civil society in public education.

Civil Society and Public Education

The history of our Congress is not written in terms of great bank balances, great presidents, or great potentates. It is written by the people, the earnest simple followers who face each day squarely and courageously, sparing not themselves.[1]

—NCCPT President Beatrice Moore Morgan, 1951

FOR YEARS I have had the joy of having a research topic that is as easy to explain to the layperson as to the professional historian—the mere mention that I was writing a book on the history of the PTA caused people to nod in immediate understanding. Yet I found myself frustrated in trying to overcome the popular culture stereotypes of a PTA composed of white, middle-class soccer moms vying for power and control in local schools. To me, the organization has meant more, despite the large measure of truth to these characterizations. Such contemporary images belie the association's past as a civic organization that has allowed for diverse members' expression of hopes and goals for public education. For me, the history of the PTA has always been about race and difference, in terms of who was included, who was excluded, and what ideals they espoused. Therefore, while I acknowledge that the National PTA has always been overwhelmingly represented by white, middle-class women, I hope that this book reveals how the racial policies and practices of the organization presented the biggest challenge to its leaders.

Among the great voluntary federations of the twentieth century, the PTA was widely accepted by citizens who saw in the organization the opportunity to lead, to serve, and to address society's most challenging issues through education, such as poverty, child welfare, health, and discrimination. Such were the advantages of membership and activism in civil society, that space between individual action and governmental oversight. While millions of members around the country studied and adhered to PTA policy as if it were gospel, the organization's federated design allowed for variance in addressing regionally, ethnically, racially, ideologically, and socioeconomically diverse needs. This was both a benefit and a drawback. While it allowed for the rapid and far-reaching growth and expansion of the organization, at times national leaders were powerless to enforce policy, as exemplified by the attempts to desegregate Southern units. One way to view this is that bridging social capital—connections among unlike groups and individuals—was as necessary as bonding social capital—links with similar individuals or groups—to bring diverse members together to span the geographic reaches of the United States. Likewise, distrust motivated members to take ownership of their roles, learn PTA policy, and develop programs to serve their communities, instead of allowing others to teach, guide, and monitor their children. The development of a strong, well-coordinated infrastructure helped individuals develop leadership skills, spread the PTA program around the country, and made members—the majority of whom were women—feel as though they were able to bring about large-scale change. Citizens from different regions, socioeconomic backgrounds, and cultures found appealing the organization's emphasis on school and social reform. Oddly enough, the organization was at its strongest numerically when it was segregated and members realized what would be lost with unification.

One of the benefits of membership in voluntary associations is the opportunity to be a part of something bigger, to meet people outside of one's geographic region and social circle, in addition to getting to know one's neighbors better. Regularly held face-to-face meetings are an important aspect of voluntary organizations, as citizens come together to discuss, debate, and even socialize. In such settings the potential exists for discourse around problems and challenges in education and other social issues. This discursive arena, found in church groups, fraternal societies, and other organizations, was not fully realized in the National PTA. In one sense, the PTA achieved a modicum of success by providing a forum for exchange of concerns, ideas, wants, and needs between black and white educators and lay activists through formal committees. There were few other arenas in the early twentieth century for these discussions to take place, particularly in regard to public education. Nonetheless, segregation proved too difficult for the organization to overcome. The National PTA could not devise a suitable structure to bring black and white members together with regularity to address issues of concern, even though the potential existed through committees and extension offices.

One of the central arguments in this book has been although the PTA was indeed run by a majority of middle-class, white women, we are well cautioned to remember that it was adapted by diverse groups of citizens who found in its design a viable means to work with the growing public education system. This feature of the PTA was a central theme in this study, as I explored the meaning and influence of civic organizations in public education. If we take parents and citizens as organized volunteers and not as individuals vested primarily in their particular interests, the landscape of the school volunteer looks much different than has been portrayed in the historiography. In other words, cooperation and conflict are not the only ways to frame this history. Therefore, this book examined how the PTA idea—that of organized groups of volunteers—took root and gave voice to those in the center as well as those on the margins of decision making in schools, understanding that the location of the margin and center depend on where one stands. In some instances, black teachers and PTA leaders—such as Narvie Harris and Clara Gay—at the hub of their communities, were on the periphery of school decision making when it came to all-white boards of education. In other cases, white nonprofessionals—state leaders such as Eunice Harper Leonard of South Carolina and Martha Rutledge of Alabama—were marginalized in schools, which led to the strengthening of a parallel educational institution that afforded them some measure of power and influence in education. Therefore, the PTA, as a federated association, defined a civic space for women volunteers. The PTA program took on different forms, purposes, and goals in different locales as ideas and skills were transferred from one place to another and changed over time. Black and white women rose through the ranks, and some activities remained constant over time, such as the emphasis on providing school lunches and holding fundraisers.

CARRYING OUT this research has been a formidable challenge. While sources on the white PTA, or NCPT, are abundant and can be found easily, it was difficult to research the black PTA because so little documentation exists. All a researcher needs to do is visit a local historical society or peruse the databases of university and public archives, and an overwhelming amount of data can be found on the NCPT. There is more than one can possibly assess for one book. Moreover, the National PTA headquarters had maintained an extensive collection of minutes, state histories, periodicals, photos, and ledgers—now housed at the University of Illinois at Chicago—yet sources on the National Congress of Colored Parents and Teachers are hard to find in that particular collection and elsewhere. A couple of treasure troves helped provide much-needed information about the black PTA's leaders and activities: two organizational histories, of the NCCPT and Georgia Colored Congress, and the extant issues of *Our National Family* and *Our Georgia Family,* housed at the Library of Congress.

The dearth of documentation, especially of state and local units, on the NCCPT is reflective of its relationship to the white association and its status as an organization in the history of American education. Since no national headquarters remains for the Colored Congress, my early research explorations had me contacting the NCPT state affiliates around the South, only to learn that little was saved for posterity. In contrast to the many collections on white PTA units found around the United States, I located only one collection of black PTA documents in Alabama, and it was thin. Thankfully, however, it was enough to help me understand and interpret the challenges of desegregating a state unit.

What I came to realize was that when Southern state and local PTA units integrated, the many documents of the black association were not kept despite one of the provisions of the unification agreement, that the white PTA would "receive all of the archives of the NCCPT . . . and will give them an honored place alongside and as part of the corresponding records of the NCPT." My find in Alabama helped me learn that the NCCPT took great care to turn over its assets, debts, and papers, but they were not catalogued appropriately, or even saved. In May 1972 former state president Tessie Nixon delivered the files of the Alabama Congress of Colored Parents and Teachers so that they could become part of the history and holdings of the newly integrated PTA. As records show, her boxes and containers were "graciously accepted by the Board of Alabama Congress of Parents and Teachers," though only one folder of materials remains in the present-day archives. The impression I obtained after these early research explorations was that the NCCPT was seen as almost an entirely separate and distinct organization by many at the local and state levels, and my fear is that much was discarded. This insight was remarkable to me because I knew the NCCPT valued the preservation of its legacy, kept careful records, and created a paper trail, the tracings of which had been scattered as Southern PTA units integrated beginning with the *Brown* decision of 1954 and ending with the unification in 1970. For example, local units maintained their own historical records, as part of PTA policy. These "procedure books" are referred to time and again in black PTA histories and periodicals, but I have not located a single one.[2]

Even though the black PTA was proportionately smaller than the white PTA, it is important to recognize how widely linked it was with civil rights and African American organizations. Moreover, it served as an integral part of the PTA infrastructure by allowing the association to find its way into African American rural and urban communities and schools. The black PTA network accomplished much throughout the duration of its existence. Most importantly, it helped create and support a system of schools in the American South and provided a network for black educators across the South during the days of segregated schools. This network united schools and educational leaders across location, and it was there for the schoolteachers, who learned about organizing citizens to support local schools from colleagues at NCCPT meetings and through other organizations with which the black PTA was net-worked, such as the American Teachers' Association, the NAACP, and the Urban League. Therefore, membership in the NCCPT afforded black women teachers and other community members leadership training, collegiality, and a means to express their hopes for public education and the school curriculum. Beyond this, it kept the white PTA honest, in a manner of speaking. In other words, the white PTA did not always act on the rhetoric on child welfare and inclusion that it espoused. This is the contribution the segregated PTA made; by its very existence it kept the idea of racial equality and inclusion on the PTA program. As these pages reveal, however, the black PTA placed race at the center of its platform, while white local and state PTA units, in most cases, chose not to address race or inequality.

Therefore, the commitment to racial inclusion in schools, society, and the organization manifested itself in vastly different ways in the two PTA branches. It appeared more frequently as slogans than actions in the white PTA, while the black PTA placed race and racial equality at the center of its program. Even though the Congress of Mothers was more forward-thinking than other wom-en's organizations about racial inclusion at the turn of the twentieth century, its leaders never did find a way to successfully bring together black and white members in one association. In these early years, white and black school-improvement associations worked separately, each focusing on the needs at hand.

After 1920, with the passage of the Nineteenth Amendment, the years of maternalist politics ended, but white and black women continued their school support efforts with increasing vigor through the 1960s. What is to account for women's activism through the middle decades of the twentieth century? Although women had the vote, they took up volunteer work in communities and schools with even greater urgency. Several conclusions may be reached. First, women's membership in the PTA and other civic associations was viewed as a part of life, parenting, and being a citizen and community member, in addition to formal political participation. Also, however, the wide appeal of parent-teacher groups cannot be overlooked, as well as the fact that the PTA idea and structure allowed for the participation of many and the expression of hopes for education and child welfare in a democracy through membership in a federated voluntary organization. Finally, it suggests that the historiography of women's political activism in the twentieth century needs to be viewed in a new light. While scholars have tended to adhere to the periodization offered by the passage of the Nineteenth Amendment, contrasting women's activism before and after they had the vote, I would like to suggest adding a different perspective. Given that membership in voluntary associations has played such a significant role in women's—and men's—lives in the twentieth century, we should reconsider women's activism according to political scientists' findings regarding the rise and fall (and even rise again) of volunteerism and membership in civic organizations. This would help explain the significant growth and influence of the National PTA through mid-century and would account for the steep declines in the 1960s.

THIS BOOK joins the growing number of scholarly works in recent years that have revealed the losses faced by black communities with the implementation of desegregation. It adds another layer to this history, moving beyond the local case study, to show the intersection of volunteer and professional roles on a broader scale, through a national network. The benefits of membership in the federation—being linked to a formidable operation that would represent local interests and offer training and leadership—continued on for most of the twentieth century. Yet, in the quest for equitable public schooling, desegregation efforts challenged the infrastructure of the organization and began to erode an important dimension of civil society, the associational link between home and school. We are learning of late how a multitude of African American teachers and principals lost their jobs after *Brown,* yet continued to fight for desegregation despite their knowledge of what was to come. Along with unemployment came the erosion of a segment of civil society that helped give agency to African Americans. The implications of these losses are not to be taken lightly and should be considered by researchers seeking to study parental involvement in today's schools.

I hope that the gaps in this study will lead other scholars to further exploration. In particular, this work focuses on a dichotomized black-white membership at the expense of investigating other ethnic, cultural, and racial groups. To a certain extent, this was a function of the available documentation, but to an even greater degree, it was the result of my own research interests in segregated schools and the networks of support that guided them in the early to mid-twentieth century. The PTA's structure as a segregated organization also led to the black-white bifurcation in this study. For the interested researcher, there were many other ethnic and cultural groups that ran affiliated parent-teacher associations around the country. Finally, one of the historian's greatest challenges is not seeing what she expects to see. At times throughout I was faced with the challenge of not resorting to oversimplification in writing about white and black PTA members, by keeping myself from painting white workers as passive about race work and black members in a sentimental light. There existed several different opinions and ideologies within each of the two groups that I hope I have portrayed with accuracy and nuance, such as the white national-level leaders who felt frustrated with segregationist state and local leaders in the South, black leaders who disagreed on whether to integrate, and white segregationists who refused to join the same association as African Americans.[3]

This history of the National PTA raises questions about the role of voluntary associations, civic engagement, and civil society in public education. What is the relationship between civic organizations, as expressions of democracy, and public schools, places where the principles of democracy and democratic life are to be taught? Where is the line between professional and volunteer support, and how does this line complicate democratic ideas about who has a say in education? In what ways do national civic organizations help or hinder local, state, and national educational reforms? Most pressing for me in this research was considering the dissolution of a federated network of black educators and volunteers and what this has meant for families, schools, and communities around the nation. It has had an impact on us all.

APPENDIX

Archives

Manuscript and Archival Material

Atlanta, Georgia
    Georgia State University
        Georgia Government Documentation Project (GGDP)
    Spelman College, Atlanta University Archives
        Selena Sloan Butler Papers, Atlanta University Center (AUC)
Berkeley, California
    Bancroft Library at the University of California, Berkeley (BLUCB)
        Phoebe Apperson Hearst Papers
Cambridge, Massachusetts
    Radcliffe Institute for Advanced Studies (RIAS)
        Elizabeth Hewes Tilton Papers
        Janet Elizabeth Hosmer Richards Papers
        Cora May Trawick Court Papers
    Gutman Library Special Collections (GLSC), Harvard Graduate School of Education
        Atlanta, Georgia Department of Education Annual Reports
        Chicago, Illinois Board of Education Annual Reports
        Des Moines, Iowa Public School Reports
        Lynn, Massachusetts School Committee Annual Reports
        North Des Moines, Iowa Public School Reports
        San Francisco, California School Board Reports
        Washington, DC, School Reports of the Board of Trustees
Chicago, Illinois
    University of Illinois at Chicago, Special Collections Department (UIC)
        PTA Records
        Quarterly Reports
Columbia, South Carolina
    Institute for Southern Studies, South Caroliniana Library (USC)
        Eunice Harper Leonard Papers

Mary K. Newton Papers
South Carolina Parent-Teacher
John's Island PTA Collection
Jamestown, New York
Fenton Historical Society
Jamestown PTA Collection
Lockport, New York
Niagara County Historical Society
Mothers' Club Records, 1898–1960
Marietta, Georgia
Cobb County Public Library
Alice M. Birney Biography Collection
Montgomery, Alabama
Auburn University at Montgomery (AUM)
Alabama Congress of Parents and Teachers (ACPT) Collection
Pocantico Hills, New York
Rockefeller Archive Center (RAC)
Anna T. Jeanes Foundation Papers
General Education Board Papers
Homemakers' Club Papers
Richmond, Kentucky
Eastern Kentucky University (EKU)
Kentucky Congress of Parents and Teachers (KCPT) Collection
Washington, DC
General Federation of Woman's Clubs Archives
GFWC minutes and proceedings
Library of Congress
National Congress of Colored Parents and Teachers (NCCPT)
Our National Family
Our Georgia Family

Newspapers and Periodicals

Child Welfare
Journal of Negro Education
National Parent-Teacher
Our National Family
Our Georgia Family

NOTES

Introduction

1. Ellen Henrotin, "The Cooperation of Woman's Clubs in the Public Schools," *Journal of Proceedings and Addresses of the Thirty-Sixth Annual Meeting of the National Education Association* (Chicago: University of Chicago, 1897), 73–82, hereafter referred to as *NEA Proceedings;* and Anne Firor Scott, *Natural Allies: Women's Associations in American History* (Urbana: University of Illinois Press, 1992), 177.

2. Alexis de Tocqueville, *Democracy in America,* ed. Harvey C. Mansfield and Delba Winthrop (Chicago: University of Chicago Press, 2000), 489. Over one hundred years later such observations continued, as Arthur Schlesinger called the United States a "nation of joiners." Arthur M. Schlesinger, Sr., "Biography of a Nation of Joiners," *American Historical Review* 50, no. 1 (1944): 1–25. More recently, the declining membership of civic associations has been lamented by scholars such as Robert D. Putnam, *Bowling Alone: The Collapse and Revival of American Community* (New York: Simon & Schuster, 2000); Robert N. Bellah, Richard Madsen, William M. Sullivan, Ann Swidler, and Steven M. Tipton, *Habits of the Heart: Individualism and Commitment in American Life* (Berkeley: University of California Press, [1985], 1996); and Theda Skocpol et al., "How Americans Became Civic," in *Civic Engagement in American Democracy,* ed. Theda Skocpol and Morris P. Fiorina (Washington, DC: Brookings Institution Press, 1999), 33. Skocpol et al. make the distinction between membership associations and voluntary groups, referring to the latter as "groups in which people did things together as members, even if they also engaged in some delivery of charitable aid to others and/or delivery of services to the broader community." Theda Skocpol, Marshall Ganz, Ruth Aguilera-Vaques, Jennifer Oser, Christine Woyshner, and David Siu, "Organizing America: Launching National Membership Associations in the United States, 1860–1920," paper presented at the American Sociological Association Annual Meeting, August 1998, 1.

3. Skocpol et al., "How Americans Became Civic," 33; and Theda Skocpol and Morris P. Fiorina, "Making Sense of the Civic Education Debate," in *Civic Engagement in American Democracy,* 2. A contemporary look at education and civil society is found in Diane Ravitch and Joseph P. Viteritti, eds., *Making Good Citizens: Education and Civil Society* (New Haven, CT: Yale University Press, 2001). However, civil society is not a neutral term.

For a discussion of its different uses and applications, see Bob Edwards and Michael W. Foley, "Civil Society and Social Capital," in *Beyond Tocqueville: Civil Society and the Social Capital Debate in Comparative Perspective*, ed. Bob Edwards, Michael W. Foley, and Mario Diani (Hanover, NH: University Press of New England, 2001), 2.

4. Among them, works that have influenced my thinking include Putnam, *Bowling Alone;* Theda Skocpol, *Diminished Democracy: From Membership to Management in American Civic Life* (Norman: University of Oklahoma Press, 2003); Theda Skocpol, Marshall Ganz, and Ziad Munson, "A Nation of Organizers: The Institutional Origins of Civic Voluntarism in the United States," *The American Political Science Review* 94, no. 3 (2000): 527–46; Elisabeth S. Clemens, *The People's Lobby: Organizational Innovation and the Rise of Interest Group Politics in the United States, 1890–1925* (Chicago: University of Chicago Press, 1997); and Gerald Gamm and Robert D. Putnam, "The Growth of Voluntary Associations in America, 1840–1940," *Journal of Interdisciplinary History* 29, no. 3 (1999): 511–57.

5. For example, see Jonathan Zimmerman, *Distilling Democracy: Alcohol Education in America's Public Schools* (Lawrence: University of Kansas Press, 1999); Wayne J. Urban, *Gender, Race, and the National Education Association: Professionalism and Its Limitations* (New York: RoutledgeFalmer, 2000); Carol F. Karpinski, *"A Visible Company of Professionals": African Americans and the National Education Association during the Civil Rights Movement* (New York: Peter Lang, 2008); and Richard Kluger, *Simple Justice: The History of Brown v. Board of Education and Black America's Struggle for Equality* (New York: Alfred A. Knopf, 1976). See also R. Scott Baker, *Paradoxes of Desegregation: African American Struggles for Educational Equity in Charleston, South Carolina, 1926–1972* (Columbia: University of South Carolina Press, 2006); David S. Cecelski, *Along Freedom Road: Hyde County, North Carolina, and the Fate of Black Schools in the South* (Chapel Hill: University of North Carolina Press, 1994); and Vanessa Siddle Walker, *Their Highest Potential: An African American School Community in the Segregated South* (Chapel Hill: University of North Carolina Press, 1996).

6. Here I am adapting Skocpol et al.'s argument that civic organizations were confident in their ability to make change at the local and national levels. See "How Americans Became Civic," 29; and Gabriel A. Almond and Sidney Verba, *The Civic Culture: Political Attitudes and Democracy in Five Nations* (Princeton, NJ: Princeton University Press, 1963). For this discussion in terms of the history of education, see Lawrence A. Cremin, "Family and Community Linkages in American Education: Some Comments on the Recent Historiography," *Teachers College Record* 79 (May 1978): 683–704.

7. Skocpol et al.'s framework of historical institutionalism calls for an examination of changing patterns of organization over time, the reallocation of resources for collective social and educational actions, and transformations in the relationship between and among diverse members of an organization and in society. See "How Americans Became Civic," 13–14. She argues, "An institutional approach to civic life suggests that state, politics, and society are—for better or worse—inevitably intertwined." Skocpol, Ganz, and Munson, "A Nation of Organizers," 542. On the institutional infrastructure of black organizations, see Michael Fultz, "Caught between a Rock and a Hard Place," unpublished paper presented at the American Educational Research Association's annual meeting, Chicago, Illinois, April 2007; and Mary S. Hoffschwelle, *The Rosenwald Schools of the American South* (Gainesville: University Press of Florida, 2006). At its peak in the mid-1960s, the PTA had approximately 12 million members. By 1980 it was down to 6 million.

8. Skocpol, Ganz, and Munson, "A Nation of Organizers." I discuss the extension of women's reform efforts beyond the Progressive era in Christine Woyshner and Anne Meis

Knupfer, "Introduction: Women, Volunteerism, and Education," in *The Educational Work of Women's Organizations, 1890–1960*, ed. Anne Meis Knupfer and Christine Woyshner (New York: Palgrave Macmillan, 2008), 3.

9. William W. Cutler III, *Parents and Schools: The 150-Year Struggle for Control in Education* (Chicago: University of Chicago Press, 2000), 7. An early work on voluntary associations and the schools is Bessie Louise Pierce's *Public Opinion and the Teaching of History in the United* States (New York: Alfred A. Knopf, 1926). According to Jonathan Zimmerman, Pierce's book and others of this era cast "lay activists as ignorant hordes who were clamoring at the schoolhouse gates." See Zimmerman, "Storm over the Schoolhouse: Exploring Popular Influences upon the American Curriculum, 1890–1941," *Teachers College Record* 100, no. 3 (1999): 602–26; quote on p. 603.

10. Reese argues, "One cannot underestimate the importance of [education professionals], but school innovation was a dynamic, interactive process involving diverse community groups. William J. Reese, *Power and the Promise of School Reform: Grassroots Movements during the Progressive Era* (New York: Teachers College Press, [1986], 2002), xxi. See also Robert H. Wiebe, *The Search for Order, 1877–1920* (New York: Hill and Wang, 1967).

11. See Cutler, *Parents and Schools;* Molly Ladd-Taylor, *Mother-Work: Women, Child Welfare and the State, 1890–1930* (Urbana: University of Illinois Press, 1997); Steven L. Schlossman, "Before Home Start: Notes toward a History of Parent Education in America," *Harvard Educational Review* 46, no. 3 (1976): 436–67; and Theda Skocpol, *Protecting Soldiers and Mothers: The Political Origins of Social Policy in the United States* (Cambridge, MA: The Belknap Press of Harvard University Press, 1992). For a contrasting view in which the author discards theories of imposition and social control, see Reese, *Power and the Promise of School Reform.*

12. Darlene Rebecca Roth, *Matronage: Patterns in Women's Organizations, Atlanta, Georgia, 1890–1940* (Brooklyn: Carlson Publishing, Inc., 1994), 11. Roth echoes Evelyn Brooks Higginbotham's point in reference to women in the black church. Higginbotham argues that women's efforts were not "dramatic protest but everyday forms of resistance to oppression and demoralization," mostly through fundraising and other volunteer contributions. *Righteous Discontent: The Women's Movement in the Black Baptist Church, 1880–1920* (Cambridge, MA: Harvard University Press, 1993), 2.

13. Some studies of the PTA focus on the organization's impact on U.S. federal policy, pointing out that the organization did "a lot more than discussing literature, holding tea parties, and supporting local schools and projects for community betterment." See Skocpol and Fiorina, "Making Sense of the Civic Engagement Debate," 15; and Clemens, *The People's Lobby.* Most of the research that examines the PTA focuses on its role in social welfare legislation and much less on how the organization influenced the school curriculum. See Robyn L. Muncy, *Creating a Female Dominion in American Reform, 1890–1935* (New York: Oxford University Press, 1991), 93; Ladd-Taylor, *Mother-Work,* 167–90; Skocpol, *Protecting Soldiers and Mothers,* 10, 494–522; and Sheila Rothman, *Woman's Proper Place: A History of Changing Ideals and Practices, 1870 to the Present* (New York: Basic Books, 1978), 136–40. The assumption is that national legislative issues are much more relevant historically than the typical activities of PTA women, considered to be "more mundane," such as organizing and staffing school lunchrooms, libraries, and health clinics. See Cutler, *Parents and Schools,* 73.

14. In this regard, I am adapting Baker's definition of "political" as women's influencing the government and local communities. See Paula Baker, "The Domestication of Politics: Women and American Political Society, 1780–1920," *American Historical Review*

89, no. 3 (1984): 620–47. On PTA work as political, see Lynn Weiner, "Motherhood, Race, and the PTA in the Postwar Era," unpublished paper presented at the annual meeting of the American Educational Research Association, April 2000, New Orleans.

15. On the new woman and the early PTA, see Schlossman, "Before Home Start." For maternalism, see Molly Ladd-Taylor, "Toward Defining Maternalism in US History," *Journal of Women's History* 5, no. 2 (1993): 111. See also Seth Koven and Sonya Michel, eds., *Mothers of a New World: Maternalist Politics and the Origins of Welfare States* (New York: Routledge, 1993); and Lynn Y. Weiner, "Maternalism as a Paradigm," *Journal of Women's History* 5, no. 2 (1993): 96–98.

16. Linda K. Kerber, "Separate Spheres, Female Worlds, and Woman's Place: The Rhetoric of Women's History," reprinted in *History of Women in the United States* (New York: K. G. Saur, 1992). See also Rosalind Rosenberg, *Beyond Separate Spheres: Intellectual Roots of Modern Feminism* (New Haven, CT: Yale University Press, 1982). I synthesize the literature on separate spheres and discuss pitfalls in Christine Woyshner, "The Education of Women for Marriage and Motherhood: Coverture, Community, and Consumerism in the Separate Spheres," *History of Education Quarterly* 43, no. 3 (2003): 410–28.

17. See, for example, research by Skocpol, *Protecting Soldiers and Mothers,* 1992; Ladd-Taylor, *Mother-Work,* 1997; and Muncy, *Creating a Female Dominion in American Reform.* The notion of multiple arenas or spheres of activities is explored in Anne Ruggles Gere, *Intimate Practices: Literacy and Cultural Work in U.S. Women's Clubs, 1880–1920* (Urbana: University of Illinois Press, 1997).

18. James L. Leloudis, "School Reform in the New South: The Woman's Association for the Betterment of Public School Houses in North Carolina, 1902–1919," *The Journal of American History* 69, no. 4 (1983): 891, 894n18. See also James L. Leloudis, *Schooling the New South: Pedagogy, Self, and Society in North Carolina, 1880–1920* (Chapel Hill: University of North Carolina Press, 1996); and William Stephenson, *Sallie Southall Cotten: A Woman's Life in North Carolina* (Greenville, NC: Pamlico Press, 1987). The "new woman" of the early twentieth century was white, college-educated, and single; she was viewed as challenging the status quo in regard to gender roles in the new century. Glenda Riley, *Inventing the American Woman: An Inclusive History,* Part II (Wheeling, IL: Harlan Davidson, Inc., 1995), 191. For a study that challenges this simplistic description, see Martha H. Patterson, *Beyond the Gibson Girl: Reimagining the American New Woman* (Urbana: University of Illinois Press, 2005).

19. Reese, *Power and the Promise of School Reform,* 40, 215. While Reese's study focused only on four medium-sized cities (Milwaukee, Toledo, Rochester, and Kansas City), its thesis can be extended to other rural, suburban, and urban regions around the country given the national network of the GFWC. Moreover, given that small cities had more voluntary associations per capita than medium-sized ones before 1910, much school reform was being undertaken by women's organizations around the nation, even if they were not members of a federated organization. Skocpol et al., "How Americans Became Civic," 52.

20. Ladd-Taylor, *Mother-Work,* 3; and Ladd-Taylor, "Toward Defining Maternalism in US History," 110. On feminism, see Nancy F. Cott, *The Grounding of Modern Feminism* (New Haven, CT: Yale University Press, 1987). See also Christine Woyshner, "Gender, Race, and the Early PTA: Civic Engagement and Public Education, 1897–1924," *Teachers College Record* 105, no. 3 (2003): 523–24.

21. Glenda Elizabeth Gilmore, *Gender and Jim Crow: Women and the Politics of White Supremacy in North Carolina, 1896–1920* (Chapel Hill: University of North Carolina Press, 1996), 37–38; and Mary Jo Deegan, ed., *The New Woman of Color: The Collected Writings*

of Fannie Barrier Williams, 1893–1918 (DeKalb: Northern Illinois University Press, 2002). On the early development of black women's clubs, see Scott, *Natural Allies,* 111–12. On black feminism, see Patricia Hill Collins, "The Social Construction of Black Feminist Thought," *Signs* 14, no. 4 (1989): 745–73; Paula Giddings, *When and Where I Enter: The Impact of Black Women on Race and Sex in America* (New York: Bantam Books, 1984); and Angela Y. Davis, *Women, Race, and Class* (New York: Vintage Books, 1983). On the use of the term "womanist" to describe middle-class black women, see Anna Julia Cooper, *A Voice from the South: By a Black Woman of the South* (Xenia, OH: Aldine Printing House, 1892).

22. Ladd-Taylor, "Toward Defining Maternalism in US History," 111–12; and Anne Meis Knupfer, *Toward a Tenderer Humanity and a Nobler Womanhood: African American Women's Clubs in Turn-of-the-Century Chicago* (New York: New York University Press, 1996), 6.

23. See, for example, Barbara J. Finkelstein, "Schooling and Schoolteachers: Selected Bibliography of Autobiographies in the Nineteenth Century," *History of Education Quarterly* 14 (Summer 1974): 293–300; Barbara Finkelstein, "In Fear of Childhood: Relationships between Parents and Teachers in Popular Primary Schools in the Nineteenth Century," *History of Childhood Quarterly* 3 (Winter 1976): 321–35; Maris Vinovskis, "Family and Schooling in Colonial and Nineteenth Century America," *Journal of Family History* 12, nos. 1–3 (1987): 19–37; and Geraldine Jonçich Clifford, "Home and School in 19th Century America: Some Personal-History Reports from the United States," *History of Education Quarterly* (Spring 1978): 3–34.

24. Cutler, *Parents and Schools,* 3; and David Tyack, *The One Best System: A History of American Urban Education* (Cambridge, MA: Harvard University Press, 1974). Reese's dialectic approach employs a similar strategy but reveals the citizen's point of view; he argues that organized volunteers worked to make schools less isolated and separate from the life of the average person. William J. Reese, "Between Home and School: Organized Parents, Clubwomen, and Urban Education in the Progressive Era," *School Review* (November 1978): 3.

25. In fact, many individuals were members of a variety of civic associations. See Skocpol et al., "How Americans Became Civic," 27–29. For membership overlap in women's associations, see Scott, *Natural Allies,* 38, 49.

26. Best known for developing the notion of social capital are Pierre Bourdieu, "The Forms of Capital," in *Handbook of Theory and Research for the Sociology of Education,* ed. John Richardson (New York: Greenwood Press, 1986), 241–58; James S. Coleman, "Social Capital in the Creation of Human Capital," *The American Journal of Sociology* 94, Supplement: Organizations and Institutions: Sociological and Economic Approaches to the Analysis of Social Structure (1988): S95–S120; and James S. Coleman, *Foundations of Social Theory* (Cambridge, MA: Harvard University Press, 1990). For a discussion of social capital as the term has been used by historians of education, see John L. Rury, *Education and Social Change: Themes in the History of American Schooling* (Mahwah, NJ: Lawrence Erlbaum Associates, 2002). If participation in civic groups, churches, and other organizations develops social capital by linking individuals to networks, the understanding is that this civic engagement fosters a healthy democracy. See Edwards and Foley, "Preface," *Beyond Tocqueville,* ix. This is also Putnam's thesis in *Bowling Alone,* that social trust is at the heart of democracy.

27. V. P. Franklin, "Introduction: Cultural Capital and African American Education," *Journal of African American History* (Spring 2002): 177. See also V. P. Franklin, *Cultural*

Capital and Black Education: African American Communities and the Funding of Black Schools (Greenwich, CT: Information Age Publishing, 2004); Walker, *Their Highest Potential; and* Cecelski, *Along Freedom Road.* See also the special issue "Cultural Capital and African American Education," *Journal of African American History* 87 (Spring 2002).

28. Putnam, *Bowling Alone,* 22–24; Mark S. Granovetter, "The Strength of Weak Ties," *The American Journal of Sociology* 78, no. 6 (1973): 1360–80; and Mark S. Granovetter, "The Strength of Weak Ties: A Network Theory Revisited," *Sociological Theory* 1 (1983): 201–33.

29. Skocpol et al., "How Americans Became Civic," 14–16.

30. Higginbotham, *Righteous Discontent,* 2, 7. See the discussion in Skocpol, *Diminished Democracy,* 78–85; and Skocpol, Ganz, and Munson, "A Nation of Organizers," 542. Not only did members in a geographic region see one another at regularly scheduled meetings but they also met others around the country at conventions and other administrative gatherings.

31. In this work I use the terms "white PTA" and "National Congress of Parents and Teachers," or NCPT, to refer to the white or majority organization. I use the terms "black PTA," "Colored Congress," or "National Congress of Colored Parents and Teachers" (NCCPT) to refer to the segregated organization. I use the acronym PTA to connote broader ideas and activities common to both associations.

32. National Congress of Colored Parents and Teachers, *Coral Anniversary History: History of the National Congress of Colored Parents and Teachers* (Dover, DE: NCCPT, 1961), 88.

33. See Claudia Keenan, "PTA Business: A Cultural History of How Suburban Women Supported the Public Schools, 1920–1960" (PhD diss., New York University, 2002).

Chapter 1

1. Clara Bliss Finley as quoted in National Congress of Parents and Teachers, *Through the Years: From the Scrapbook of Mrs. Mears* (Washington, DC: National Congress of Parents and Teachers, 1932), 43–44. Finley was a medical doctor who spoke on hygiene and played a key role in the founding of the National Congress of Mothers. She was influential in educating the first Board of Managers in rules of order. See National Congress of Mothers Minutes, April 5, 1897, and September 16, 1897, PTA Records, University of Illinois at Chicago, Special Collections Department, hereafter referred to as PTA Records, UIC. Toward the completion of this manuscript, the historical collection of the National PTA was moved from the organization's headquarters to the University of Illinois at Chicago. Therefore, I cite the records as they were catalogued by the PTA, but cite them as being housed at UIC.

2. *Washington Star,* 13 February 1897, in "The National PTA/National PTA Newspaper Clippings, 1897–1898," PTA Records, UIC. See also *The Philadelphia Record,* 15 February 1897. On dress reform, see Amy Kesselman, "The 'Freedom Suit': Feminism and Dress Reform in the United States, 1848–1975," *Gender and Society* 5, no. 4 (1991): 495–510; Gayle V. Fischer, "'Pantalets' and 'Turkish Trousers': Designing Freedom in the Mid-Nineteenth Century United States," *Feminist Studies* 23, no. 1 (1997): 110–40; and Gayle V. Fischer, *Pantaloons and Power: A Nineteenth Century Dress Reform in the United States* (Kent, OH: Kent State University Press, 2001). Walker was known for wearing men's attire, and her appearance at the NCM drew some attention, though Congress officers

tried to keep her from stealing the spotlight and detracting from their agenda. At least one newspaper kept its observations to a minimum, noting, "Dr. Mary Walker is conspicuous at the Congress." *The Evening Star,* 18 February 1897, as reprinted in NCPT, *Through the Years,* 48. Another was less discreet and reported that Walker tried to address the crowd on dress reform but "finally sat down amid laughter, hisses, and applause." *The Washington Post,* 20 February 1897. On the Congress of Mothers' position on corsets, see Alice McLellan Birney, "The Twentieth Century Girl: What We Expect of Her," *Harper's Bazaar* (May 26, 1900): 224–27.

3. For example, see Gunther Barth, *City People: The Rise of Modern City Culture in Nineteenth Century America* (New York: Oxford University Press, 1980); Sean D. Cashman, *America in the Gilded Age: From the Death of Lincoln to the Rise of Theodore Roosevelt* (New York: New York University Press, 1993); Charles W. Calhoun, ed., *The Gilded Age: Perspectives on the Origins of Modern America* (Lanham, MD: Rowman & Littlefield, Publishers, 2007); and Rayford W. Logan, *The Negro in American Life and Thought: The Nadir, 1877–1901* (New York: Dial Press, 1954).

4. Rothman, *Woman's Proper Place;* Ruth Schwartz Cowan, *More Work for Mother: The Ironies of Household Technology from the Open Hearth to the Microwave* (New York: Basic Books, 1983); and Scott, *Natural Allies,* 118. See also Skocpol, Ganz, and Munson, "A Nation of Organizers," 529.

5. Skocpol, *Protecting Soldiers and Mothers,* 328–29; and Rothman, *Woman's Proper Place,* 65–66. Though the focus of this chapter is on white women's associations, it should be noted that middle-class black women were just as active in forming organizations. I discuss the role of the National Association of Colored Women's Clubs in shaping the black PTA in the next chapter.

6. Scott, *Natural Allies,* 81. For social reform, see Karen Blair, *The Clubwoman as Feminist: True Womanhood Redefined, 1868–1914* (New York: Holmes and Meier Publishers, Inc., 1980); and for self-education, see Theodora Penny Martin, *The Sound of Our Own Voices: Women's Study Clubs, 1860–1910* (Boston: Beacon Press, 1987).

7. Rothman, *Woman's Proper Place,* 67–68. Skocpol calls the WCTU women's first "mass movement" in *Protecting Soldiers and Mothers,* 326. Julia Grant explains that club women of the late nineteenth century were enthusiastic about kindergartens and lobbied to make them part of the public school systems. Grant, *Raising Baby by the Book: The Education of American Mothers, 1890–1960* (New Haven, CT: Yale University Press, 1998), 35. See also Barbara Beatty, *Preschool Education in America: The Culture of Young Children from the Colonial Era to the Present* (New Haven, CT: Yale University Press, 1995).

8. Scott explains that "over and over clubwomen spoke of their enterprise as a way of building bridges among women who tended to stick closely to people who shared their own religious, political, or family connections." *Natural Allies,* 120.

9. *The Washington Post,* 19 February 1897, as reprinted in NCPT, *Through the Years,* 57–58; *The Philadelphia Record,* 20 February 1897; and *The Evening Star,* 18 February 1897, as reprinted in NCPT, *Through the Years,* 49. For hats staying on, see *The Boston Journal,* 21 February 1897; and *Union Springfield,* 23 February 1897. At least one report has Birney asking her audience whether she should remove her hat, and their voting no. See *Boston Herald,* 20 February 1897. The same event, as reported on in the *Chicago Tribune,* has Birney speaking from "under her violet-trimmed chapeau," while the audience exposed their heads (20 February 1897).

10. *New York [illegible] Sunday,* 30 January 1898. Located in scrapbook titled "The National PTA/National PTA Newspaper Clippings, 1897–1898," PTA Records, UIC. See

also *West Chester [Pennsylvania] News,* 18 February 1897. In the early twentieth century, the right hat commanded respect because it connoted a woman's class position.   .

11. Several years later, the issue was still discussed by NCM leaders. National Congress of Mothers, *Quarterly Report* 1, no. 1 (1900): 69, PTA Records, UIC. A PTA organizer from Illinois, Cora C. Bright, believed that she needed to represent herself in an appropriate manner to the public, and this involved selecting the appropriate hat for the occasion. See Bright's recollections on finding the right hat to wear to "a high tea in honor of visiting educational dignitaries" and her relief that she "went to the tea in a borrowed hat, without disgracing the Congress" in Bright, "As It Was in the Beginning," unpublished manuscript, 1932, 28–30, PTA Records, UIC.

12. Schlossman, "Before Home Start," 436–67. Muncy refers to the time between 1900 and 1920 as the "era of educated motherhood because women were professionalizing their maternal work just as they were systematizing their charitable activities." *Creating a Female Dominion in American Reform,* 56; see also Rothman, *Woman's Proper Place,* 98–111; Ladd-Taylor, *Mother-Work,* 4; and Barbara Beatty, Emily D. Cahan, and Julia Grant, eds., *When Science Encounters the Child: Education, Parenting, and Child Welfare in 20th Century America* (New York: Teachers College Press, 2006).

13. NCPT, *Through the Years,* 44; and Ladd-Taylor, *Mother-Work,* 55. Educated motherhood was the Progressive Era ideal that made mothering a public duty. Rothman, *Woman's Proper Place,* 97. See also chapter 3, "The Ideology of Educated Motherhood." Rothman argues that Elizabeth Harrison, the noted kindergarten educator, gave educated motherhood the status of a profession (103). See also Skocpol, *Protecting Soldiers and Mothers,* 353; and Caroll Smith-Rosenberg, *Disorderly Conduct: Visions of Gender in Victorian America* (New York: Knopf, 1985).

14. Ladd-Taylor, *Mother-Work,* 3, 55. Skocpol sets the parameters for the maternalist era as 1900 to 1920. See *Protecting Soldiers and Mothers,* 11. Anne Firor Scott argues that the rare women's association of this era tested boundaries of acceptability, but did not breech them, in *Natural Allies,* 81.

15. Skocpol has called the WCTU, the GFWC, and the PTA the "three great modern [women's] federations." See "Casting Wide Nets: Federalism and Extensive Associations in the Modernizing United States," paper presented at Bertelsmann Science Foundation conference on the decline of social capital, Berlin, Germany, June 1997, 23, in author's possession. In 1897, the year the NCM was organized, the GFWC had around 60,000 members, and the WCTU 143,000. In 1925, the GFWC had approximately 400,000 members, the WCTU 356,000, and the PTA 875,000. Data from Civic Engagement Project (CEP), under the direction of Theda Skocpol and Marshall Ganz, Harvard University, in author's possession. Hereafter referred to as CEP Data.

16. Scott, *Natural Allies,* 3.

17. Therefore, my analysis challenges Cutler's assertion that the parent-teacher movement began in rural regions. See *Parents and Schools,* 20, 141. On the early organization of the National Congress of Mothers, see Skocpol, *Protecting Soldiers and Mothers,* 333–36. Skocpol argues that the NCM coopted local clubs, bringing them into its membership in the early years. On the founding of the National Congress of Mothers, see Ladd-Taylor, *Mother-Work,* 46–50; and Schlossman, "Before Home Start," 443–52.

18. Mrs. Theodore W. Birney, "Address of Welcome," in *The Work and Words of the National Congress of Mothers (First Annual Session)* (New York: D. Appleton and Company, 1897), 6. On women's study clubs, see Martin, *The Sound of Our Own Voices.*

19. Scott, *Natural Allies,* 154. Joan Marie Johnson provides a cogent argument about how southern women's education at northern institutions shaped their public activism in

"Job Market or Marriage Market? Life Choices for Southern Women Educated at Northern Colleges, 1875–1915," *History of Education Quarterly* 47, no. 2 (2007): 149–72. Also, challenging the assumption in biography that "average people are simply average," Glenda Elizabeth Gilmore argues that every person's story holds potential interest. See *Gender and Jim Crow*, 4. On biography and women's lives see Carolyn Heilbrun, *Writing a Woman's Life* (New York: W. W. Norton, 1988); and Sara Alpern, Joyce Antler, Elisabeth Israels Perry, and Ingrid Winther Scobie, *The Challenge of Feminist Biography: Writing the Lives of Modern American Women* (Urbana: University of Illinois Press, 1992). Among the many PTA histories that offer biographical sketches of Alice Birney, see in particular Harry Overstreet and Bonaro Overstreet, *Where Children Come First: A Study of the P.T.A. Idea* (Chicago: National Congress of Parents and Teachers, 1949), 42; Alice Birney Robert, "Great-Grandmother Birney and I," *National Parent-Teacher* 54, no. 6 (1960): 12; and Alonsita Walker, "My Mother," *National Parent-Teacher* 37, no. 6 (1943): 15. Family members I contacted knew little of Birney other than what they had read in these accounts.

20. Author unknown, "Mrs. Theodore Weld Birney: An Editorial Sketch," *Coming Age* 2, no. 3 (1899): 247, Harvard University Widener Library. On Marietta and the McLellan Family, see Sarah Blackwell Gober Temple, *The First Hundred Years: A Short History of Cobb County, Georgia* (Atlanta: Cherokee Publishing Company, [1935] 1980), 635; Kenneth Coleman, ed., *A History of Georgia* (Athens: University of Georgia Press, 1977); and Lewis Nicholas Wynne, *The Continuity of Cotton: Planter Politics in Georgia, 1865–1892* (Macon, GA: Mercer University Press, 1986). At the end of the 1850s, over a dozen manufacturing mills for flour, cotton, leather, and paper were built in Marietta. Perhaps most important, the town drew many to its restorative surroundings, many of whom wished to rid themselves of illnesses such as malaria. Temple, *Short History of Cobb County*, 119, 149, 154, 297.

21. Temple, *Short History of Cobb County*, 94, 176; Virginia Bernhard, Betty Brandon, Elizabeth Fox-Genovese, and Theda Purdue, eds., *Southern Women: Histories and Identities* (Columbia: University of Missouri Press, 1992), 6; Margaret A. Nash, *Women's Education in the United States, 1780–1840* (New York: Palgrave Macmillan, 2005); Kim Tolley and Nancy Beadie, eds., *Chartered Schools: Two Hundred Years of Independent Academies in the United States, 1727–1925* (New York: RoutledgeFalmer, 2002); Anne Firor Scott, *The Southern Lady: From Pedestal to Politics, 1830–1930* (Chicago: University of Chicago Press, 1970), 13, 68, 111–12; and Johnson, "Job Market or Marriage Market?" 156–57.

22. Christine Anne Farnham, *The Education of the Southern Belle: Higher Education and Student Socialization in the Antebellum South* (New York: New York University Press, 1994), 3. Though Birney was educated in the postbellum South, little had changed for women, despite the war and Reconstruction. See Scott, *The Southern Lady*, x–xi. On Birney attending Marietta Female College, see Temple, *Short History of Cobb County*, 178, 416.

23. Scott, *The Southern Lady*, 68. See also Steven Stowe, "The Not-So-Cloistered Academy: Elite Women's Education and Family Feeling in the Old South," in Walter J. Fraser, Jr., R. Frank Saunders, Jr., and Jon L. Wakely, eds., *The Web of Southern Social Relations: Women, Family, and Education* (Athens: University of Georgia Press, 1985), 91.

24. Temple, *Short History of Cobb County*, 418–19; Tillman, "Alice Josephine McLellan Birney," in Edward T. James, Janet Wilson James, and Paul S. Boyer, eds., *Notable American Women: A Biographical Dictionary*, Vol. I (Cambridge, MA: The Belknap Press of Harvard University Press, 1971), 147–48; Farnham, *The Education of the Southern Belle*, 112; and Johnson, "Job Market or Marriage Market?" 150–51, 164. On Mount Holyoke, see Nash, *Women's Education in the United States*, 70. Nash discusses other historians' conflicting

views of Mount Holyoke and its founder as to whether it was conservative or not. See her discussion on p. 128, n38. See also Barbara Miller Solomon, *In the Company of Educated Women: A History of Women and Higher Education in America* (New Haven, CT: Yale University Press, 1985); Linda Eisenmann, "Reconsidering a Classic: Assessing the History of Women's Higher Education a Dozen Years after Barbara Solomon," *Harvard Educational Review* 67, no. 4 (Winter 1997): 689–717; Elizabeth Alden Green, *Mary Lyon and Mount Holyoke: Opening the Gates* (Hanover, NH: University Press of New England, 1979); and Amanda Porterfield, *Mary Lyon and the Mount Holyoke Missionaries* (New York: Oxford University Press, 1997).

25. Alonsita Walker as quoted in Yolande Gwin, "It's Alice Birney's Day," *Atlanta Journal*, 17 February 1952, in the Alice M. Birney Biography Collection, Cobb County Public Library. The corset was not abandoned by women on a wide-scale basis until the early decades of the twentieth century. See Barbara Ehrenreich and Deirdre English, *For Her Own Good: 150 Years of the Experts' Advice to Women* (Garden City, NY: Anchor Press, 1978), 98. More information on Birney can be found in Alice Birney Robert, "Great-grandmother Birney and I," *National Parent-Teacher* 54, no. 6 (1960): 12–13; Janet M. Millard, "Alice McLellan Birney," *A Woman's Place: 52 Women of Cobb County, Georgia, 1850–1981* (Marietta: Cobb Marietta Girls' Club, 1981), 16; Marvina W. Northcutt, "Alice McLellan Birney—One of Marietta's Gems," 1963, unpublished document in the Alice M. Birney Biography Collection, Cobb County Public Library; Gwin, "It's Alice Birney's Day"; Tillman, "Alice Josephine McLellan Birney," 147; and Ladd-Taylor, *Mother-Work*, 47–48. James Gillespie Birney ran for president on the Free Soil Party ticket in 1840 and then again in 1844. Theodore's father, William Birney, was born in 1819 in Huntsville, Alabama, and later attended Yale University. William Birney was a general in the Civil War for the North. He enlisted slaves in his troops, counter to governmental policy. After the war, he retired to Washington, DC, to practice law. He continued his race work there, as he supported the education of blacks. He later had a school named for his efforts on behalf of freeing the enslaved peoples. See Mrs. Theodore Weld Birney, "An Editorial Sketch," *Coming Age* 2, no. 3 (1899): 247; unpublished Birney family genealogy and miscellaneous papers, in possession of the author; and "James Gillespie Birney," in *Dictionary of American Biography*, ed. Dumas Malone (New York: Charles Scribner's Sons, 1933), vol. 2, 291–94. I am grateful to Mr. Arthur Birney for sharing his family's genealogical information with me.

26. As quoted in Mildred White Wells, *Unity in Diversity: The History of the General Federation of Women's Clubs* (Washington, DC: General Federation of Women's Clubs, 1953), 7–8; Dr. Sarah Hackett Stevenson, "Address of Welcome," Convention Records (Addresses and Papers), 1892, 7, General Federation of Women's Clubs Archives, Washington, DC, hereafter referred to as GFWC Archives; and Scott, *Natural Allies*, 141. For women reformers, the community meant the nation. See also Muncy, *Creating a Female Dominion in American Reform*, 36; Skocpol, *Protecting Soldiers and Mothers*, 324; and Rothman, *Woman's Proper Place*, 4, 69. Three histories of the GFWC offer thorough but sympathetic portraits of the associations. See Jane Cunningham Croly, *The History of the Women's Club Movement in America* (New York: Henry G. Allen, 1898); Wells, *Unity in Diversity*; and Mary I. Wood, *The History of the General Federation of Women's Clubs* (New York: The General Federation of Women's Clubs, 1912).

27. Skocpol, "Casting Wide Nets," 23. The history of the founding of the Woman's Christian Temperance Union is somewhat similar. In 1874 during the temperance crusades in the Midwest, a group of Sunday school teachers met in Chautauqua to discuss their shared interest in temperance. Within a year they held the first convention in Cleve-

land, Ohio, and then organized a national association to further the cause of temperance on the local level, while at the national level it initiated petitions in the U.S. Congress calling for an investigation of liquor trafficking and for national prohibition. See Anna Gordon, *The Beautiful Life of Frances E. Willard* (Chicago: Woman's Temperance Publishing Association, 1898); Ruth Bordin, *Woman and Temperance: The Quest for Power and Liberty, 1873–1900* (Philadelphia: Temple University Press, 1981); Ruth Bordin, *Frances Willard: A Biography* (Chapel Hill: University of North Carolina Press, 1986); and Jack S. Blocker, *"Give to the Winds They Fears": The Women's Temperance Crusade, 1873–1874* (Westport, CT: Greenwood Press, 1985). For an examination of the WCTU's role in temperance education in the schools, see Zimmerman, *Distilling Democracy.*

28. National Congress of Parents and Teachers, *Golden Jubilee History, 1897–1947* (Chicago: National Congress of Parents and Teachers, 1947), 28–29. On Chautauqua, see Harry P. Harrison, *Culture under Canvas: The Story of Tent Chautauqua* (Westport, CT: Greenwood Press, 1978); and John E. Tapia, *Circuit Chautauqua: From Rural Education to Popular Entertainment in Early Twentieth Century America* (Jefferson, NC: McFarland & Co., 1997). National Congress of Parents and Teachers, *A New Force in Education* (Baltimore: The Lord Baltimore Press, 1929), 23; Winifred King Rugg, "The Founding of the Congress," *National Parent-Teacher* 29, no. 5 (1935): 13–15, 35.

29. As quoted in NCPT, *Through the Years,* 23. Hearst received much correspondence asking for assistance for one project or another, many of which she refused. See Phoebe A. Hearst Papers, Bancroft Library at University of California at Berkeley, hereafter referred to as BLUCB. On Hearst, see Rodman Wilson Paul, "Phoebe Apperson Hearst," in *Notable American Women,* ed. James and James, 171–73; William Randolph Hearst, *The Life and Personality of Phoebe Apperson Hearst,* n.d., PTA Records, UIC; and Amalie Hofer, "National Congress of Mothers: Every Father and Every Mother in the Land a Participant," as reproduced in NCPT, *Through the Years,* 22.

30. The cabinet ladies are listed in Rugg, "The Founding of the Congress," 14; and Ladd-Taylor, *Mother-Work,* 49.

31. Alice Birney to Phoebe Hearst, September 11, 1896, Phoebe A. Hearst Papers, BLUCB; emphasis in the original. Membership in the GFWC grew exponentially through the 1910s and doubled in the 1920s, going from 197,831 members in 1920 to 421,934 members just two years later (CEP data, in author's possession). See Scott, *Natural Allies,* 131, on state units of GFWC doubling under Henrotin's leadership. Skocpol contrasts the two associations (GFWC and NCM), noting that the NCM was "rapidly organized from the top down," unlike the GFWC. *Protecting Soldiers and Mothers,* 334.

32. Emma J. Masters to Alice Birney, March 30, 1896, scrapbook, "The National PTA/National PTA Newspaper Clippings, 1896–1911," PTA Records, UIC; Janet T. Richards, "Reveille 1897: 'I Heard Them Promise,'" *National Parent-Teacher* 36, no. 6 (1942): 16; and Ellen M. Henrotin to Phoebe Hearst, November 2, 1896, Phoebe A. Hearst Papers, BLUCB. On the ways women's clubs unified diverse members see Scott, *Natural Allies,* 120.

33. Alice M. Birney to Phoebe A. Hearst, September 11, 1896, Phoebe A. Hearst Papers, BLUCB. On the ideals of the kindergarten movement, see Beatty, *Preschool Education in America.*

34. *The New York Journal,* 9 December 1896; *The New York Sun,* 9 December 1896; and Mrs. Theodore W. Birney, "Scope and Aims of the National Congress of Mothers," *Mothers' Magazine* 1, no. 1 (1898): 1–21; from PTA Scrapbook, 1897, 1898. Unlike other women's association leaders, NCM organizers exploited the press to their advantage,

according to Skocpol, "Casting Wide Nets," 9. Women's organization leaders, however, understood the value of public relations through women's magazines. See Muncy, *Creating a Female Dominion in American Reform,* 56. On the growth of William Randolph Hearst's newspaper chain, see Redman Wilson Paul, "Phoebe Apperson Hearst," in *Notable American Women: A Biographical Dictionary,* Vol. II, ed. Edward T. James, Janet Wilson James, and Paul A. Boyer (Cambridge, MA: The Belknap Press of Harvard University Press), 172. Helen Townsend Conway Birney (1856–1946) ended up playing an integral role in the early Congress of Mothers nationally and in the Washington, DC, area. She was married to Arthur Alexis Birney, older brother of Theodore, who served as U.S. Attorney under presidents Harrison and Cleveland. Helen Birney was the first president of the District of Columbia Congress of Mothers from 1905 to 1916. Birney Family Genealogy, in possession of the author; and *The History of the District of Columbia Congress of Parents and Teachers, 1905–1955,* unpublished manuscript, PTA Records, UIC, 5.

35. Grant, *Raising Baby by the Book,* 15. NCPT, *Through the Years,* 17; NCM Minutes, January 22, 1897, and January 29, 1897, PTA Records, UIC. The letter-writing strategy was a common way of organizing large-scale associations in the nineteenth century. See Skocpol, "Casting Wide Nets," and Richard R. John, *Spreading the News: The American Postal System from Franklin to Morse* (Cambridge, MA: Harvard University Press, 1995). On this tactic in the WCTU, see Bordin, *Woman and Temperance,* 50. She explains, "Willard wrote prominent clergyman in every state and territory asking for the names and addresses of women active or committed to the temperance cause. . . . Her travel and her letter-writing not only facilitated the growth of the Union but enhanced her personal prestige as well."

36. Hofer, "National Congress of Mothers," as quoted in NCPT, *Through the Years,* 21. Congress minutes note the receipt of around a half-dozen letters per day asking about its work. NCM Minutes, March 9, 1897; and NCM Minutes, January 15, 1897, PTA Records, UIC.

37. NCPT, *Golden Jubilee History,* 36, 45. The NCM relied on prominent men, in addition to Theodore Roosevelt, to help publicize the Mothers' Congress. Muncy argues that women reformers needed the help of prominent men to succeed on the national level. *Creating a Female Dominion in American Reform,* 41. See also Skocpol, *Protecting Soldiers and Mothers,* 337.

38. NCM Minutes, December 29, 1902, 87, PTA Records, UIC. Robyn Muncy argues that Kelley's relationship with the Congress of Mothers was symbiotic, as her relationship with the NCM and GFWC "drew the leadership of those bodies and their millions of members into the network [of women reformers such as Kelley, Lillian Wald, and Jane Addams] as well." Muncy, *Creating a Female Dominion in America Reform, 1890–1935,* 35. For more on Kelley's activism, see Kathryn Kish Sklar, *Florence Kelley and the Nation's Work: The Rise of Women's Political Culture, 1830–1900* (New Haven, CT: Yale University Press, 1995).

39. National Congress of Mothers, *Work and Words,* 273–74. NCM Minutes, March 30, 1897, 4; and April 5, 1897, 47, PTA Records, UIC.

40. Schlossman, "Before Home Start," 448; and Grant, *Raising Baby by the Book,* 56. On the history of eugenics, see Steven Selden, *Inheriting Shame: The Story of Eugenics and Racism in America* (New York: Teachers College Press, 1999). See also C. Vann Woodward, *The Strange Career of Jim Crow* (New York: Oxford University Press, 1974); and Richard Hofstadter, *Social Darwinism in American Thought* (Boston: Beacon Press, 1955).

41. Mothers' Club of Lockport [New York] Minutes, Oct. 1907. In Minutes Book Oct. 2, 1903–May 23, 1908; Mothers' Club Records Collection, Niagara County Historical Society, Lockport, NY. Kohut was an educator and social welfare leader from Hungary. She was educated at a normal school and studied at the University of California at Berkeley before moving to New York City. There she campaigned for better sanitation and educational activities. See Norma Fain Pratt, "Rebekah Bettelheim Kohut," in *Notable American Women: The Modern Period,* ed. Barbara Sicherman and Carol Hurd Green (Cambridge, MA: The Belknap Press of Harvard University Press, 1980), 403–4.

42. Mrs. Theodore W. Birney, "The Power of Organized Motherhood to Benefit Humanity," *Quarterly Report* 1, no. 1 (1900): 32; and Mrs. Theodore W. Birney, "Address of Welcome," *National Congress of Mothers Third Annual Convention* (Philadelphia: Geo. F. Lasher, Printer and Binder, 1899), 198. See also Edmond Demolins, *Anglo-Saxon Supremacy: To What It Is Due,* trans. Louis Bert Lavigne (New York: Fenno, 1898); Ladd-Taylor, *Mother-Work,* 55; and Gilmore, *Gender and Jim Crow,* 50.

43. Oscar Chrisman, "The Science of Child Study," *Quarterly Report* 1, no. 1 (1900): 38, 41, 44, PTA Records, UIC. Iowa Congress of Parents and Teachers, *A History of the Iowa Congress of Parents and Teachers* (Des Moines: Iowa Congress of Parents and Teachers, n.d.), 29; National Congress of Mothers, *Quarterly Report* 1, no. 1 (1900): 46, 49; and NCM Minutes, May 26, 1900, 64, PTA Records, UIC.

44. Rothman, *Woman's Proper Place,* 131; and Birney as quoted in NCPT, *Through the Years,* 29. On clubwomen supporting suffrage, see Reese, *Power and the Promise of School Reform,* 32; Blair, *The Clubwoman as Feminist;* and Cutler, *Parents and Schools.*

45. Joyce Antler, "'After College, What?': New Graduates and the Family Claim," *American Quarterly* 32 (Fall 1980): 412–13; Alice M. Birney, "Address of Welcome," *The Work and Words of the National Congress of Mothers (First Annual Session)* (New York: D. Appleton and Company, 1897), 7; and Birney, "The Power of Organized Motherhood to Benefit Humanity," 31. For the debate on women's higher education during this era, see Antler, "'After College What?'"; Solomon, *In the Company of Educated Women;* and Eisenmann, "Reconsidering a Classic." For southern college-educated women, see Johnson, "Job Market or Marriage Market?" 153–55.

46. See Schlossman, "Before Home Start," 444. Many works address this curricular shift. Those that have influenced my thinking are David L. Angus and Jeffrey E. Mirel, *The Failed Promise of the American High School, 1890–1995* (New York: Teachers College Press, 1999); Herbert M. Kliebard, *Forging the American Curriculum: Essays in Curriculum History and Theory* (New York: Routledge, 1992), 10–12; Kliebard, *The Struggle for the American Curriculum, 1893–1958* (Boston: Routledge and Keegan Paul, 1986); and Herbert M. Kliebard, *Schooled to Work: Vocationalism and the American Curriculum, 1876–1946* (New York: Teachers College Press, 1999). Julie A. Reuben adds that changing definitions of citizenship also aided this sea change in the curriculum, in "Beyond Politics: Community Civics and the Redefinition of Citizenship in the Progressive Era," *History of Education Quarterly* 37, no. 4 (1997): 399–420.

47. Reese, *Power and the Promise of School Reform,* 45. On the "new education," see also Schlossman, "Before Home Start," 444. The NCM and GFWC sought to bring "systematic moral instruction" into the schools. *Fifth Biennial of the General Federation of Women's Clubs,* (Detroit: John Bornman & Son, 1900), 17, GFWC Archives, Washington, DC. On the history of moral education, see B. Edward McClellan, *Moral Education in America: Schools and the Shaping of Character from Colonial Times to the Present* (New York: Teachers College Press, 1999).

48. Kliebard, *Forging the American Curriculum*, 32, 39–40. See also Charles W. Eliot, "Introduction," in *Essays on Education, etc. by Herbert Spencer* (New York: E. P. Dutton & Co., Inc., [1911] 1949), vii.

49. Mrs. Theodore W. Birney, "Sympathetic Parenthood," in National Congress of Mothers, *The Child in Home, School, and State: Report of the National Congress of Mothers* (Washington, DC: National Congress of Mothers, 1905), 165. Spencer's five criteria that categorized the leading life activities that were to determine school curriculum were the following: "1. those activities which directly minister to self-preservation; 2. those activities which, by securing the necessaries of life, indirectly minister to self-preservation; 3. those activities which have for their end the rearing and discipline of offspring; 4. those activities which are involved in the maintenance of proper social and political relations; 5. those miscellaneous activities which fill up the leisure part of life, devoted to the gratification of tastes and feelings." *Essays on Education, etc by Herbert Spencer*, 7. See also Kliebard, *Forging the American Curriculum*, 31.

50. Schlossman, "Before Home Start," 441. See also Dorothy Ross, *G. Stanley Hall: The Psychologist as Prophet* (Chicago: University of Chicago Press, 1972), 126, 131, 260, 293, 305, 306; Kliebard, *Struggle for the American Curriculum*, 37; Kliebard, *Forging the American Curriculum*, 42–43; and Grant, *Raising Baby by the Book*, 36–38.

51. Mrs. Montford C. Holley, (n.d.), 4, Mothers' Club of Lockport Vertical File, Niagara County Historical Society, Lockport, New York; Mrs. Charles Henrotin, "Address," General Federation of Women's Clubs Convention Records, May 12, 1892, 49; Kliebard, *Struggle for the American Curriculum*, 41, 93–94; G. Stanley Hall, "Some Practical Results of Child Study," *The Work and Words of the First National Congress of Mothers (First Annual Session)* (New York: D. Appleton and Company, 1897), 165; and Birney, "The Power of Organized Motherhood to Benefit Humanity," 30. Emphases in the original. See also *NEA Proceedings*, 1903, 446–51; and Reese, *Power and the Promise of School Reform*, chapter 3, on the municipalization of motherhood.

52. Charlotte Hawkins Brown, "President's Address," GFWC Convention Records, May 11, 1892; GFWC and Birney, "Power of Organized Motherhood," 31–32.

53. Bordin, *Woman and Temperance*, 64; and NCM Minutes, April 5, 1897, 81, and September 16, 1897, 133, PTA Records, UIC. Hearst moved to California in September 1897, and the Board of Managers asked her to continue as its president, but she declined. Hearst did not even want her photo used in connection with the Congress; see NCM Minutes, September 15, 1897, PTA Records, UIC; and Alice M. Birney to Phoebe A. Hearst, May 14, 1900, Phoebe A. Hearst Papers, BLUCB.

54. NCM, *Second and Third Annual Conventions*, 153, Chicago, PTA Records, UIC.

55. Birney as quoted in NCM, *The Child in Home, School, and State*, 11. Unlike the GFWC, in the early years the PTA did not set term limits for its presidents.

56. See Alice M. Birney to Mary Mears, October 23, 1899, as reprinted in NCPT, *Through the Years*, 124; Pennsylvania Congress of Parents and Teachers, *History of the Pennsylvania State Congress of Parents and Teachers* (Philadelphia: Pennsylvania Congress of Parents and Teachers, n.d.), 5–6; NCPT, *Golden Jubilee*, 57; Elvena B. Tillman, "Hannah Kent Schoff," in *Notable American Women*, 237. On the development of juvenile courts by settlement house women, see Muncy, *Creating a Female Dominion in American Reform*, 18–19; and Cutler, *Parents and Schools*, 99–100.

57. As reprinted in Pennsylvania Congress of Parents and Teachers, *History of the Pennsylvania Congress of Parents and Teachers* (Philadelphia: Pennsylvania Congress of Parents and Teachers, n.d.), 8; NCPT, *Golden Jubilee*, 43; Mrs. Ellen M. Henrotin, "The Co-operation of Woman's Clubs in the Public Schools," in *NEA Proceedings*, 1897, 76.

58. CEP data, in author's possession.

59. Reese, *Power and the Promise of School Reform,* 35. Reese's book thoroughly details the activities of women's clubs in four medium-sized Midwestern cities but refers to them as "grassroots." As I argue in this chapter, the activities of women's organizations, owing to their top-down coordination through major federations and the NEA, cannot necessarily be considered grassroots movements.

60. Scott, *Natural Allies,* 185–86. In the appendix, Scott organized Beard's data. For Beard's discussion of educational reforms, see *Woman's Work in Municipalities* ([New York: D. Appleton and Company, 1915] New York: Arno Press, 1972), 40.

61. Rothman argues that clubwomen wanted to "transform public policy, to move from personal and private encounter to state action, to bring about compulsory legislation of one sort or another." Rothman, *Woman's Proper Place,* 135.

62. Skocpol, *Protecting Soldiers and Mothers,* 482. In making this assertion, Skocpol points out that she disagrees with Muncy's instrumental-professional and bureaucratic interpretation, in *Creating a Female Dominion,* that assumes that smaller groups of professionals were able to direct women's federations. See Skocpol, *Protecting Soldiers and Mothers,* 683n9. Tyack, *One Best System,* 6–8; Reese, *Power and the Promise of School Reform;* and Wayne J. Urban, *Gender, Race, and the National Education Association: Professionalism and Its Limitations* (New York: RoutledgeFalmer, 2000).

63. Wayne J. Urban argues that women teachers were marginalized until 1917, when they began to enjoy a "relatively symbiotic" though not equitable relationship with the association. See Urban, "Courting the Woman Teacher," 140. See also Urban, *Gender, Race, and the National Education Association.* In the 1960s the NEA became the trade union we know it to be today.

64. Mary Codding Bourland, "Parents as Child Students," *NEA Proceedings,* 1897, 860; and Proceedings of the New Board of Directors, *NEA Proceedings,* 1907, 51–52. See also Address by Mrs. Charles Henrotin of the Congress Auxiliary Woman's Branch of the World's Fair, GFWC Convention Records, May 12, 1892, GFWC Archives; and Mrs. O. Shepard Barnum, "The Past, Present, and Future of the Patrons' Department," *NEA Proceedings,* 1917, 639. Educators around the country took note of the educational work of white women's clubs at the turn of the twentieth century. See, for example, "Twenty-Seventh Annual Report from the Department of Education to the General Assembly of the State of Georgia," (Atlanta: Geo. W. Harrison, State Printer, 1899), 178–84; "Public Schools of the City of Chicago Forty-Fourth annual Report of the Board of Education" (Chicago: John F. Higgins, Print, 1898), 68–69; "1901 Report of Public Schools of North Des Moines, Iowa" (Des Moines: Talbott-Koch Printing Company, 1901), 65; and "Annual Report of the Public Schools of the City and County of San Francisco" (San Francisco: W. M. Hinton & Co., 1898), 26; all, Cambridge, MA, Gutman Library Special Collections, Cambridge, MA, Gutman Library Special Collections.

65. Mrs. O. Shepard Barnum, "Women's Work in the Socialization of the Schools," *NEA Proceedings,* 1908, 1236. All membership figures from CEP data, in author's possession. In 1908, the combined membership of the three major women's federations was roughly 260,000 (GFWC—63,000; PTA—10,000; WCTU—187,000). Adding the membership of the other organizations in the DWO brings the total close to 300,000.

66. Helen Grenfell, "The Influence of Women's Organizations in Public Education," *NEA Proceedings,* 1907, 128.

67. Minutes, Department of National Organizations of Women, *NEA Proceedings,* 1908, 1217–18.

68. Elmer Ellsworth Brown, "The Work of Women's Organizations in Education:

Suggestions for Effective Co-Operation," *NEA Proceedings*, 1908, 1220; and Minutes, Department of National Organizations of Women, *NEA Proceedings*, 1908, 1217.

69. Laura Drake Gill, "The Scope of the Department of Women's Organizations," *NEA Proceedings*, 1909, 71; and "Membership of the National Education Association," *NEA Proceedings*, 1900, 4. See also Grant, *Raising Baby by the Book*, on women's special capacity as mothers and as women to carry out reform work; and Scott, *Natural Allies*, on why and how women's organizations gave them power in the public arena when men did not need such associations. For a contrasting view on the efforts of men's voluntary membership associations in Progressive-Era educational reform, see Reese, *Power and the Promise of School Reform*.

70. Mrs. O. Shepard Barnum, "Women's Work in the Socialization of the Schools," *NEA Proceedings*, 1908, 1231–38. See also Mrs. Henry J. Hersey, "The Parents' Obligation to the School," *NEA Proceedings*, 1909, 1012–16; Laura Drake Gill, "The Scope of the Department of Women's Organizations," *NEA Proceedings*, 1909, 70–75; and Dorothy Sparks, *Strong is the Current: History of the Illinois Congress of Parents and Teachers, 1900–1947* (Chicago: Illinois Congress of Parents and Teachers, 1948), 18–19.

71. Mary Frances Farnham, *NEA Proceedings*, 1911, 1109. Men had been welcomed to join the Department of Women's Organizations, but it is unknown how many were members. See Gill, "The Scope of the Department of Women's Organizations," *NEA Proceedings*, 1909, 70–71; and Rothman, *Woman's Proper Place*, 170.

72. Helen L. Grenfell, "The Constitution of the Ideal School Board and the Citizen's Duty Toward It," *NEA Proceedings*, 1909, 994; and Laura Drake Gill, "The Work of the Department of School Patrons," *NEA Proceedings*, 1910, 1075–77; quote on p. 1076. See also "Summary of State Reports of Joint Committees and Affiliated Organizations, 1910–1911," *NEA Proceedings*, 1911, 1097–103; and "Summary of State Reports of Joint Committees and Affiliated Organizations, 1911–1912, *NEA Proceedings*, 1912, 1341–50.

73. Carolyn Terry Bashaw, "Ella Flagg Young," in *Historical Dictionary of Women's Education in the United States*, ed. Linda Eisenmann (Westport, CT: Greenwood Press, 1998), 496–98; Judy Suratt, "Ella Flagg Young," in *Notable American Women*, ed. Edward T. James, Janet Wilson James, and Paul S. Boyer (Cambridge, MA: The Belknap Press of Harvard University Press, 1981); and Joan K. Smith, *Ella Flagg Young: Portrait of a Leader* (Ames, IA: Educational Studies Press, 1979).

74. Barnum, "The Work of the Coming Year," *NEA Proceedings*, 1910, 1078. See also Jackie M. Blount, "Ella Flagg Young and the Chicago Schools," in *Founding Mothers and Others: Women Educational Leaders during the Progressive Era*, ed. Alan R. Sadovnik and Susan F. Semel (New York: Palgrave, 2002).

75. Helen Hefferan, "Report of School Revenue Committee of the Department of School Patrons," *NEA Proceedings*, 1911, 1094–96. Young enjoyed a close relationship with women's associations. Women's organizations helped reinstate her to the superintendency in Chicago in 1912–13 after she resigned because of a disagreement over textbook adoption and teacher rights. See Bashaw, "Ella Flagg Young," 497; and Beard, *Woman's Work in Municipalities*, 6–7.

76. Francis G. Blair, as quoted in Helen M. Hefferan, "Report of the Committee on School Revenue," *NEA Proceedings*, 1912, 1339; and Hefferan, "Report of School Revenue Committee," 1911, 1096.

77. "Summary of State Reports of Joint Committees and Affiliated Organizations [of the Department of School Patrons], 1910–1911," *NEA Proceedings*, 1911, 1101.

78. "Summary of State Reports of Joint Committees and Affiliated Organizations [to the Department of School Patrons], 1910–1911," *NEA Proceedings*, 1911, 1098, 1101;

"Secretary's Minutes, Department of School Patrons," *NEA Proceedings*, 1916, 799; and Reese, *Power and the Promise of School Reform*, 218, 221.

79. "Summary of State Reports of Joint Committees and Affiliated Organizations, 1911–1912," *NEA Proceedings*, 1912, 1341. See also Mrs. O. Shepard Barnum, "The Past, Present, and Future of the Patrons' Department," *NEA Proceedings*, 1917, 640; and "Summary of State Reports of Joint Committees and Affiliated Organizations, 1911–1912," *NEA Proceedings*, 1912, 1342–43.

80. "Summary of State Reports of Joint Committees and Affiliated Organizations [of the Department of School Patrons], 1910–1911," *NEA Proceedings*, 1911, 1098.

81. Barnum, "Women's Work in the Socialization of the Schools," 1236; Mrs. Henry J. Hersey, "The Parents' Obligation to the Schools," *NEA Proceedings*, 1909, 1015–16; and "Summary of State Reports of Joint Committees and Affiliated Organizations, 1911–1912, *NEA Proceedings*, 1912," 1342–43. See also Rothman, *Woman's Proper Place*, 105.

82. Mrs. O. Shepard Barnum, "The Past, Present, and Future of the Patrons' Department," *NEA Proceedings*, 1917, 641–42. The U.S. Congress had organized the Woman's Committee both to study wartime preparedness among citizens and to coordinate volunteers' efforts. See Muncy, *Creating a Female Dominion in American Reform*, 97; and William J. Breen, *Uncle Sam at Home: Civilian Mobilization, Wartime Federalism, and the Council of National Defense, 1917–1919* (Westport, CT: Greenwood Press, 1984).

83. Reese, *Power and the Promise of School Reform*, 205; and Cutler, *Parents and Schools*. Membership figures on the PTA and GFWC from CEP data, in author's possession. NEA membership figures from "Membership of the National Education Association," *NEA Proceedings*, 1930, 4. See also Urban, "Courting the Woman Teacher," 143. Urban writes that this era signaled the beginning of the modern NEA and that James W. Crabtree, the organization's secretary in 1917, is responsible for enlisting the support of women teachers, which resulted in the exponential growth in membership. By 1931, the NEA had 220,149 members.

84. Urban, *Gender, Race, and the National Education Association*, 18. Some confusion seems to have resulted from the phasing out of the department, because the PTA sent its dues in 1923, but they were promptly returned. See Minutes of the Board of Managers of the National Congress of Mothers and Parent-Teacher Associations, April 23, 1923, p. 2, Elizabeth (Hewes) Tilton Papers, Folder 223, Box 7, Schlesinger Library, Radcliffe Institute for Advanced Studies, hereafter referred to as RIAS.

85. Muncy, *Creating a Female Dominion in American Reform*, 103–4. The organizations included the GFWC, the National Consumers' League, the National League of Women Voters, the National Women's Trade Union League, the PTA, the AAUW, the WCTU, the National Federation of Business and Professional Women's Clubs, the National Council of Jewish Women, and the American Home Economics Association, and, as Muncy explains, their top priority in 1920, when they were first organized, was the Sheppard-Towner Maternity and Infancy Act.

86. Rothman, *Woman's Proper Place*, 187, 188. See also Grant, *Raising Baby by the Book*, 39; and Kathleen D. McCarthy, "Parallel Power Structures: Women and the Voluntary Sphere," in *Lady Bountiful Revisited: Women, Philanthropy, and Power*, ed. Kathleen D. McCarthy (New Brunswick, NJ: Rutgers University Press, 1990), 6.

87. Reese argues that women's organization's reform efforts died down after the war, but I disagree. Women's volunteerism in schools continued well into the twentieth century. Reese, *Power and the Promise of School Reform*, 227–29; and Woyshner and Knupfer, "Introduction: Women, Volunteerism, and Education," 3–4. Putnam, *Bowling Alone*; and Skocpol, *Diminished Democracy*.

21. Don Shoemaker, ed., *With All Deliberate Speed: Segregation-Desegregation in Southern Schools* (New York: Harper & Brothers, 1957), 152; NCCPT, *Coral Anniversary,* 76; and *Our National Family* (March 1958): 15. One report in *Our National Family* explained that because of the "rapid progress of integration" in DC, a workshop was postponed because all school personnel were being utilized for the effort. See *Our National Family* (March 1955): 20. The actual figure by which the integrated DC Congress grew was 12,744 from 1955 to 1956, which was one thousand members fewer than the total in the District's Colored Congress. It is unclear what happened to the extra thousand members, though the record suggests that they protested the merger and decided to remain independent. PTA membership data, CEP, in possession of the author.

22. NCCPT, *Coral Anniversary,* 69. Although separate records were not kept on the numbers of black and white members, in 1961 it was estimated that 6,000 African Americans belonged to Missouri's Congress of Parents and Teachers. *Our National Family* (Sept. 1955): 15; and *Our National Family* (June 1955).

23. See *Our National Family* (June 1956): 7; and *Our National Family* (Sept. 1956): 9. Most of the available documentation on the PTA is of white units, which not only tell only one side of the story but also often fail to include accounts of the process of unification. For example, nearly all of the self-published histories of southern state PTAs leave out the integration of their PTA. Kentucky's *Diamond Jubilee History* reports on many activities and accomplishments of the KCPT during the administration of Mrs. George C. Spoonamore, Jr. (1969–71). The theme of her administration was "Facing Up to a Changing World," which KCPT historians describe as a focus on "Children's Emotional Health, Judicial Concern for Children in Trouble, Smoking and Health, and Financing Public Education." Not once is the integration of the state unit with the Kentucky Colored Congress mentioned in this history. See KCPT, *Diamond Jubilee 1918–1993* (KCPT, n.d.). In perusing the *South Carolina Parent-Teacher,* I noted that although an entire issue was devoted to the ESEA, there was no mention of desegregation. See *South Carolina Parent-Teacher* 31, no. 5 (Feb. 1966). Likewise, I could not locate discussions of race, the *Brown* decision, or desegregation of schools in the journal from 1950 to 1970 despite its inclusion of such topics as school consolidation, world citizenship, and international relations. A discussion of Brotherhood Week in 1967 referred only to religious diversity and cooperation "among different groups." The pattern is repeated in other collections.

24. NCCPT, *Coral Anniversary,* 79–80; and CEP data, in possession of the author. The last recorded membership figure for the Kentucky Colored Congress was 1,620 in 1957. In the extensive KCPT collection housed at Eastern Kentucky University, the only references to its segregated association I could locate were in the minutes of the Board of Managers meetings. The black and white state organizations did not unify until 1966, and it is difficult to establish the point at which the white organization included the membership figures of the Colored Congress.

25. KCPT, Pre-Convention Meeting of Board of Managers, Monday, April 25, 1955, Box 4, Executive Committee Minutes, January 1954–April 1956, EKU.

26. KCPT, Minutes of the Executive Committee Meeting, September 14, 1955, Box 4, Executive Committee Minutes, January 1954–April 1956, EKU; and Coleman, "Desegregation of the Public Schools in Kentucky," 254. Coleman argues that the "favorable state context" was due to the low percentage of African Americans in the population, its location as a border state, and its history of less-restrictive segregation (258). Louisville appears to present a unique case, however, since it was considered a "mecca" for black teachers who had lost their jobs in other school districts and the larger percentage of

blacks in the municipality. The city by 1960 had come to be considered a model of desegregation. See Eddie W. Morris, "Facts and Factors of Faculty Desegregation in Kentucky, 1955–1965," *Journal of Negro Education* 36, no. 1 (1967): 75–77; and James W. Vander Zanden, "Turmoil in the South," *Journal of Negro Education* 29, no. 4 (1960): 445–52.

27. KCPT, Executive Committee Meeting, Frankfort, Kentucky, July 18, 1956, Box 5, Executive Committee Minutes, July 18, 1956–April 23, 1970, EKU. See also KCPT, Minutes of the Pre-Convention Board of Managers Meeting, April 30–May 1, 1956, Box 4, Executive Committee Minutes, January 1954–April 1956, EKU.

28. KCPT, Minutes, Board of Managers of the Kentucky Congress of Parents and Teachers, Sept. 18, 1956, Box 5, Executive Committee Minutes, July 18, 1956–April 23, 1970, EKU; Coleman, "Desegregation of the Public Schools in Kentucky," 257; "West Virginia PTA Workshop [held at] Bluefield State College," *Our National Family* (March 1955): 20; KCPT, Minutes of the Meeting of the Board of Managers, January 16, 1957, Box 5, Executive Committee Minutes, July 18, 1956–April 23, 1970, EKU; Morris, "Facts and Factors of Faculty Desegregation in Kentucky, 1955–1965," 75; and KCPT, Minutes of the Executive Committee Meeting, January 21, 1958, Box 5, Executive Committee Minutes, July 18, 1956–April 23, 1970, EKU. A parallel in resistance to integration can be found in the NEA-ATA merger. See Karpinski, *"A Visible Company of Professionals,"* chapter 9.

29. KCPT, Minutes of the Board of Managers, January 11, 1961, Box 5, Executive Committee Minutes, July 18, 1956–April 23, 1970; and KCPT, Report of the Special Committee on Group Relations, April 6, 1961, Box 5, Executive Committee Minutes, July 18, 1956–April 23, 1970, EKU.

30. Minnie J. Hitch, "President's Message," *Our National Family* (Sept. 1966): 3; and KCPT, Minutes of the Executive Committee Meeting, April 25, 1966, Box 5, Executive Committee Minutes, July 18, 195–April 23, 1970, EKU.

31. Cecelski, *Along Freedom Road,* 9. Cecelski argues that "strong undercurrents of ambivalence toward school desegregation emerged among southern blacks in the late 1960s and early 1970s."

32. Nasstrom, "Women and the Civil Rights Movement," 146–47, 153, 179. On race relations in Atlanta, see Virginia H. Hein, "The Image of 'A City Too Busy to Hate': Atlanta in the 1960s," *Phylon* 33 (Third Quarter, 1972): 205–21; and Alton Hornsby, Jr., "A City That Was Too Busy to Hate: Atlanta Businessmen and Desegregation," in *Southern Businessmen and Desegregation,* ed. Elizabeth Jacoway and David R. Colburn (Baton Rouge: Louisiana State University Press, 1981), 120–36.

33. Horace Mann Bond, *Negro Education in Alabama: A Study in Cotton and Steel* (New York: Atheneum, 1939), 159–63, 255–56; Leroy F. Box, *Laws Relating to the Public School System of Alabama* (Montgomery, AL: Barrett and Brown, 1878), 23; *Acts of the General Assembly of Alabama, Passed at the Session of 1890–1891* (Montgomery: Allred and Company, 1891), 554; and Montgomery, "Activities of Parent-Teacher Associations in the Negro Schools of Alabama," 6–7.

34. In the 1930s it adopted the platform "Legislation, Citizenship, and Education," and in 1957 it started an annual Conference on Citizenship. Fannie Mitchell Nelson, "The Alabama PTA Story, 1911–1968," 1969, Folder 48, Box 25, AUM; and NCCPT, *Coral Anniversary History,* 60–62.

35. Orfield, *The Reconstruction of Southern Education,* 47–48.

36. *Our National Family* (June 1954): 16; Olin H. Horton, Memorandum to PTA Members, Dec. 1, 1954, Folder 26, Box 16, AUM; Inez V. Hepburn as quoted in column "Tell It to Old Grandma," *Montgomery Advertiser* of the *Alabama Journal,* 2 September 1956,

Folder 26, Box 16, AUM; Mary N. Sellers to Mrs. Rollin Brown, March 1, 1956, Folder 26, Box 16, AUM; and Mrs. Rollin Brown to Mrs. Sellers, March 27, 1956, Folder 6, Box 14, AUM.

37. Alabama Congress of Parents and Teachers to Executive Committee of the National Congress of Parents and Teachers, September 14, 1956, Folder 6, Box 14, emphasis added; and ACPT, "For Your Information," September 14, 1956, Folder 6, Box 14, AUM. See also "Integration Stand Revised by P-TA," *Alabama Journal,* 28 September 1956, Folder 26, Box 16, AUM.

38. As quoted in ACPT, "For Your Information," September 14, 1956, Folder 6, Box 14, AUM; emphasis in original. Further research will determine the extent to which the NCPT worked with the NAACP on desegregation. See Richard Kluger, *Simple Justice,* especially chapter 24.

39. Narvie J. Harris interview, 11 June 1992, 53–56, GGDP. For example, PTA president Mayme Williams was an NAACP member. See *Our National Family* (Sept. 1953): 3. See Nasstrom, "Women and the Civil Rights Movement," 169; and Fairclough, *A Class of Their Own,* 382. See also Cecelski, *Along Freedom Road* and *Our National Family,* on the fact that most African Americans supported the NAACP (10).

40. Nasstrom, "Women and the Civil Rights Movement," 128. She argues that the NAACP was led by black Baptist ministers, and women were relegated to supporting roles.

41. Baker, *Paradoxes of Desegregation,* 113–14; and CEP data, in possession of the author. See also Kluger, *Simple Justice,* 173–86, 195–97.

42. *Our National Family* (March 1958): 12. For examples of NAACP reports, see *Our National Family* (Aug. 1952): 6. The West Virginia Congress of Colored Parents and Teachers reported on the activities of the NAACP in that state. See also greetings from the NAACP reported in *Our National Family* (Sept. 1954): 18; and *Our National Family* (Sept. 1957): 6.

43. Betty Baldwin McLaurine, Letter of Resignation, July 24, 1956, in Folder 26, Box 16; "PTA Leader Resigns Post in Race Row," *Montgomery Advertiser,* 25 July 1956, Folder 26, Box 16; Fanny [Mitchell Nelson] to Mrs. J. H. Rutledge, July 27, 1956, Folder 26, Box 16, AUM. *N.B.:* Nelson's first name is spelled alternately "Fanny" and "Fannie" in the documentation.

44. E. L. White to Fanny Nelson, July 30, 1956, Folder 26, Box 16; and Mrs. Harry Nelson to Mr. E. L. White, August 1, 1956, Folder 26, Box 16, AUM.

45. Mrs. J. H. Rutledge to Dear Council President, August 1, 1956, Folder 26, Box 16, AUM.

46. "P-TA Chapters to Get Letter on National Group's Stand," *Alabama Journal,* 2 August 1956, Folder 26, Box 16; Mrs. G. J. Simpkin to "Gentlemen," August 27, 1956, Folder 26, Box 6; and Mary to Martha [Rutledge], August 25, 1956, Folder 26, Box 6, AUM.

47. R. J. Lawrence to Mrs. James Hepburn, August 9, 1956, Folder 26, Box 6, AUM.

48. Mrs. J. H. Rutledge to "Dear PTA Member," August 1956, Folder 26, Box 6, AUM. Perhaps because she did not give a clear denial, or as she put it, "I believe that would be better [to leave it out] because it might stir up trouble," Rutledge deleted the paragraph from the final version, but left it in only for the members of the Montgomery County Council PTA, since she wanted to challenge McLaurine's leadership in that district. Martha [Rutledge] to Fanny [Mitchell Nelson], August 27, 1956, Folder 26, Box 6, AUM.

49. "Cloverdale P-TA Group Votes to Stay with National Group," *The Montgomery Advertiser,* 28 August 1956, Folder 26, Box 16, AUM.

50. "State Not Bound by National PTA Integration Moves, Chief Asserts," *The Anniston Star,* 29 August 1956, Folder 26, Box 16; and "Alabama PTA Head Cites Separate School Stand," *The Birmingham News,* 31 August 1956, Folder 26, Box 16, AUM.

51. "PT-A Councils Battle over Integration," *Montgomery Advertiser,* 2 September 1956, Folder 26, Box 16; and McLaurine, "Why? Independent Parent Teacher Alliance?" September 4, 1956, Folder 26, Box 16, AUM.

52. As quoted in "Integration Stand Revised by P-TA," *Alabama Journal,* 28 September 1956, Folder 26, Box 16; and "Citizens' Council Urges Local PTA Secession Move," *The Selma Times-Journal,* Sept. 1956, Folder 26, Box 16, AUM. The council included representatives from each PTA group in Selma, according to the article. For more on white Citizen Councils, see Numan V. Bartley, *The Rise of Massive Resistance: Race and Politics in the South in the* 1950s (Baton Rouge: Louisiana State University Press, 1969); and Neil R. McMillen, *The Citizens' Council: Organized Resistance to the Second Reconstruction, 1954-1964* (Chicago: University of Chicago Press, 1971).

53. "Integration Stand Revised by P-TA," *Alabama Journal,* 28 September 1956, Folder 26, Box 16; "Two More Montgomery Units to End National P-TA Link," *Montgomery Advertiser,* 10 October 1956, Folder 26, Box 16; and "To Break Original County Unit," *Montgomery Advertiser,* 11 October 1956, Folder 26, Box 16, AUM. See also "Martin PTA Decides to Join National Body Again," *The Birmingham News,* Folder 26, Box 16, AUM.

54. Membership in 1956 was 212,923; and in 1957 it was 190,450. During the Depression, ACPT membership had dropped from 21,000 to 13,000 (1932 to 1933), only to return to the original figure the following year. In 1960 ACPT membership was 215,391 and grew to an all-time high of 232,462 in 1966 before it began to decline again. CEP data, in possession of the author.

55. *Our National Family* (Dec. 1956): 8. Alabama's Colored Congress grew by 30 percent from 1953 to 1958 amid the controversy in the white units, increasing its membership from 23,000 to 33,000. Kathryn Nasstrom explains that it was difficult even to conduct an anonymous poll of white PTA workers on whether or not they supported the desegregation of Atlanta's public schools, which revealed "how the controversial nature of school desegregation discouraged open discussion." In "Women, the Civil Rights Movement, and the Politics of Historical Memory in Atlanta, 1946-1973," 145.

56. Kluger, *Simple Justice,* 751; Nasstrom, "Women and the Civil Rights Movement," 115-17; and Mrs. Drayton Duck to Fan[ny] Nelson, Nov. 5, 1963, Folder 6, Box 14, AUM. In 1971 the ACPT recorded a membership of 160,450 members. CEP membership data, in possession of the author.

57. Another source claims the black Georgia State PTA was founded in 1911. See Georgia Congress of Colored Parents and Teachers, *Our Georgia Family* 16, no. 1 (1957): 26. Program, Forty-Third Annual Session of the Alabama Colored Congress of Parents and Teachers, April 25 and 26, 1957, Folder 47, Box 12, AUM. On voter registration drives, see Steven F. Lawson, *Black Ballots: Voting Rights in the South, 1944-1969* (New York: Columbia University Press, 1976).

58. See *Coral Anniversary,* 62; and *Our National Family,* the publication of the National Congress of Colored Parents and Teachers. Membership data are scant and sometimes contradictory on the black PTA. "Dedication to Ethel Woodrick Kight," *Our Georgia Family* 27, no. 2 (1968): 15. See also *Our National Family* (Sept. 1957): 3.

59. "State News," *Our Georgia Family* (June 1967): 26. See also CEP data, in possession of the author. For additional reports on the Tennessee Congress of Colored Parents and Teachers and its mergers with the white Congress, see *Our National Family* (Dec. 1966):

20; and *Our National Family* (March 1967): 22. Educational leaders in Tennessee were also unsuccessful in visiting white PTA meetings right after the *Brown* decision to promote the benefits of desegregation. See Shoemaker, *With All Deliberate Speed,* 51.

60. *Our National Family* (June 1959): 22.

61. Nasstrom, "Women, the Civil Rights Movement, and the Politics of Historical Memory in Atlanta, 1946–1973," 68.

62. GCCPT, *Golden Anniversary History,* 144, PTA Records, UIC. In contrast, the NCPT magazine, *National Parent-Teacher,* throughout the 1960s and 1970s made little mention of the black PTA or the merger.

63. *Our Georgia Family* (Fall 1967): 3; and "Two Georgia Congresses Existing Side by Side," *Our Georgia Family* 29, no. 4 (1970): 9, 10. Announcements of joint conferences between Atlanta's black and white PTAs appear in the pages of the NCCPT's journal. For example, see *Our National Family* (Dec. 1966): 20.

64. North Carolina Congress of Parents and Teachers, "Guidelines," n.d., Folder 47, Box 12, AUM. In 1954, North Carolina's state legislature passed the Pupil Assignment Act, giving local districts the right to deny blacks admission to white schools without citing race as a reason. See Cecelski, *Along Freedom Road,* 25.

65. See, for example, Mrs. Jerome Z. Morris to Mrs. Harry Nelson, January 29, 1963; and Mrs. Jerome Z. Morris to Mrs. Harry Nelson, March 27, 1963, in Folder 47, Box 12, AUM. In this correspondence Morris, the president of the Congress of Colored Parents and Teachers, apologizes to the president of the white Congress, Nelson, for the "constant flow of mail to you from our units."

66. "Statement of Joint Policy: National Congress of Parents and Teachers and National Congress of Colored Parents and Teachers," ca. 1966, Folder 47, Box, 12, AUM.

67. See Alabama Congress of Parents and Teachers [white], Executive Committee Minutes, 1965. The outgoing ACPT president listed information to be passed on to her successor, Mrs. John R. Lathram, as "Committees considered but not to be announced or listed" in her notes for the meeting that year. The Group Relations Committee was listed with the white members Mrs. H. C. Wright, Mr. W. T. McKee, and Dr. Kermit A. Johnson, the superintendent of the Jefferson County Public Schools. See Folder 1, Box 4, AUM. As a result of the secretive nature of these meetings, the minutes—if there were any—were not archived with the rest of the Alabama PTA collection.

68. *Our National Family* (Dec. 1966): 20; and Mrs. Harry Nelson to Mr. Thomas, January 22, 1968, Folder 47, Box 12, ACPT Collection, AUM. Even with all the tumult around them, leaders sought to avoid controversy on the public stage. Ethel Bell, president of the Alabama Colored Congress, assured Lathram that she did not expect her to "get on the spot, or wave out into controversial issues of our times." Mrs. Ethel L. Bell to Mrs. John R. Lathram, March 10, 1966, Folder 47, Box 12, ACPT Collection, AUM. This kind of relationship was common in the southern units with segregated congresses. See also "Convention Highlights," *Our Georgia Family* 29, no. 7 (1970): 8; and "Two Georgia Congresses Existing Side by Side," *Our Georgia Family* 29, no. 4 (1970): 10.

69. Jennelle Moorhead, "Prime Time for PTA Action," *Our National Family* (Sept. 1966): 12; and *Our National Family* (Dec. 1967): 5.

70. Mrs. John R. Lathram to Mrs. Jennelle Moorhead, ca. Feb. 6, 1967, Folder 47, Box 12; and Ethel L. Bell to Mrs. John R. Lathram, February 6, 1967, Folder 47, Box 12, AUM.

71. Bell later explained to Lathram why she had invited the national officers: "We did that because we felt there were [*sic*] some information that would have been pertinent to

our thinking. That made the committee larger than we wanted it to be. I sincerely hope that [white state president] Mrs. Nelson can understand that it was not an intention to 'over do' the thing." Ethel L. Bell to Mrs. John R. Lathram, March 9, 1967, Folder 47, Box 12, AUM.

72. Mrs. Forte, Minutes of the Intergroup Relations Committee Meeting, March 8, 1967, Folder 47, Box 12; Questionnaire on Intergroup Relations Committee, ca. March 1967, Folder 47, Box 12, ACPT Collection; and Mrs. William O. Jones to Mrs. John R. Lathram, September 25, 1969, Folder 47, Box 12, ACPT Collection, AUM.

73. Mrs. Irvin R. Hendryson to "Presidents of the Following [white] State Congresses . . . ," May 1, 1969, Folder 47, Box 12, ACPT Collection, AUM. Tennessee and Maryland merged their segregated PTAs in 1967, while the state units in Texas and Arkansas integrated in 1969. Rev. R. L. Hope to All Principals, Presidents, and Principals of PTA Council, White, October 1, 1969, Folder 47, Box 12; and Dot to Fan, September 25, 1969, Folder 47, Box 12, ACPT Collection, AUM; emphasis in original.

74. "Why We Exist and the Direction We Take 1965," *Our National Family* (Sept. 1967): 12; and Our *Georgia Family* (Fall 1967): 10.

75. Clara Gay, "President's Message," *Our National Family* (Dec. 1967): 3; *Our National Family* (June 1968): 21; *Our National Family* (Dec. 1967): 15; Baker, *Paradoxes of Desegregation,* 169–71; and *South Carolina Parent-Teacher,* December 1954, 5.

76. Clara Gay, "President's Message," *Our National Family* (March 1968): 3; and (June 1968): 3; Clara Gay, "Unity as We Disunite," *Our National Family* (Oct. 1968): 6; Clara Gay, "President's Message," *Our National Family* (Oct. 1968): 3; and Dot to Fan, n.d., Folder 47, Box 12, AUM; emphasis in original.

77. Rev. R. L. Hope to All Principals, Presidents, and Principals of PTA Council, White, October 1, 1969, Folder 47, Box 12, AUM.

78. Mrs. H. Eugene Gibbons to Dr. Cranford H. Burns, October 1969, Folder 7, Box 12, AUM. On the job losses teachers and principals faced, see Fultz, "The Displacement of Black Educators Post-*Brown.*"

79. Ethel Kight, "The Target—Aspiring for One World," *Our National Family* (March 1967): 4; Ethel Kight, "The Parent-Teacher Congress Serving as a Lighthouse," *Our National Family* (June 1968): 4; and *Our National Family* (June 1968): 10–12, 13, 14–16.

80. "Two Georgia Congresses Existing Side by Side," *Our Georgia Family* 29, no. 4 (1970): 10; and "President's Message," *Our Georgia Family* 29, no. 4 (1970): 3. See *Our National Family* (Sept. 1955), in which the Kansas Colored Congress votes to be dissolved (15) and Missouri's leaders are listed as members of a "dissolved" organization (17); and Narvie J. Harris, "Projecting," in GCCPT, *Golden Anniversary History,* 1969, 143.

81. Mrs. L. M. Gill to Mrs. W. O. Jones, March 14, 1970, Folder 47, Box 12; Mrs. W. O. Jones to Mrs. L. M. Gill, March 26, 1970, Folder 47, Box 12; and Mrs. W. O. Jones to Mrs. L. M. Gill, April 3, 1970, Folder 47, Box 12, AUM.

82. Alabama Congress of Colored Parents and Teachers, Proposed Resolutions, April 4, 1970, Folder 47, Box 12, AUM.

83. Alabama Congress of Parents and Teachers, Minutes, Pre-Convention Board of Managers' Meeting, April 22, 1970, Folder 48, Box 12, emphasis in original; and Alabama Congress of Parents and Teachers, "A Statement of Position," April 24, 1970, Folder 48, Box 12, AUM.

84. National Congress of Parents and Teachers, "Plan for Unification of the National Congress of Colored Parents and Teachers with the National Congress of Parents and Teachers," 1970, Folder 47, Box 12, ACPT Collection, AUM. All life members in the

NCCPT also were automatically made life members in the NCPT. See "Golden Anniversary Convention," *Our Georgia Family* 29, no. 4 (1970): 4.

85. Fultz, "African American Teachers in the South, 1890–1940: Powerlessness and the Ironies of Expectations and Protest," 421; and "National Congress of Colored Parents and Teachers Convene in Historic Convention," *Our Georgia Family* 29, no. 4 (1970): 7–8.

86. National PTA, "Convention Resolutions," *National PTA Bulletin,* Summer 1970, 2; National PTA News Release, June 22, 1970, Folder 47, Box 12, AUM; and "Two Georgia Congresses Existing Side by Side," *Our Georgia Family* 29, no. 4 (1970): 10. Another source claims that the PTA units in Texas and Arkansas desegregated in 1969.

87. Victoria Radaviche to L. M. Gill, September 4, 1970, Folder 47, Box 12; and Mrs. Wm. O. Jones to Mrs. L. M. Gill, September 5, 1970, Folder 47, Box 12, ACPT Collection, AUM. See also L. M. Gill to Mrs. Leon S. Price, August 28, 1970, Folder 47, Box 12, ACPT Collection, AUM.

88. L. M. Gill to Mrs. W. O. Jones, September 21, 1970, Folder 47, Box 12; L. M. Gill to District Presidents of the Alabama Congress of Colored Parents and Teachers, September 26, 1970, Folder 47, and Box 12; Mrs. William O. Jones to Mrs. Gill, October 7, 1970, Folder 47, Box 12, ACPT Collection, AUM. See also "Golden Anniversary Convention," *Our Georgia Family* 29, no. 4 (1970): 5. On the Virginia Colored Congress Parents and Teachers decision to retain its officers, called an "unprecedented move" by black PTA members, see *Our National Family* (March 1958): 12.

89. Mrs. L. M. Gill to Mrs. Leon S. Price, October 26, 1970, Folder 47, Box 12; and Mrs. Leon S. Price to Mrs. L. M. Gill, November 3, 1970, Folder 47, Box 12, ACPT Collection, AUM.

90. Charles S. Bullock III and Joseph Stewart, Jr., "The Justice Department and School Desegregation: The Importance of Developing Trust," *The Journal of Politics* 39, no. 4 (1977): 1043; Jones, "Desegregation and Social Reform since 1954," 165–70; Marian Wright Edelman, "Southern School Desegregation, 1954–1973: A Judicial-Political Overview," *Annals of the American Academy of Policy and Social Science* 407 (May 1973): 38–41; and Faustine C. Jones, "Ironies of School Desegregation," *Journal of Negro Education* 47, no 1 (1978): 9–10.

91. See Mrs. W. O. Jones to Mrs. L. M. Gill, January 14, 1971; Gill to Jones, January 17, 1971; and Gill to Jones, February 1, 1971, Folder 47, Box 12, ACPT Collection, AUM.

92. Gill to Jones, March 1, 1970, Folder 47, Box 12, ACPT Collection; and L. M. Gill to P.T.A. Co-Workers, February 5, 1971, Folder 47, Box 12, ACPT Collection, AUM.

93. L. M. Gill, "The President's Message," in Fifty-Seventh Annual Convention of the Alabama Congress of Colored Parents and Teachers," April 1971, Folder 22, Box 30; and Mrs. Harry Nelson, "Directions for the Continued Implementation of P.T.A. Work," ca. 1971, Folder 47, Box 12, ACPT Collection, AUM.

94. Gill to Jones, March 17, 1971, Folder 47, Box 12; and Mrs. William O. Jones to Mrs. C. G. Watkins, March 29, 1971, Folder 47, Box 12, ACPT Collection, AUM.

95. Mrs. Leon S. Price to Mrs. William O. Jones, April 5, 1971, Folder 47, Box 12; and L. M. Gill to Mrs. W. O. Jones, April 19, 1971, Folder 48, Box 12, ACPT Collection, AUM.

96. Clara Gay, "Unity—Our Challenge," *Our National Family* (Sept. 1967): 4; and Kight, "Joining Hands for World Peace," *Our National Family* (Sept. 1967): 5. The theme in this particular issue was the representation of African Americans in the newly united PTA.

97. Fultz, "Caught between a Rock and a Hard Place." See also Fairclough, *A Class of Their Own,* 411; and Walker, *Their Highest Potential,* especially chapter 7.

98. Minnie J. Hitch, "President's Message," *Our National Family* (June 1967): 3; and *Our National Family* (Oct. 1968): 6.

99. "National Congress of Colored Parents and Teachers Convene in Historic Convention," *Our Georgia Family* 29, no. 4 (1970): 8; and Harris and Taylor, *African-American Education in DeKalb County*, 32–33. The Narvie Harris Traditional Theme School in DeKalb County is her legacy, and one of its guiding principles is parental and community involvement. See http://www.dekalb.k12.ga.us/narvieharris/.

100. South Carolina Congress of Parents and Teachers, "Fiftieth Anniversary Celebration: South Carolina Congress of Parents and Teachers," April 27–28, 1973; Folder 35, Box 1, National Congress of Parents and Teachers, 1952–1973, Eunice Harper Leonard Papers, South Caroliniana Library, USC.

Epilogue

1. Beatrice Moore Morgan, "President's Message," *Our National Family* (Feb. 1951): 3.

2. "Plan for Unification of the National Congress of Colored Parents and Teachers with the National Congress of Parents and Teachers," 1970, Folder 47, Box 12, AUM.

3. On the assumption of finding what one is looking for, see Joan Burstyn, "History as Image: Changing the Lens," *History of Education Quarterly* 27, no. 2 (1987): 166–80. On sentimentalization of black educators in the history of education, see Thomas V. O'Brien, "Perils of Accommodation: The Case of Joseph W. Holley," *American Educational Research Journal* 44, no. 4 (2007): 806–52. O'Brien writes, "Black women and men [school] founders are often presented as savvy, courageous fighters who consistently outwitted their oppressors" (807).

WORKS CITED

Theses and Dissertations

Buchholz, Corrina A. "The Ruffin Incident and Other Integration Battles in Women's Clubs, 1890–1920." Master's thesis, Sarah Lawrence College, 2000.

Cowing, W. Thornton. "An Evaluation of a Parent Teacher Association." Master's thesis, Massachusetts State College, 1933.

Crehan, Anne M. "The Parent-Teacher Association in the Buffalo Public Schools." Master's thesis, Canisius College, 1948.

Fermoile, Margaret L. "A History of the Parent Teacher Association in Amherst [NY] #18 and Its Contribution to the School and the Community." EdM thesis, Canisius College, 1948.

Keenan, Claudia. "PTA Business: A Cultural History of How Suburban Women Supported the Public Schools, 1920–1960." PhD diss., New York University, 2002.

Montgomery, Bishop Marteinne. "The Activities of Parent-Teacher Associations in the Negro Schools of Alabama." Master's thesis, University of Chicago, 1940.

Nasstrom, Kathryn L. "Women, the Civil Rights Movement, and the Politics of Historical Memory in Atlanta, 1946–1973." PhD diss., University of North Carolina–Chapel Hill, 1993.

Rota, Tiziana. "Between 'True Women' and 'New Women': Mount Holyoke Students, 1837 to 1908." PhD diss., University of Massachusetts, 1983.

Shivery, Louie D. "The History of Organized Social Work among Negroes in Atlanta, 1890–1935." Master's thesis, Atlanta University, 1936.

Taylor, Marguerite Smith. "Evaluation of the Program of the Colored Parent-Teachers Association in Missouri." Master's thesis, Lincoln University, August 1954.

Published Works

Almond, Gabriel A., and Sidney Verba. *The Civic Culture: Political Attitudes and Democracy in Five Nations.* Princeton, NJ: Princeton University Press, 1963.

Alpern, Sara, Joyce Antler, Elisabeth Israels Perry, and Ingrid Winther Scobie. *The Challenge of Feminist Biography: Writing the Lives of Modern American Women.* Urbana: University of Illinois Press, 1992.

Anderson, Eric, and Alfred Moss. *Dangerous Donations. Northern Philanthropy and Southern Black Education, 1902–1930.* Columbia: The University of Missouri Press, 1999.

Anderson, James D. *The Education of Blacks in the South, 1860–1935.* Chapel Hill: University of North Carolina Press, 1988.

Angus, David L., and Jeffrey E. Mirel. *The Failed Promise of the American High School, 1890–1955.* New York: Teachers College Press, 1999.

Antler, Joyce. "'After College, What?': New Graduates and the Family Claim." *American Quarterly* 32 (Fall 1980): 409–34.

Arlitt, Ada Hart. *Parent Education Guidebook.* Chicago: National Congress of Parents and Teachers, 1937.

Baker, Paula. "The Domestication of Politics: Women and American Political Society, 1780–1920." *American Historical Review* 89, no. 3 (1984): 620–47.

Baker, R. Scott. *Paradoxes of Desegregation: African American Struggles for Educational Equity in Charleston, South Carolina, 1926–1972.* Columbia: University of South Carolina Press, 2006.

Barth, Gunther. *City People: The Rise of Modern City Culture in Nineteenth Century America.* New York: Oxford University Press, 1980.

Bartlett, Irving H. *The American Mind in the Mid-Nineteenth Century,* second edition. Arlington Heights, IL: Harlan Davidson, Inc., 1982.

Bartley, Numan V. *The Rise of Massive Resistance: Race and Politics in the South during the 1950s.* Baton Rouge: Louisiana State University Press, 1969.

Beard, Mary Ritter. *Woman's Work in Municipalities.* New York: D. Appleton and Company, 1915. New York: Arno Press, 1972.

Beatty, Barbara. *Preschool Education in America: The Culture of Young Children from the Colonial Era to the Present.* New Haven, CT: Yale University Press, 1995.

Beatty, Barbara, Emily D. Cahan, and Julia Grant, eds. *When Science Encounters the Child: Education, Parenting, and Child Welfare in 20th Century America.* New York: Teachers College Press, 2006.

Bellah, Robert N., Richard Madsen, William M. Sullivan, Ann Swidler, and Steven M. Tipton. *Habits of the Heart: Individualism and Commitment in American Life.* Berkeley: University of California Press, [1985], 1996.

Bernhard, Virginia, Betty Brandon, Elizabeth Fox-Genovese, and Theda Purdue, eds. *Southern Women: Histories and Identities.* Columbia: University of Missouri Press, 1992.

Birney, Alice McLellan. "The Twentieth Century Girl: What We Expect of Her." *Harper's Bazaar* (May 26, 1900): 224–27.

Birney, Mrs. Theodore W. "Address of Welcome." *The Work and Words of the National Congress of Mothers (First Annual Session),* 7. New York: D. Appleton and Company, 1897.

———. "Scope and Aims of the National Congress of Mothers." *Mothers' Magazine* 1, no. 1 (1898): 1–21.

———. "Address of Welcome." *National Congress of Mothers Third Annual Convention,* 198. Philadelphia: Geo. F. Lasher, Printer and Binder, 1899.

———. "The Power of Organized Motherhood to Benefit Humanity." *Quarterly Report* 1, no. 1 (1900): 29–35.

Blair, Karen. *The Clubwoman as Feminist: True Womanhood Redefined, 1868–1914.* New York: Holmes and Meier Publishers, Inc., 1980.

Blocker, Jack S. *"Give to the Winds Thy Fears": The Women's Temperance Crusade, 1873–1874.* Westport, CT: Greenwood Press, 1985.

Blount, Jackie M. "Ella Flagg Young and the Chicago Schools." In *Founding Mothers and Others: Women Educational Leaders during the Progressive Era,* edited by Alan R. Sadovnik and Susan F. Semel, 163–76. New York: Palgrave, 2002.

Bond, Horace Mann. *Negro Education in Alabama: A Study in Cotton and Steel.* New York: Atheneum, [1939], 1969.

Bordin, Ruth. *Frances Willard: A Biography.* Chapel Hill: University of North Carolina Press, 1986.

———. *Woman and Temperance: The Quest for Power and Liberty, 1873–1900.* Philadelphia: Temple University Press, 1981.

Bourdieu, Pierre. "The Forms of Capital." In *Handbook of Theory and Research for the Sociology of Education,* edited by John Richardson, 241–58. New York: Greenwood Press, 1986.

Box, Leroy F. *Laws Relating to the Public School System of Alabama.* Montgomery, AL: Barrett and Brown, 1878.

Breen, William J. *Uncle Sam at Home: Civilian Mobilization, Wartime Federalism, and the Council of National Defense, 1917–1919.* Westport, CT: Greenwood Press, 1984.

Brock, William R. *Welfare, Democracy, and the New Deal.* Cambridge: Cambridge University Press, 1988.

Buchanan, Linda R., and Philo A. Hutcheson. "Reconsidering the Washington-Du Bois Debate: Two Black Colleges in 1910–1911." In *Essays in Twentieth-Century Southern Education: Exceptionalism and Its Limits,* edited by Wayne J. Urban, 77–99. New York: Garland Publishing, Inc., 1999.

Bullock, Charles S., III, and Joseph Stewart, Jr. "The Justice Department and School Desegregation: The Importance of Developing Trust." *The Journal of Politics* 39, no. 4 (1977): 1036–43.

Burstyn, Joan. "History as Image: Changing the Lens," *History of Education Quarterly* 27, no. 2 (1987): 166–80.

Butchart, Ronald. *Northern Schools, Southern Blacks, and Reconstruction: Freedman's Education, 1862–1875.* Westport, CT: Greenwood Press, 1980.

Butterworth, Julian. *The Parent-Teacher Association and Its Work.* New York: Macmillan, 1928.

Butts, R. Freeman. "Historical Perspective on Citizenship Education in the United States." In *Education for Responsible Citizenship,* National Task Force on Citizenship Education, 47–68. St. Louis, MO: Institute for Development of Educational Activities, 1977.

Calhoun, Charles W., ed. *The Gilded Age: Perspectives on the Origins of Modern America.* Lanham, MD: Rowman & Littlefield, Publishers, 2007.

Callejo-Pérez, David M. *Southern Hospitality: Identity, Schools, and the Civil Rights Movement in Mississippi, 1964–1972.* New York: Peter Lang Publishers, 2001.

Cashman, Sean D. *America in the Gilded Age: From the Death of Lincoln to the Rise of Theodore Roosevelt.* New York: New York University Press, 1993.

Cecelski, David S. *Along Freedom Road: Hyde County, North Carolina, and the Fate of Black Schools in the South.* Chapel Hill: University of North Carolina Press, 1994.

Clemens, Elisabeth S. *The People's Lobby: Organizational Innovation and the Rise of Interest*

Group Politics in the United States, 1890–1925. Chicago: University of Chicago Press, 1997.

Clifford, Geraldine Jonçich. "Home and School in 19th Century America: Some Personal-History Reports from the United States." *History of Education Quarterly* (Spring 1978): 3–34.

Coleman, A. Lee. "Desegregation of the Public Schools in Kentucky—The Second Year after the Supreme Court's Decision." *Journal of Negro Education* 25, no. 3 (1956): 254–61.

Coleman, James S. "Social Capital in the Creation of Human Capital." *The American Journal of Sociology* 94, Supplement: Organizations and Institutions: Sociological and Economic Approaches to the Analysis of Social Structure (1988): S95–120.

———. *Foundations of Social Theory.* Cambridge, MA: Harvard University Press, 1990.

Coleman, Kenneth, ed. *A History of Georgia.* Athens: University of Georgia Press, 1977.

Collins, Patricia Hill. "The Social Construction of Black Feminist Thought." *Signs* 14, no. 4 (1989): 745–73.

Commission on the Reorganization of Secondary Education. *Cardinal Principles of Secondary Education,* Bulletin 1918, no. 35, Department of the Interior, Bureau of Education. Washington, DC: U.S. Government Printing Office, 1918.

Cook, Lloyd Allen. "Intergroup Education." *Review of Education Research* 17, no. 4 (1947): 266–78.

Cooper, Anna Julia. *A Voice from the South: By a Black Woman of the South.* Xenia, OH: Aldine Printing House, 1892.

Cott, Nancy F. *The Grounding of Modern Feminism.* New Haven, CT: Yale University Press, 1987.

Cott, Nancy F., Jeanne Boydston, Ann Braude, Lori Ginzberg, and Molly Ladd-Taylor, eds. *Root of Bitterness: Documents of the Social History of American Women.* Boston: Northeastern University Press, 1996.

Cowan, Ruth Schwartz. *More Work for Mother: The Ironies of Household Technology from the Open Hearth to the Microwave.* New York: Basic Books, 1983.

Crawford, Susan, and Peggy Levitt. "Social Change and Civic Engagement: The Case of the PTA." In *Civic Engagement in American Democracy,* edited by Theda Skocpol and Morris P. Fiorina, 249–96. Washington, DC: Brookings Institution Press, 1999.

Cremin, Lawrence A. "Family and Community Linkages in American Education: Some Comments on the Recent Historiography." *Teachers College Record* 79 (May 1978): 683–704.

Croly, Jane Cunningham. *The History of the Women's Club Movement in America.* New York: Henry G. Allen, 1898.

"Cultural Capital and African American Education," *Journal of African American History* 87 (Spring 2002).

Cutler, William W., III. *Parents and Schools: The 150-Year Struggle for Control in Education.* Chicago: University of Chicago Press, 2000.

Davis, Angela Y. *Women, Race, and Class.* New York: Vintage Books, 1983.

Davis, Elizabeth Lindsay. *Lifting as They Climb.* New York: G. K. Hall & Co., [1933], 1996.

Davis, O. L. "Rachel Davis DuBois: Intercultural Education Pioneer." In *"Bending the Future to Their Will": Civic Women, Social Education, and Democracy,* edited by Margaret Smith Crocco and O. L. Davis, Jr., 169–84. Lanham, MD: Rowman & Littlefield Publishers, 1999.

Deegan, Mary Jo, ed. *The New Woman of Color: The Collected Writings of Fannie Barrier Williams, 1893-1918.* DeKalb: Northern Illinois University Press, 2002.

Demolins, Edmond. *Anglo-Saxon Supremacy: To What It is Due,* Translated by Louis Bert. Lavigne. New York: Fenno, 1898.

Dorn, Charles. "'The World's Schoolmaster': Educational Reconstruction, Grayson Kefauver, and the Founding of UNESCO, 1942-1946." *History of Education* 35, no. 3 (2006): 297-320.

DuBois, Rachel Davis. *All This and Something More: Pioneering in Intercultural Education.* Bryn Mawr, PA: Dorrance & Company, Inc., 1984.

———. *The Art of Group Conversation: A New Breakthrough in Social Communication.* New York: Association Press, 1963.

Du Bois, W. E. B. *The Souls of Black Folk: Essays and Sketches.* Chicago: A. G. McClurg, 1903.

———. *The Autobiography of W. E. B. Du Bois: A Soliloquy on Viewing My Life from the Last Decade of Its First Century.* New York: International Publishers, 1968.

Edelman, Marian Wright. "Southern School Desegregation, 1954-1973: A Judicial-Political Overview." *Annals of the American Academy of Policy and Social Science* 407 (May 1973): 32-42.

Edwards, Bob, and Michael W. Foley. "Civil Society and Social Capital." In *Beyond Tocqueville: Civil Society and the Social Capital Debate in Comparative Perspective,* edited by Bob Edwards, Michael W. Foley, and Mario Diani, 1-16. Hanover, NH: University Press of New England, 2001.

Ehrenreich, Barbara, and Deirdre English. *For Her Own Good: 150 Years of the Experts' Advice to Women.* Garden City, NY: Anchor Press, 1978.

Eisenmann, Linda. "Reconsidering a Classic: Assessing the History of Women's Higher Education a Dozen Years after Barbara Solomon." *Harvard Educational Review* 67, no. 4 (1997): 689-717.

———, ed. *Historical Dictionary of Women's Education in the United States.* Westport, CT: Greenwood Press, 1998.

Eliot, Charles W. "Introduction." In *Essays on Education, etc. by Herbert Spencer.* New York: E. P. Dutton & Co., Inc., [1911], 1949.

Fairclough, Adam. "'Being in the Field of Education and Also Being a Negro . . . Seems Tragic': Black Teachers in the Jim Crow South." *Journal of American History* no. 1 (June 2000): 65-91.

———. *Teaching Equality: Black Schools in the Age of Jim Crow.* Athens, GA: University of Georgia Press, 2001.

———. "The Costs of *Brown:* Black Teachers and School Integration." *The Journal of American History* 91, no. 1 (2004): 43-55.

———. *A Class of Their Own: Black Teachers in the Segregated South.* Cambridge, MA: The Belknap Press of Harvard University Press, 2007.

Farnham, Christine Anne. *The Education of the Southern Belle: Higher Education and Student Socialization in the Antebellum South.* New York: New York University Press, 1994.

Fields, Mamie Garvin, with Karen Fields. *Lemon Swamp and Other Places: A Carolina Memoir.* New York: Free Press, 1983.

Finkelstein, Barbara J. "Schooling and Schoolteachers: Selected Bibliography of Autobiographies in the Nineteenth Century." *History of Education Quarterly* 14 (Summer 1974): 293-300.

————. "In Fear of Childhood: Relationships between Parents and Teachers in Popular Primary Schools in the Nineteenth Century." *History of Childhood Quarterly* 3 (Winter 1976): 321–35.

Fischer, Gayle V. "'Pantalets' and 'Turkish Trousers': Designing Freedom in the Mid-Nineteenth Century United States." *Feminist Studies* 23, no. 1 (1997): 110–40.

————. *Pantaloons and Power: A Nineteenth Century Dress Reform in the United States.* Kent, OH: Kent State University Press, 2001.

Franklin, V. P. *Black Self-Determination: A Cultural History of African-American Resistance.* Brooklyn, NY: Lawrence Hill Books, 1992.

————. "Introduction: Cultural Capital and African American Education." Special issue, *Journal of African American History* (Spring 2002): 175–81.

————. *Cultural Capital and Black Education: African American Communities and the Funding of Black Schools.* Greenwich, CT: Information Age Publishing, 2004.

Fraser, Walter J., R. Frank Saunders, Jr., and Jon L. Wakely, eds. *The Web of Southern Social Relations: Women, Family, and Education.* Athens: University of Georgia Press, 1985.

Fuchs, Eckhardt. "Educational Sciences, Morality and Politics: International Educational Congresses in the Early Twentieth Century." *Paedagogica Historica* 40, nos. 5–6 (2004): 757–84.

Fultz, Michael. "African-American Teachers in the South, 1890–1940: Growth, Feminization, and Salary Discrimination." *Teachers College Record* 96, no. 3 (1995): 544–68.

————. "African American Teachers in the South, 1890–1940: Powerlessness and the Ironies of Expectation and Protest." *History of Education Quarterly* 35, no. 4 (1995): 401–22.

————. "The Displacement of Black Educators Post-*Brown*: An Overview and Analysis." *History of Education Quarterly* 44, no. 1 (2004): 11–45.

————. "Caught between a Rock and a Hard Place," unpublished paper presented at the American Educational Research Association's annual meeting, Chicago, Illinois, April 2007.

Gamm, Gerald, and Robert D. Putnam. "The Growth of Voluntary Associations in America, 1840–1940." *Journal of Interdisciplinary History* 29, no. 3 (1999): 511–57.

Gere, Anne Ruggles. *Intimate Practices: Literacy and Cultural Work in U.S. Women's Clubs, 1880–1920.* Urbana: University of Illinois Press, 1997.

Giddings, Paula. *When and Where I Enter: The Impact of Black Women on Race and Sex in America.* New York: Bantam Books, 1984.

Gill, Peggy B. "Community, Commitment, and African American Education: The Jackson School of Smith County, Texas, 1925–1954." *Journal of African American History* (Spring 2002): 256–68.

Gilmore, Glenda Elizabeth. *Gender and Jim Crow: Women and the Politics of White Supremacy in North Carolina, 1896–1920.* Chapel Hill: University of North Carolina Press, 1996.

Gold, Kenneth M. *School's In: The History of Summer Education in American Public Schools.* New York: Peter Lang Publishers, 2002.

Gordon, Anna. *The Beautiful Life of Frances E. Willard.* Chicago: Woman's Temperance Publishing Association, 1898.

Gordon, Linda. *Pitied But Not Entitled: Single Mothers and the History of Welfare, 1890–1935.* New York: The Free Press, 1994.

Gordon, Lynn D. "Race, Class, and the Bonds of Womanhood at Spelman Seminary, 1881–1923." *History of Higher Education Annual* 9 (1989): 7–32.

Gordon, William M. "The Implementation of Desegregation Plans since *Brown.*" *Journal of Negro Education* 63, no. 3 (1994): 310–22.

Gorrell, Donald K. *The Age of Social Responsibility: The Social Gospel in the Progressive Era, 1900–1920.* Macon, GA: Mercer University Press, 1988.

Gould, Joseph E. *The Chautauqua Movement: An Episode in the Continuing American Revolution.* New York: State University of New York, 1961.

Granovetter, Mark S. "The Strength of Weak Ties." *The American Journal of Sociology* 78, no. 6 (1973): 1360–80.

———. "The Strength of Weak Ties: A Network Theory Revisited." *Sociological Theory* 1 (1983): 201–33.

Grant, Julia. *Raising Baby by the Book: The Education of American Mothers, 1890–1960.* New Haven, CT: Yale University Press, 1998.

Green, Elizabeth Alden. *Mary Lyon and Mount Holyoke: Opening the Gates.* Hanover, NH: University Press of New England, 1979.

Haney, James E. "The Effects of the *Brown* Decision on Black Educators." *Journal of Negro Education* 47, no. 1 (1978): 88–95.

Harlan, Louis R. *Booker T. Washington: The Making of a Black Leader, 1856–1901,* vol. 1. New York: Oxford University Press, 1972.

———. *Booker T. Washington: The Wizard of Tuskegee, 1901–1915,* vol. 2. New York: Oxford University Press, 1983.

Harris, Narvie J., and Dee Taylor. *African-American Education in DeKalb County: From the Collection of Narvie J. Harris.* Charleston, SC: Arcadia Publishing, 1999.

Harrison, Harry P. *Culture under Canvas: The Story of Tent Chautauqua.* Westport, CT: Greenwood Press, 1978.

Heilbrun, Carolyn. *Writing a Woman's Life.* New York: W. W. Norton, 1988.

Hein, Virginia H. "The Image of 'A City Too Busy to Hate': Atlanta in the 1960s." *Phylon* 33 (Third Quarter, 1972): 205–21.

Higginbotham, Evelyn Brooks. *Righteous Discontent: The Women's Movement in the Black Baptist Church, 1880–1920.* Cambridge, MA: Harvard University Press, 1993.

Hill, Ruth Edmonds, ed. *The Black Women Oral History Project: From the Arthur and Elizabeth Schlesinger Library on the History of Women in America.* Westport, CT: Meckler, 1991.

Hine, Darlene Clark, Elsa Barkley Brown, and Rosalyn Terborg-Penn, eds. *Black Women in America,* vol. 1. Bloomington: Indiana University Press, 1993.

Hine, Darlene Clark, and Kathleen Thompson. *A Shining Thread of Hope: The History of Black Women in America.* New York: Broadway Books, 1998.

Hoffschwelle, Mary S. *Rebuilding the Rural Southern Community: Reformers, Schools, and Homes in Tennessee, 1900–1930.* Knoxville: University of Tennessee Press, 1998.

———. "'Better Homes on Better Farms': Domestic Reform in Rural Tennessee." *Frontiers: A Journal of Women's Studies* 22, no. 1 (2001): 51–73.

———. *The Rosenwald Schools of the American South.* Gainesville: University Press of Florida, 2006.

Hofstadter, Richard. *Social Darwinism in American Thought.* Boston: Beacon Press, 1955.

Holbeck, Elmer. *An Analysis of the Activities and Potentialities for Achievement of the Parent-Teacher Association with Recommendations.* New York: Teachers College Bureau of Publications, 1934.

Hollinger, David A. *In the American Province: Studies in the History and Historiography of Ideas.* Baltimore: Johns Hopkins University Press, 1989.

Hope, John. "Trends in Patterns of Race Relations in the South since May 17, 1954." *Phylon* 17, no. 2 (1956): 103–18.

Hopkins, Charles Howard. *The Rise of the Social Gospel in American Protestantism, 1865–1915.* New Haven, CT: Yale University Press, 1940.

Hornsby, Jr., Alton. "A City That Was Too Busy to Hate: Atlanta Businessmen and Desegregation." In *Southern Businessmen and Desegregation,* edited by Elizabeth Jacoway and David R. Colburn, 120–36. Baton Rouge: Louisiana State University Press, 1981.

Horowitz, H. W., and K. L. Karst. *Law, Lawyers, and Social Change.* Indianapolis, IN: Bobbs-Merrill, 1969.

Iowa Congress of Parents and Teachers [ICPT]. *A History of the Iowa Congress of Parents and Teachers, 1900–1941.* Des Moines: Iowa Congress of Parents and Teachers, n.d.

James, Edward T., Janet Wilson James, and Paul S. Boyer, eds. *Notable American Women: A Biograpical Dictionay,* vol. I. Cambridge, MA: The Belknap Press of Harvard University Press, 1971.

John, Richard R. *Spreading the News: The American Postal System from Franklin to Morse.* Cambridge, MA: Harvard University Press, 1995.

Johnson, Joan Marie. *Southern Ladies, New Women: Race, Region, and Clubwomen in South Carolina, 1890–1930.* Gainsville: University of Florida Press, 2004.

———. "Job Market or Marriage Market? Life Choices for Southern Women Educated at Northern Colleges, 1875–1915." *History of Education Quarterly* 47, no. 2 (2007): 149–72.

Jones, Beverly Washington. *Quest for Equality: The Life and Writings of Mary Eliza Church Terrell, 1863–1954.* Brooklyn, NY: Carlson Publishing, 1990.

Jones, Faustine C. "Ironies of School Desegregation." *Journal of Negro Education* 47, no. 1 (1978): 2–27.

Jones, Jacqueline. *Soldiers of Light and Love: Northern Teachers and Georgia Blacks, 1865–1873.* Chapel Hill: University of North Carolina Press, 1980.

———. *Labor of Love, Labor of Sorrow: Black Women, Work, and the Family from Slavery to the Present.* New York: Basic Books, Inc., 1985.

Jones, Leon. "Desegregation and Social Reform since 1954." *Journal of Negro Education* 43, no. 2 (1974): 155–71.

Jones, Lewis W. "Two Years of Desegregation in Alabama." *Journal of Negro Education* 25, no. 3 (1956): 205–11.

Kallen, Horace. *Culture and Democracy in the United States.* New York: Arno, [1924], 1970.

Karpinski, Carol F. *"A Visible Company of Professionals": African Americans and the National Education Association during the Civil Rights Movement.* New York: Peter Lang, 2008.

Keenan, Claudia. "The Suburban PTA and the Good Life." In *The Educational Work of Women's Organizations, 1890–1960,* edited by Anne Meis Knupfer and Christine Woyshner, 235–50. New York: Palgrave-Macmillan, 2008.

Kelley, Robin D. G. "'We Are Not What We Seem': Rethinking Black Working-Class Opposition in the Jim Crow South," *Journal of American History* 80, no. 1 (1993): 76, 78.

Kerber, Linda K. "Separate Spheres, Female Worlds, and Woman's Place: The Rhetoric of Women's History." Reprinted in *History of Women in the United States,* xx–xx. New York: K. G. Saur, 1992.

Kesselman, Amy. "The 'Freedom Suit': Feminism and Dress Reform in the United States, 1848–1975." *Gender and Society* 5, no. 4 (1991): 495–510.

Kliebard, Herbert M. *The Struggle for the American Curriculum, 1893–1958.* Boston: Routledge and Keegan Paul, 1986.

———. *Forging the American Curriculum: Essays in Curriculum History and Theory.* New York: Routledge, 1992.

———. *Schooled to Work: Vocationalism and the American Curriculum, 1876–1946.* New York: Teachers College Press, 1999.

Kluger, Richard. *Simple Justice: The History of* Brown v. Board of Education *and Black America's Struggle for Equality.* New York: Alfred A. Knopf, 1976.

Kohlstedt, Sally Gregory. "'A Better Crop of Boys and Girls': The School Gardening Movement, 1890–1920." *History of Education Quarterly* 48, no. 1 (2008): 58–93.

Koven, Seth, and Sonya Michel, eds. *Mothers of a New World: Maternalist Politics and the Origins of Welfare States.* New York: Routledge, 1993.

Knupfer, Anne Meis. *Toward a Tenderer Humanity and a Nobler Womanhood: African American Women's Clubs in Turn-of-the-Century Chicago.* New York: New York University Press, 1996.

Krug, Edward A. *The Secondary School Curriculum.* New York: Harper Brothers, 1960.

Ladd-Taylor, Molly. *Mother-Work: Women, Child Welfare and the State, 1890–1930.* Urbana: University of Illinois Press, 1993.

———. "Toward Defining Maternalism in US History." *Journal of Women's History* 5, no. 2 (1993): 110–13.

Lasch-Quinn, Elisabeth. *Black Neighbors: Race and the Limits of Reform in the American Settlement House Movement, 1890–1945.* Chapel Hill: University of North Carolina Press, 1993.

Lattimore, Florence. *A Palace of Delight (The Locust Street Settlement for Negroes in Hampton, Virginia).* Hampton, VA: Press of the Hampton Normal and Agricultural Institute, 1915.

Lawson, Steven F. *Black Ballots: Voting Rights in the South, 1944–1969.* New York: Columbia University Press, 1976.

Leloudis, James L. "School Reform in the New South: The Woman's Association for the Betterment of Public School Houses in North Carolina, 1902–1919." *The Journal of American History* 69, no. 4 (1983): 886–909.

———. *Schooling the New South: Pedagogy, Self, and Society in North Carolina, 1880–1920.* Chapel Hill: University of North Carolina Press, 1996.

Lerner, Gerda, ed. *Black Women in White America: A Documentary History.* New York: Vintage Books, 1972.

———. "Community Work of Black Club Women." In *The Majority Finds Its Past,* 93. New York: Oxford University Press, 1979.

———. *The Majority Finds Its Past.* New York: Oxford University Press, 1979.

Lewis, David L. *W. E. B. Du Bois: Biography of a Race, 1868–1919.* New York: Henry Holt, 1993.

Littlefield, Valinda. "A Yearly Contract with Everybody and His Brother: Durham County, North Carolina Black Female Public School Teachers, 1885–1927." *Journal of Negro History* 79, no. 1 (1994): 37–53.

———. "'To Do the Next Needed Thing': Jeanes Teachers in the Southern United States, 1908–1934." In *Telling Women's Lives: Narrative Inquiries in the History of Women's Education,* edited by Kathleen Weiler and Sue Middleton, 130–46. Philadelphia: Open University Press, 1999.

Locust Street Settlement: Founded and Managed by Colored People. Hampton, VA: Press of the Hampton Normal and Agricultural Institute, 1912.

Logan, Rayford W. *The Negro in American Life and Thought: The Nadir, 1877–1901.* New York: Dial Press, 1954.

Lowe, Robert. "Retrospective: Richard Kluger's *Simple Justice* after 29 Years." *History of Education Quarterly* 44, no. 1 (2004): 125–32.

Malone, Dumas, ed. *Dictionary of American Biography,* vol. 2. New York: Charles Scribner's Sons, 1933.

Martin, Theodora Penny. *The Sound of Our Own Voices: Women's Study Clubs, 1860–1910.* Boston: Beacon Press, 1987.

Mason, Martha Sprague, ed. *Parents and Teacher: A Survey of Organized Cooperation of Home, School, and Community.* Boston: Ginn and Company, 1928.

McCarthy, Kathleen D. *Lady Bountiful Revisited: Women, Philanthropy, and Power.* New Brunswick, NJ: Rutgers University Press, 1990.

McClellan, B. Edward. *Moral Education in America: Schools and the Shaping of Character from Colonial Times to the Present.* New York: Teachers College Press, 1999.

McMillen, Neil R. *The Citizens' Council: Organized Resistance to the Second Reconstruction, 1954–1964.* Chicago: University of Chicago Press, 1971.

McPherson, James M. *The Abolitionist Legacy: From Reconstruction to the NAACP.* Princeton, NJ: Princeton University Press, 1975.

Meier, August. *Negro Thought in America, 1880–1915: Racial Ideologies in the Age of Booker T. Washington.* Ann Arbor: University of Michigan Press, 1963.

Menchan, W. McKinley. "Adult Education Programs of Negro Parent-Teacher Associations." *Journal of Negro Education* 14, no. 3 (1945): 412–17.

Millard, Janet M. "Alice McLellan Birney." *A Woman's Place: 52 Women of Cobb County, Georgia, 1850–1981.* Marietta: Cobb Marietta Girls' Club, 1981.

Mirel, Jeffrey. "Civic Education and Changing Definitions of American Identity, 1900–1950." *Educational Review* 54, no. 2 (2002): 143–52.

Montalto, Nicholas V. *A History of the Intercultural Educational Movement, 1924–1941.* New York: Garland Publishing, 1982.

Morris, Eddie W. "Facts and Factors of Faculty Desegregation in Kentucky, 1955–1965." *Journal of Negro Education* 36, no. 1 (1967): 75–77.

Morris, Robert C. *Reading, 'Riting, and Reconstruction: The Education of the Freedmen in the South, 1861–1870.* Chicago: University of Chicago Press: 1981.

Morris, Vivian Gunn, and Curtis L. Morris. *The Price They Paid: Desegregation in an African American Community.* New York: Teachers College Press, 2002.

"Mrs. Theodore Weld Birney: An Editorial Sketch." *Coming Age* 2, no. 3 (1899): 247. Harvard University Widener Library.

Muncy, Robyn L. *Creating a Female Dominion in American Reform 1890–1935.* New York: Oxford University Press, 1991.

NASC Interim History Writing Committee. *The Jeanes Story: A Chapter in the History of American Education, 1908–1968.* Atlanta, GA: Southern Education Foundation, 1979.

Nash, Margaret A. "'Patient Persistence': The Political and Educational Values of Anna Julia Cooper and Mary Church Terrell." *Educational Studies* 35, no. 2 (2004): 122–36.

———. *Women's Education in the United States, 1780–1840.* New York: Palgrave Macmillan, 2005.

National Congress of Colored Parents and Teachers [NCCPT]. *Coral Anniversary: History of the National Congress of Colored Parents and Teachers.* Dover, DE: NCCPT, 1961.

National Congress of Mothers [NCM]. *The Work and Words of the National Congress of Mothers (First Annual Session).* New York: D. Appleton and Company, 1897.

————. *The Child in Home, School, and State: Report of the National Congress of Mothers.* Washington, DC: NCM, 1905.

National Congress of Parents and Teachers [NCPT]. *Through the Years: From the Scrapbook of Mrs. Mears.* Washington, DC: National Congress of Parents and Teachers, 1932.

————. *A New Force in Education.* Baltimore: The Lord Baltimore Press, 1929.

————. *Golden Jubilee History, 1897–1947.* Chicago: National Congress of Parents and Teachers, 1947.

————. *The Rural PTA: Suggestions for Organizing and Conducting a Parent-Teacher Association.* Washington, DC: NCPT, 1935.

National PTA [NCPT]. *The PTA Story: A Century of Commitment to Children.* Chicago: National PTA, 1997.

Neverdon-Morton, Cynthia. *Afro-American Women of the South and the Advancement of the Race.* Knoxville: University of Tennessee Press, 1989.

Nieman, Donald, ed. *African Americans and Education in the South, 1865–1900.* New York: Garland Publishing, Inc., 1994.

O'Brien, Thomas V. "Perils of Accommodation: The Case of Joseph W. Holley." *American Educational Research Journal* 44, no. 4 (2007): 806–52.

Orfield, Gary. *The Reconstruction of Southern Education: The Schools and the 1964 Civil Rights Act.* New York: Wiley-Interscience, 1969.

U.S. Census Bureau, "Thirteenth Census of the United States: 1910," vol. 4.

Overstreet, Harry, and Bonaro Overstreet. *Where Children Come First: A Study of the P.T.A. Idea.* Chicago: National Congress of Parents and Teachers, 1949.

Patterson, Martha H. *Beyond the Gibson Girl: Reimagining the American New Woman.* Urbana: University of Illinois Press, 2005.

Paul, Redman Wilson. "Phoebe Apperson Hearst," in *Notable American Women: A Biographical Dictionary,* vol. II, ed. Edward T. James, Janet Wilson James, and Paul A. Boyer. Cambridge, MA: The Belknap Press of Harvard University Press, 1971.

Pennsylvania Congress of Parents and Teachers. *History of the Pennsylvania State Congress of Parents and Teachers.* Philadelphia: Pennsylvania Congress of Parents and Teachers, n.d.

Perkins, Linda M. "The Role of Education in the Development of Black Feminist Thought, 1860–1920." *History of Education* 22, no. 3 (1993): 265–75.

Perry, Thelma D. *History of the American Teachers Association.* Washington, DC: National Education Association, 1975.

Pierce, Bessie Louise. *Public Opinion and the Teaching of History in the United States.* New York: Alfred A. Knopf, 1926.

Porterfield, Amanda. *Mary Lyon and the Mount Holyoke Missionaries.* New York: Oxford University Press, 1997.

Powdermaker, Hortense. *After Freedom: A Cultural Study in the Deep South.* New York: Russell & Russell, 1939, 1968.

Pratt, Norma Fain. "Rebekah Bettelheim Kohut," in *Notable American Women: The Modern Period,* ed. Barbara Sicherman and Carol Hurd Green, 403–4. Cambridge, MA: The Belknap Press of Harvard University Press, 1980.

Putnam, Robert D. *Bowling Alone: The Collapse and Revival of American Community.* New York: Simon & Schuster, 2000.

Ravitch, Diane. *The Troubled Crusade: American Education, 1945–1980.* New York: Basic Books, 1983.

Ravitch, Diane, and Joseph P. Viteritti, eds. *Making Good Citizens: Education and Civil Society*. New Haven, CT: Yale University Press, 2001.

Reese, William J. "Between Home and School: Organized Parents, Clubwomen, and Urban Education in the Progressive Era." *School Review* (November 1978): 3–28.

———. *Power and the Promise of School Reform: Grassroots Movements during the Progressive Era*. New York: Teachers College Press, [1986], 2002.

Reuben, Julie A. "Beyond Politics: Community Civics and the Redefinition of Citizenship in the Progressive Era." *History of Education Quarterly* 37, no. 4 (1997): 399–420.

Richards, Janet T. "Reveille 1897: 'I Heard Them Promise.'" *National Parent-Teacher* 36, no. 6 (1942): 16–18.

Riley, Glenda. *Inventing the American Woman: An Inclusive History*, Part II. Wheeling, IL: Harlan Davidson, Inc., 1995.

Robert, Alice Birney. "Great-Grandmother Birney and I." *National Parent-Teacher* 54, no. 6 (1960): 12–13.

Rosenberg, Rosalind *Beyond Separate Spheres: Intellectual Roots of Modern Feminism*. New Haven, CT: Yale University Press, 1982.

Rosenthal, Jonas O. "Negro Teachers' Attitudes toward Desegregation." *Journal of Negro Education* 26, no. 1 (1957): 63–71.

Ross, Dorothy. *G. Stanley Hall: The Psychologist as Prophet*. Chicago: University of Chicago Press, 1972.

Roth, Darlene Rebecca. *Matronage: Patterns in Women's Organizations, Atlanta, Georgia, 1890–1940*. Brooklyn, NY: Carlson Publishing, Inc., 1994.

Rothman, Sheila M. *Woman's Proper Place: A History of Changing Ideals and Practices, 1870 to the Present*. New York: Basic Books, 1978.

Rouse, Jacqueline Ann. *Lugenia Burns Hope: Black Southern Reformer*. Athens: University of Georgia Press, 1989.

———. "Atlanta's African-American Women's Attack on Segregation, 1900–1920." In *Gender, Class, Race & Reform in the Progressive Era*, edited by Noralee Frankel and Nancy S. Dye, 10–23. Lexington: University Press of Kentucky, 1991.

Rugg, Winifred King. "The Founding of the Congress." *National Parent-Teacher* 29, no. 5 (1935): 13–15, 35.

Rury, John L. *Education and Social Change: Themes in the History of American Schooling*. Mahwah, NJ: Lawrence Erlbaum Associates, 2002.

Russett, Cynthia Eagle. *Sexual Science: The Victorian Construction of Womanhood*. Cambridge, MA: Harvard University Press, 1989.

Russo, Charles J., J. John Harris, and Rosetta F. Sandidge. "*Brown v. Board of Education* at 40: A Legal History of Equal Educational Opportunities in American Public Education." *Journal of Negro Education* 63, 3 (1994): 297–309.

Savage, Carter Julian. "Cultural Capital and African American Agency: The Economic Struggle for Effective Education for African Americans in Franklin, Tennessee, 1890–1967." *The Journal of African American History* 87 (Spring 2002): 206–35.

Schlesinger, Sr., Arthur M. "Biography of a Nation of Joiners." *American Historical Review* 50, no. 1 (1944): 1–25.

Schlossman, Steven. "Before Home Start: Notes toward a History of Parent Education in America, 1897–1929." *Harvard Educational Review* 46, no. 3 (1976): 436–67.

Scott, Anne Firor. *The Southern Lady: From Pedestal to Politics, 1830–1930*. Chicago: University of Chicago Press, 1970.

———. *Natural Allies: Women's Associations in American History*. Urbana: University of Illinois Press, 1992.

Selden, Steven. *Inheriting Shame: The Story of Eugenics and Racism in America.* New York: Teachers College Press, 1999.

Shaw, Stephanie J. *What a Woman Ought to Be and Do: Black Women Professional Workers During the Jim Crow Era.* Chicago: University of Chicago Press, 1997.

Shoemaker, Don, ed. *With All Deliberate Speed: Segregation-Desegregation in Southern Schools.* New York: Harper & Brothers, 1957.

Sitkoff, Harvard. *A New Deal for Blacks: The Emergence of Civil Rights as a National Issue.* New York: Oxford University Press, 1978.

Sklar, Kathryn Kish. *Florence Kelley and the Nation's Work: The Rise of Women's Political Culture, 1830–1900.* New Haven, CT: Yale University Press, 1995.

Skocpol, Theda. *Protecting Soldiers and Mothers: The Political Origins of Social Policy in the United States.* Cambridge, MA: The Belknap Press of Harvard University Press, 1992.

———. "Casting Wide Nets: Federalism and Extensive Associations in the Modernizing United States." Unpublished paper prepared for a conference on *The Decline of Social Capital,* Berlin, Germany, June 3–5, 1997.

———. *Diminished Democracy: From Membership to Management in American Civic Life.* Norman: University of Oklahoma Press, 2003.

Skocpol, Theda, and Morris P. Fiorina, eds. *Civic Engagement in American Democracy.* Washington, DC: Brookings Institution Press, 1999.

Skocpol, Theda, Marshall Ganz, Ruth Aguilera-Vaques, Jennifer Oser, Christine Woyshner, and David Siu. "Organizing America: Launching National Membership Associations in the United States, 1860–1920." Paper presented at the American Sociological Association Annual Meeting, August 1998.

Skocpol, Theda, Marshall Ganz, and Ziad Munson. "A Nation of Organizers: The Institutional Origins of Civic Voluntarism in the United States." *The American Political Science Review* 94, no. 3 (2000): 527–46.

Smith, Alice Brown. *Forgotten Foundations: The Role of Jeanes Teachers in Black Education.* New York: Vantage Press, 1997.

Smith, Joan K. *Ella Flagg Young: Portrait of a Leader.* Ames, IA: Educational Studies Press, 1979.

Smith-Rosenberg, Caroll. *Disorderly Conduct: Visions of Gender in Victorian America.* New York: Knopf, 1985.

Solomon, Barbara Miller. *In the Company of Educated Women: A History of Women and Higher Education in America.* New Haven, CT: Yale University Press, 1985.

Solomon, W. E. "Desegregation in Public Education in South Carolina." *Journal of Negro Education* 24, no. 3 (1955): 327–32.

Sparks, Dorothy. *Strong is the Current: History of the Illinois Congress of Parents and Teachers, 1900–1947.* Chicago: Illinois Congress of Parents and Teachers, 1948.

Stephenson, William. *Sallie Southall Cotten: A Woman's Life in North Carolina.* Greenville, NC: Pamlico Press, 1987.

Stowe, Steven. "The Not-So-Cloistered Academy: Elite Women's Education and Family Feeling in the Old South." In *The Web of Southern Social Relations: Women, Family, and Education,* edited by Walter J. Fraser, Jr., R. Frank Saunders, Jr., and Jon L. Wakelyn. Athens: University of Georgia Press, 1985. 90–106.

Suggs, Henry Lewis. *The Black Press in the South, 1865–1979.* Westport, CT: Greenwood Press, 1983.

Tanner, Daniel, and Laurel Tanner. *History of the School Curriculum.* New York: Macmillan, 1990.

Tapia, John E. *Circuit Chautauqua: From Rural Education to Popular Entertainment in Early Twentieth Century America.* Jefferson, NC: McFarland & Co., 1997.

Temple, Sarah Blackwell Gober. *The First Hundred Years: A Short History of Cobb County, Georgia,* second edition. Atlanta: Cherokee Publishing Company, 1980.

de Tocqueville, Alexis. *Democracy in America.* Edited by Harvey C. Mansfield and Delba Winthrop. Chicago: University of Chicago Press, 2000.

Tolley, Kim, and Nancy Beadie, eds. *Chartered Schools: Two Hundred Years of Independent Academies in the United States, 1727–1925.* New York: RoutledgeFalmer, 2002.

Tushnet, Mark V. *The NAACP's Legal Strategy against Segregated Education, 1925–1950.* Chapel Hill: University of North Carolina Press, 1987.

Tyack, David. *The One Best System: A History of American Urban Education.* Cambridge, MA: Harvard University Press, 1974.

Tyack, David, and Larry Cuban. *Tinkering Toward Utopia: A Century of Public School Reform.* Cambridge, MA: Harvard University Press, 1995.

Tyack, David, and Elisabeth Hansot. *Learning Together: A History of Coeducation in American Public Schools.* New Haven, CT: Yale University Press, 1990.

Tyack, David, Robert Lowe, and Elisabeth Hansot. *Public Schools in Hard Times: The Great Depression and Recent Years.* Cambridge, MA: Harvard University Press, 1984.

Urban, Wayne J. *Gender, Race, and the National Education Association: Professionalism and Its Limitations.* New York: RoutledgeFalmer, 2000.

———. "Courting the Woman Teacher: The National Education Association, 1917–1970." *History of Education Quarterly* 41, no. 2 (2001): 139–66.

Vinovskis, Maris. "Family and Schooling in Colonial and Nineteenth Century America." *Journal of Family History* 12, nos. 1–3 (1987): 19–37.

Walker, Alonsita. "My Mother." *National Parent-Teacher* 37, no. 6 (1943): 14–16.

Walker, Vanessa Siddle. *Their Highest Potential: An African American School Community in the Segregated South.* Chapel Hill: University of North Carolina Press, 1996.

Washington, Booker T. *Up from Slavery: An Autobiography.* New York: Doubleday, Page, 1902.

Watkins, William H. *The White Architects of Black Education: Ideology and Power in America, 1865–1954.* New York: Teachers College Press, 2001.

Wells, Mildred White. *Unity in Diversity: The History of the General Federation of Women's Clubs.* Washington, DC: General Federation of Women's Clubs, 1953.

Weiler, Kathleen. "Corrine Seeds and the Avenue 21 School: Toward a Sensuous History of Citizenship Education." *Historical Studies in Education* 14, no. 2 (2002): 191–218.

Weiner, Lynn Y. "Maternalism as a Paradigm." *Journal of Women's History* 5, no. 2 (1993): 96–98.

———. "Motherhood, Race, and the PTA in the Postwar Era," unpublished paper presented at the annual meeting of the American Educational Research Association, New Orleans, April 2000.

Wells, Mildred White. *Unity in Diversity: The History of the General Federation of Women's Clubs.* Washington, DC: General Federation of Women's Clubs, 1953.

Wiebe, Robert H. *The Search for Order, 1877–1920.* New York: Hill and Wang, 1967.

Wolseley, Roland E. *The Black Press, USA,* second edition. Ames: Iowa State University Press, 1992.

Wood, Mary I. *The History of the General Federation of Women's Clubs.* New York: The General Federation of Women's Clubs, 1912.

Woodward, C. Vann. *The Strange Career of Jim Crow.* New York: Oxford University Press, 1974.

———. *Thinking Back: The Perils of Writing History.* Baton Rouge: University of Louisiana Press, 1986.

Woyshner, Christine. "The Education of Women for Marriage and Motherhood: Coverture, Community, and Consumerism in the Separate Spheres." *History of Education Quarterly* 43, no. 3 (2003): 410–28.

———. "Gender, Race, and the Early PTA: Civic Engagement and Public Education, 1897–1924." *Teachers College Record* 105, no. 3 (2003): 523–24.

———. "From Assimilation to Cultural Pluralism: The PTA and Civic Education, 1900–1950." In *Social Education in the Twentieth Century: Curriculum and Context for Citizenship,* edited by Christine Woyshner, Joseph Watras, and Margaret Smith Crocco, 93–109. New York: Peter Lang, 2004.

Woyshner, Christine, and Anne Meis Knupfer. "Introduction: Women, Volunteerism, and Education." In *The Educational Work of Women's Organizations, 1890–1960,* 1–16. New York: Palgrave Macmillan, 2008.

Wynne, Lewis Nicholas. *The Continuity of Cotton: Planter Politics in Georgia, 1865–1892.* Macon, GA: Mercer University Press, 1986.

Zanden, James W. Vander. "Turmoil in the South." *Journal of Negro Education* 29, no. 4 (1960): 445–52.

Zimmerman, Jonathan. *Distilling Democracy: Alcohol Education in America's Public Schools.* Lawrence: University of Kansas Press, 1999.

———. "Storm over the Schoolhouse: Exploring Popular Influences upon the American Curriculum, 1890–1941." *Teachers College Record* 100, no. 3 (1999): 602–26.

———. *Whose America? Culture Wars in the Public Schools.* Cambridge, MA: Harvard University Press, 2002.

INDEX

Alabama State Mothers' League, 80, 166
American Association of University
    Women, 132
American Cancer Society, 129, 132
American Child Health Association, 100
American Legion, 92, 134, 139
American States' Rights Association,
    168–69
American Teachers Association, 105, 132,
    199. *See also* National Association for
    Teachers in Colored Schools
Anderson, James D., 56, 59, 70, 222n5,
    224n14
Association of Collegiate Alumni, 41–42,
    48, 130
Association for the Study of Negro Life
    and History, 147
Atlanta Neighborhood Union, 78

Baptist church, 60–61, 82
Bell, Ethel, 181–82
Birney, Alice McLellan, 20, 22–27, 29,
    31–38, 98, 106, 127, 211n9
Birney, Helen T., 65, 77, 216n34
Birney, Theodore Weld, 25, 214n25
Blocker, Mary W., 104, 107
Bond, Horace Mann, 146
Boy Scouts of America, 92, 96, 177,
    233n17
Briggs v. Elliott, 148

Bright, Cora, 42, 44, 50, 212n11
Brown v. Board of Education, 2, 16, 151,
    153–59, 168–69, 171, 173, 175, 178;
    Brown II, 154, 198, 200
Brown, Ethel G., 169
Butler, Selena Sloan, 77–78, 82–84, 90,
    100–102, 104, 106–7, 111–12, 121, 177
Butterworth, Julian, 108, 110–12, 114
Button, F. C., 69

"cabinet ladies," 27–28, 30, 37
canning clubs, 67, 71, 75, 168. *See also*
    Homemakers' clubs
Cardinal Principles of Education, 16,
    89–90, 119–23, 126, 133, 137, 239n10
character education, 15–16, 44, 63–64, 74,
    119, 122, 146. *See also* moral educa-
    tion
Child Labor Act, 131
Citizens' Council, 163, 174
citizenship: in the school curriculum, 34,
    44, 67; as a PTA initiative, 7, 89–90,
    119, 127, 133, 137–39, 141, 146, 148.
    See also civic education
civic education, 16, 43, 67, 126, 137–38,
    168. *See also* citizenship
Civil Rights Act, 156–57, 160, 168, 176
Civil Rights movement, 11, 156
civil society, 3, 6, 43, 77, 99, 142, 192, 195,
    200

Committee on Extension of Parent-
    Teacher Associations among Colored
    People, 82–83, 90, 100, 104–5, 113
Committee on Interracial Cooperation,
    102
consolidation of schools, 183
cooperation: between PTA and schools,
    8, 31, 48, 50–51, 73, 91, 128; as a cat-
    egory of analysis, 10–11, 57, 197
cultural capital, 11. *See also* social capital
cultural pluralism, 137–38, 140
curriculum, 6, 43, 56, 72, 144, 188;
    agricultural, 56–57, 67, 69, 71, 73–74;
    functional, 5, 34–37, 44, 90, 118–22;
    industrial, 56, 59, 67, 69–74; influence
    of PTA on, 4, 6, 13, 15, 16, 49, 88–89,
    91, 98, 110, 126, 136, 147; for women,
    23–24

Daddy's meetings, 97, 149
Daughters of the American Colonists, 132
Daughters of the American Revolution
    (DAR), 41, 98
Davis, Jackson, 72–73, 227n46
Declaration of Unification, 188–89, 191
desegregation: of schools, 16, 154, 156–58,
    160, 162–63, 166, 175–77, 179–80,
    184, 186, 200; of the PTA, 152–94
dress reform, 18–19, 24
DuBois, Rachel Davis, 144–46
Du Bois, W. E. B., 32, 59, 64
DuVaul, Charles W., 98

Elementary and Secondary Education Act
    (ESEA), 156–57, 168, 176

farm demonstration project, 69, 71
Favrot, Leo M., 72
federal aid to education, 131–32
federated organizational structure:
    benefits of, 5, 96, 99, 143, 156, 173,
    200; of PTA, 2, 12, 13, 15, 21–22, 34,
    38, 41, 54, 83, 88, 91–92, 100–101,
    105–6, 112, 122–23, 130, 153, 160,
    165, 171–75, 192, 195–97; of women's
    organizations, 40, 60, 66
Founders Day, 95, 106, 125
fundraising, 5, 7, 15, 50, 63, 89, 91, 95–96,

106–18, 122–25, 149–50, 197, 237n66.
    See also philanthropy

Gay, Clara B., 152, 179, 183, 188, 191–93,
    197
gender, as a category of analysis, 7–10, 33
General Education Board (GEB), 58–60,
    69–73, 75–76, 78
General Federation of Women's Clubs
    (GFWC), 1, 2, 8, 15, 21, 26, 29, 34, 36,
    39–41, 47–48, 50, 52, 54, 60, 65–66,
    98, 130, 142, 217n47; membership in,
    28, 48, 212n15, 215n31
Gill, Laura Drake, 42–43
Gill, Lonia, 186, 188–91
Godard, George, 73

Hall, G. Stanley, 35–36
Harper, Frances Watkins, 32, 52–53, 55,
    62, 64
Harris, Narvie Jordan, 85–88, 90, 99, 107,
    114–15, 138, 170, 180, 186, 188, 193,
    197
Hastings, Minetta, 133, 141–43
health: in the school curriculum, 35, 40,
    43–44, 46, 89–90, 237n65; healthful
    living, 7; PTA programs in, 4, 49, 67,
    83, 95, 105–6, 120–22, 126, 129–37,
    143, 168, 182, 238n71
Hearst, Phoebe Apperson, 27–28, 30,
    37–38, 98, 106, 215n29, 218n53
Henrotin, Ellen, 1, 28–29
Hitch, Minnie, 164–65
Holbeck, Elmer, 97, 110, 112, 114
Holland, Annie W., 76
Homemakers' clubs, 56, 69–77, 84, 135,
    226n37, 228n54. *See also* canning
    clubs
Hoover, Herbert, 104

intercultural education, 16, 140, 143–46,
    243n38. *See also* intergroup relations
intergroup relations, 127, 159, 245n56;
    committee of the PTA, 144–46,
    149, 151, 153, 155, 159–65, 178–82,
    189–91, 253n67. *See also* intercultural
    education
international understanding, 16, 140–50

Jamestown (New York) PTA, 139
Jeanes teachers, 54, 70–73, 76–77, 85–86, 88, 106, 193, 227n41, 231n5
John's Island (South Carolina) PTA, 95–97, 110–11
Jones, Mary Edith, 186, 189–91
Junior PTA, 128

Kight, Ethel, 147, 177, 185, 192
kindergartens, 20, 27, 32, 35–36, 41, 43, 50, 52, 63–64, 66, 110, 118; organizers of, 26–27, 29, 35, 63, 77

Lambert, J. S., 80
leadership, development of through PTA work, 91, 95, 97, 115, 128, 164, 196
League of Women Voters, 98
legislation: PTA influence on, 6, 16, 109, 124, 127, 130–36, 150, 194, 240n20
Leonard, Eunice Harper, 120, 132–33, 135, 137, 197
Lockport (NY) Mothers' Club, 32, 36

Mack, Essie D., 108
manual training, 43, 59. See also vocational education
March of Dimes, 129
Marietta Female College, 23–24
Marshall, Thurgood, 154, 156
maternalism, 8, 9, 21, 32, 49, 55, 63, 130, 138, 199. See also sentimental maternalist
McDavid, Mary Foster, 108
McLaurine, Betty Baldwin, 170–73, 175
membership, of the PTA, 39, 48–50, 84, 89, 92–94, 98–99, 102–6, 112–13, 123–24, 150, 153, 156–59, 168, 170, 174–78, 180, 185, 193–94, 234n25, 246n2; drives, 95, 123–24, 129, 149–50, 158, 186; overlapping in women's organizations, 22, 50, 60, 89, 98; state units, 48–49, 92–93, 103–4, 155–57, 162, 165, 177
Moorhead, Jennelle, 181
moral education, 15–16, 35, 40, 44, 69. See also character education
Morgan, Beatrice Moore, 127, 129, 147, 149–50, 195

Morris, Thelma M., 177
Mount Holyoke Seminary (College), 24, 34
Murray, Anna J., 62–64

National Association for the Advancement of Colored Persons (NAACP), 3, 5, 14, 67, 132, 144, 148–49, 154, 169–70, 173, 176, 199, 251n42
National Association of Colored Women (NACW), 1, 2, 9, 14, 53–54, 60–63, 66–70, 77–78, 80–81, 132; Nashville branch, 101
National Association for Teachers in Colored Schools (NATCS), 14, 60, 70, 72, 82, 101, 105, 225n22; Kentucky branch, 69; Georgia branch, 106. See also American Teachers' Association
National Congress of Mothers (NCM), 2, 15, 18–39, 41, 50, 52, 54–55, 62–64, 77–78, 88, 106, 110, 138, 199, 217n47, 244n43; constitution, 38; Declaration of Principles, 31
National Council of Christians and Jews, 141
National Council of Jewish Women, 41; in Kentucky, 47–48
National Defense in Education Act (NDEA), 126
National Education Association (NEA), 1, 3, 35, 39–49, 51, 65, 88, 142, 155; Committee on the Reorganization of Secondary Education, 16, 89–90, 119, 123, 126, 137; Department of School Patrons, 44–51, 84; Department of Women's Organizations, 15, 39, 41–44, 65; Kindergarten Department, 40–41; membership, 41, 48
National Federation of Business and Professional Women's Clubs, 142
National Kindergarten Association, 103
National Negro Health Week, 129
National Youth Administration, 134
Nelson, Fannie Mitchell, 171, 180–81, 184
Newbold, N. C., 76, 114
Newton, Mary K., 96
"new woman," 8–9
Nineteenth Amendment, 3, 5, 9, 49, 199. See also suffrage

Our National Family, 106–7, 112–13, 117, 125, 147, 149, 152, 155, 170, 178, 181, 183, 185, 231n4

Palmetto Education Association, 148–49
Parent-Teacher Alliance, 171, 173–75
Partridge, Deborah, 145–46
patriotism, 48, 64, 126, 138–40
philanthropy, 15, 56, 58–60, 67, 69–71, 75. *See also* fundraising
Plessy v. Ferguson, 53, 154
Presson, J. A., 72
Price, Pearl, 152, 188–91

Randolph, Virginia, 73, 75, 228n47, 228n49
Reese, William J., 6, 8, 39, 133, 207n10, 208n19, 209n24, 219n59, 221n87
Reeve, Margaretta Willis, 49, 51, 82, 88, 118
Rosenwald Schools, 70, 80
Ruffin, Josephine St. Pierre, 60, 80
Rutledge, Martha, 171–74, 197

salaries for teachers, 43, 45, 109, 114, 131
Sanders, W. W., 81, 230n68
Schoff, Hannah Kent, 38–39, 49, 113
scholarships, 115–16, 168
school equalization efforts, 131–32, 148–49
school facilities, 43, 80–81
school funding, 45–46, 88, 108, 114, 117, 194
school gardens, 45, 48, 135
school improvement societies, 53, 56–57, 66, 70, 73–74, 76–77, 81, 91–92, 95, 199; in Kentucky, 47
School Lunch Act, 5, 131–37
school lunches, 5, 44, 46, 78, 110, 114, 118, 121, 123, 126, 130, 132–37, 150, 197. *See also* School Lunch Act
sentimental maternalist, 9, 38. *See also* maternalism
Service Bureau for Intercultural Education, 144–45
Sheppard-Towner Infancy and Maternity Protection Act, 130, 132, 136

singing at PTA meetings, 94, 96, 177
Skocpol, Theda, 3, 4, 12, 40, 205n2, 206n6, 206n7, 212n15, 215n31, 219n62
Smith-Hughes Act, 75–76
Smith-Lever Act, 71, 75
social capital, 8, 11–12, 89; differences between bridging and bonding, 11, 196. *See also* cultural capital
South Carolina Federation of Women's Clubs, 95, 132
Southern Association of College Women, 41, 48
Southern Education Board (SEB), 47, 58–59, 70
Spencer, Herbert, 35–36, 90, 218n49
Strong, Anna, 128
suffrage for women, 33–34, 130. *See also* Nineteenth Amendment

Tennessee Interracial Commission, 102
Terrell, Mary Church, 32, 60, 62–64
Tilton, Elizabeth Hewes, 130
de Tocqueville, Alexis, 2–3
tree planting, 95–96, 168
Trenholm, H. Councill, 80
Tuskegee, 71, 136, 145, 156

United Daughters of the Confederacy, 139
United Nations, 16, 131, 140, 142–43, 146, 150
United Nations Educational, Scientific, and Cultural Organization (UNESCO), 4, 140
Urban League, 14, 78, 82, 88, 103, 178, 199

vocational education, 48, 59, 75, 103, 118, 120–21
voter registration, 106–7, 138, 148, 177

Walker, Vanessa Siddle, 11, 116, 234n24
Washington, Booker T., 59, 63–64, 129, 145
Wessels, Adeline, 83, 90, 100–101, 104, 113, 116
White House Conference on Child Welfare, 102, 104, 128, 154

Williams, Fannie Barrier, 61

Williams, Mayme, 151, 155

Woman's Association for the Betterment of Public Schools (WABPS), 8

Woman's Christian Temperance Union (WCTU), 1, 3, 19–21, 29, 32, 34, 37, 41, 212n15, 214n27, 216n35

Woman's Joint Congressional Committee, 49, 131

women's club movement, 15, 16, 19, 22, 25–26, 84, 110

Women's Committee of the Council of National Defense, 48

Women's Work in Municipalities (Beard), 39–40

Woodson, Carter G., 147

Works Progress Administration, 134

workshops for PTA members, 96–97, 108, 114, 128–29, 136, 150, 157, 159, 178, 233n19

world understanding, 139–40, 143–44, 147, 150

Yonge Street PTA, 78–79

Young, Ella Flagg, 45, 220n75

Young Woman's Christian Association (YWCA), 19, 77–78, 82, 92, 152, 178